THE IMMATERIAL SELF

INTERNATIONAL LIBRARY OF PHILOSOPHY
Editor: Ted Honderich
Grote Professor of the Philosophy of Mind and Logic
University College London

Recent books in the series include:

* CONTENT AND CONSCIOUSNESS
Daniel C. Dennett

STATE PUNISHMENT
Nicola Lacey

NEEDS
Garrett Thompson

MODERN ANTI-REALISM AND MANUFACTURED TRUTH
Gerald Vision

* PHILOSOPHY OF ECONOMICS:
ON THE SCOPE OF REASON IN ECONOMIC INQUIRY
Subroto Roy

* WITTGENSTEIN'S PHILOSOPHY OF PSYCHOLOGY
Malcolm Budd

SCIENTISM: PHILOSOPHY AND THE
INFATUATION WITH SCIENCE
Tom Sorrell

* Also available in paperback

THE IMMATERIAL SELF

A defence of the Cartesian dualist conception of the mind

John Foster

London and New York

First published 1991
by Routledge
11 New Fetter Lane, London EC4P 4EE

Simultaneously published in the USA and Canada
by Routledge
a division of Routledge, Chapman and Hall, Inc.
29 West 35th Street, New York, NY 10001

Typeset in 10/12pt Baskerville by
Ponting–Green Publishing Services, London
Printed and bound in Great Britain by
TJ Press (Padstow) Ltd, Padstow, Cornwall

British Library Cataloguing in Publication Data
Foster, John
The immaterial self: a defence of the Cartesian dualist
conception of the mind. – (International Library of
Philosophy)
1. Dualism
I. Title   II. Series
147.4

Library of Congress Cataloging in Publication Data
Foster, John
The immaterial self: a defence of the Cartesian dualist
conception of the mind / John Foster.
p.   cm. – (International library of philosophy)
Includes bibliographical references and index.
1. Philosophy of mind.   2. Dualism.   3. Mind and body.
4. Descartes, René, 1596–1650–Contributions in dualist
doctrine of mind.   I. Title.   II. Series.
BD418.3.F67   1991
128'.2–dc20   09-26357

ISBN 0-415-02989-9

To the memory of
Leonard Purkiss Foster
and
Reginald Thomas Munns

CONTENTS

vii

PREFACE

Dualism is a doctrine which is engaged on two fronts. It affirms a thesis about the mind, in opposition to the various forms of materialism and mental reductionism, and also affirms a thesis about the physical world, in opposition to the various forms of mentalism and idealism. My aim in this book is only to examine and defend the dualist account of the *mind*, and, in particular, to argue for its *Cartesian* (non-Humean) version, which assigns the immaterial contents of the mind to an immaterial mental subject.

In thinking about these issues, I have benefited from discussions with a number of colleagues, pupils, and friends. My particular thanks are due to Howard Robinson, who read an earlier draft of the book and gave me some helpful advice.

1

THE DUALIST DOCTRINE

1 THE FIVE CLAIMS

Dualism is a doctrine about the mental and the physical realms and the relationship between them. We can represent it as the conjunction of five claims:

[1] There is a mental realm.
[2] The mental realm is fundamental.
[3] There is a physical realm.
[4] The physical realm is fundamental.
[5] The two realms are ontologically separate.

These claims are naturally seen as falling into two overlapping groups – [1], [2], and [5] combining to form the dualist's thesis about the mind (and its relation to the physical world), and [3], [4], and [5] combining to form his thesis about the physical world (and its relation to the mind). We shall look into this division presently. But we must start by trying to get clear about what the claims themselves mean.

2 THE INTERPRETATION OF THE CLAIMS

Claim [1], which asserts the existence of a mental realm, is fairly straightforward and needs little in the way of clarification. The only point which needs to be stressed (in case too much is read into the word 'realm') is that the claim is to be interpreted in its weakest sense, whereby the existence of any mind or the occurrence of any mental event would suffice for its truth. In practice, of course, nearly all dualists will accept a variety of stronger claims of the same general kind. Thus virtually all

1

will accept that, except in cases of very severe brain-damage, human beings of sufficient maturity have minds. Most will also be prepared to ascribe a modest degree of mentality to certain kinds of non-human animal. And some will accept the existence of non-embodied minds, such as those of God, angels, and departed spirits. But commitments over the size and composition of the mental realm are not essential to the dualist position as such. Thus if someone were to insist that his was the only mind, or, still more restrictively, that there was no mentality beyond his own current consciousness, he could still be classified as a dualist, so long as he accepted the other components of the dualist doctrine. I make this point for reasons of precision, rather than because I want to make much of it in my subsequent discussion. In practice, the dualist positions which I shall be taking seriously are ones which, at least in the sphere of human mentality, endorse our ordinary assumptions about the scope and makeup of the mental realm.

Thus weakly interpreted, claim [1] is likely to strike us as uncontroversial. After all, how could anyone deny his own current mentality without manifest absurdity? But, for the moment, we must put questions of evaluation on one side and concentrate on providing an exposition of the dualist doctrine. This means moving on to a consideration of claim [2].

This second claim, which presupposes the existence of a mental realm and characterizes it as fundamental, is more complicated than the first. Put roughly, what it is asserting is that mentality is not *reducible* to something else. But to see exactly what this means, we need to begin by exploring the notion of reduction. In particular, we need to draw a distinction between two forms of reduction, one of which is concerned with concepts and statements, the other with facts or states of affairs. To help us draw this distinction, I am going to start by focusing on a quite different case in which the possibility of reduction arises – one which has no direct bearing on the issue of dualism. The case in question is that of physical colour.

Opaque physical objects appear coloured to their visual percipients. In appearing coloured, an object appears to possess, to be characterized by, an 'intrinsic' quality – a quality which pertains to how the object is in itself, in contrast with its dispositional properties and its relations to other things.

Because objects appear coloured, we ordinarily assume that they are. Of course, we recognize that when the conditions of observation are unfavourable (for example, under poor illumination), or when the the subject's powers of colour-vision are impaired (for example, he is colour-blind), an object's apparent colour may differ from its real colour. But at least we assume that any opaque object has *some* colour, and that its real colour is as it appears to be to the normal percipient who views it in standard conditions.

The trouble is that this common-sense assumption seems to get undermined by the findings of science. In the first place, science reveals that an object's colour-appearance is entirely due to the character of the light which it reflects and to the way in which our visual systems respond to it. Secondly, it also reveals that, given a certain kind of illumination, an object's disposition to reflect light of a certain character is entirely due to the arrangement and functional properties of its surface-atoms, and so has nothing to do with any intrinsic colour which it or its atoms might happen to possess. Putting both these points together, we seem forced to the conclusion that our attribution of colour to physical objects is wholly unwarranted: our only grounds for making this attribution are that physical objects look coloured; but if their looking coloured is to be causally explained in terms of factors which do not involve their possession of colour, then it seems that colour-appearance provides no evidence at all for colour-possession. Moreover, even if, perchance, objects are coloured, and even if they happen to be coloured in the ways they standardly appear, we seem forced to conclude that their colours are never visible to us. For we can hardly be said to see some feature of an object if that feature is causally irrelevant to the object's visual appearance.

In an attempt to avoid these unpalatable conclusions, many philosophers, following the lead of John Locke,[1] have accepted a 'dispositional' account of physical colour, which represents an object's possession of colour as consisting in, and nothing over and above, its disposition to look coloured to (produce the appropriate colour-experiences in) the human observer. Thus, in line with common sense, they acknowledge that ripe tomatoes are red and that fresh grass is green. But they insist that this redness and this greenness amount to nothing more than the dispositions of these objects to have the appropriate sorts of colour-appearance to the normal human percipient who views them in standard conditions. This removes any conflict with the scientific findings, since the obtaining of these dispositions is perfectly compatible with, and indeed explicable in terms of, the facts which science reveals. In offering this account, of course, these philosophers are not claiming that the sensible colours which characterize visual appearance – the colours which feature in the content of our visual experiences – are themselves dispositional; and in this respect they are likely, in deference to science, to recognize a systematic discrepancy between the way objects visually appear to us and the way they really (or at any rate fundamentally-really[2]) are. Their claim is simply that when we ordinarily ascribe a colour-property to a physical object – for example, redness to a tomato – the truth or falsity of our ascription depends solely on that object's dispositions to colour-appearance, irrespective of what the object is like (or is fundamentally like) in itself.

Whether or not this dispositional account is correct is not something I want to discuss. The point I want to stress is that it can be developed in two quite different ways, and it is this difference which will serve to bring out the relevant distinction between the two forms of reduction.

Take the case of the ripe tomato. According to the dispositional account, the tomato is red and its being so consists in, and is nothing over and above, its disposition to look red to the normal human observer in standard conditions. But how exactly is the dispositionalist to defend this view? On what basis does he take the object's redness to consist in this phenomenal disposition? Well, one thing he might argue is that our very ascription of redness to the tomato is to be construed in dispositional terms – that when we say that the tomato is red, what we really mean, or what our statement really means, is that the tomato is disposed to produce the appropriate kind of colour-experience in the relevant class of observers in the relevant sorts of condition. On this approach, the dispositional account would be represented as implicit in our actual concept of physical colour – as something which can be established by conceptual analysis alone, without reference to the scientific findings or to any other kind of evidence concerning the nature of physical objects and the causes of visual experience. The claim would be that, irrespective of what the tomato is like in itself, and irrespective of what endows it with its red-appearance, our ordinary ascription of redness to it turns out, on analysis, to be an ascription of a phenomenal disposition rather than an attempt to characterize its intrinsic nature.

This would be the dispositionalist's most straightforward approach. But it is not the only one available. Let us say that a fact F is wholly constituted by a fact or set of facts F' if and only if the following two conditions hold: (i) F obtains in virtue of F' (in some way that makes the obtaining of F asymmetrically dependent on the obtaining of F'), and (ii) the obtaining of F is nothing over and above the obtaining of F'. Exactly what these conditions amount to is something which I shall cover in more detail later.[3] For the moment, let us just settle for a simple and trivial example. Thus if we suppose that John weighs 14 stone and Mary weighs 10 stone, and if we let F_1 be the weight-fact about John and F_2 be the weight-fact about Mary, we can say that John's being heavier than Mary is wholly constituted by the combination of F_1 and F_2. For obviously the weight-relationship between two objects is entirely derived from, and nothing over and above, the obtaining of their specific weights.

Now someone might concede that our actual concept of physical colour represents it as something intrinsic, and so is not amenable to a dispositional analysis, but still insist that physical-colour facts are wholly constituted by dispositional facts. Thus he might deny that our ordinary ascription of redness to tomatoes is to be construed dispositionally (deny that the statement 'tomatoes are red' can be re-expressed as 'tomatoes are disposed to ...'[4]), but still maintain that a tomato's being red is something derivative from, and nothing over and above, its disposition to look intrinsically red to the normal percipient in standard conditions. Someone who endorsed the dispositional account in this form would, in effect, be assigning the colour-facts and the dispositional facts to different metaphysical levels of reality. On the one hand, he would be acknowledging that physical objects have colour and that the colour-facts about them cannot be expressed in any but colour-ascriptive terms. On the other hand, he would be claiming that the whole domain of physical-colour facts is sustained by, and nothing over and above, an underlying reality from which all such facts are absent – a reality in which the only relevant facts are ones about phenomenal dispositions or the factors in terms of which these dispositions are scientifically explained. Such a position will only be available, of course, if our actual concept of physical colour, though representing it as something intrinsic and non-dispositional, does *not* represent it as metaphysically fundamental. If our ordinary colour-ascriptions are to be counted as true, despite the exclusion of physical colour from the metaphysically basic reality, then it is crucial that their content be sufficiently neutral on metaphysical questions to allow the philosopher to represent the facts which they record as constituted by facts of a quite different kind.

Now both these versions of the dispositional account can be described as *reductionist* with respect to physical colour: each, in its own way, is claiming that physical colour is reducible to something else. But they are reductionist in quite different ways. The first version represents physical colour as reducible to phenomenal dispositions at the level of concept and meaning. The claim is that a correct analysis of our ordinary colour-ascriptions reveals them to be disposition-ascriptions: if they seem to be ascriptions of an intrinsic quality, this is only an illusion sustained by their overt form – an illusion which disappears when their real content is made clear by conceptual analysis. The second version represents physical colour as reducible to phenomenal dispositions at the level of facts or states of affairs. The claim is that, while colour-ascriptions have their own distinctive meaning and cannot be re-expressed in any other terms, the facts which they record are wholly constituted by dispositional facts, an object's possession of colour being derivative from, and nothing over and above, its disposition to look intrinsically coloured to the human observer. In the first case, we may speak of the postulated reduction as 'conceptual' or (the term I shall normally use) 'analytical', since it is a matter of reducing one class of statements to another class of statements by conceptual analysis. In the second case, we may speak of the postulated reduction as 'factual' or (the term I shall normally use) 'metaphysical', since it is a matter of reducing one class of facts to another class of facts by metaphysical stratification. In the one case, it is a matter of unpacking what is implicit in our ordinary colour-ascriptions. In the other, it is a matter of assigning the colour-facts and the dispositional facts to their appropriate levels in the metaphysical hierarchy.

This distinction between the analytical and metaphysical forms of reduction is not confined to the case of physical colour. It is a purely general distinction, which can be applied to any case where an issue of reduction arises. In particular then – and it is here that we rejoin the main theme of our discussion – we can apply it to the case of *mental* reduction, which arises in connection with claim [2]. Thus when considering the issue of whether mentality is reducible to something else, we can distinguish between (i) the position of the *analytical* reductionist, who claims that the very content, or subject-matter, of our ordinary statements about the mind turns out, on conceptual analysis, to be non-mentalistic, and (ii) the position of the *metaphysical* reductionist, who concedes that such statements are irreducibly mentalistic, but insists that the facts which they record are wholly constituted by facts of a quite different kind. Thus defined, the two forms of mental reductionism are, of course, incompatible, since the metaphysical form explicitly includes a denial of the analytical. But this does not mean that analytical reductionists are committed to taking mental facts, or some selection of them, as metaphysically basic. There is nothing to prevent someone from first subjecting psychological concepts to a non-mentalistic analysis and then claiming that, thus non-mentalistically construed, mental facts are reducible to non-mental facts by relations of constitution. Indeed, as we shall see, this is a common reductionist approach.[5]

The issue of mental reductionism is one which we shall examine in detail in due course. The point I want to make now is that claim [2] is to be interpreted as excluding mental reductionism of both types. It is to be taken as asserting both (i) that the mental realm is *conceptually* fundamental, i.e. that the subject-matter of statements about the mind is always irreducibly mentalistic, and (ii) that the mental realm is *metaphysically* fundamental, i.e. that mental facts are never wholly constituted by non-mental facts. Thus if Smith is in pain at time *t*, claim [2] commits the dualist to saying two things: first, that the concept of pain is not to be analysed in such a way that, in its fully analysed form, the statement that Smith is in pain at *t* loses its explicitly psychological content; and second, that there is no set of non-mental facts such that Smith's being in pain at *t* is derivative from, and nothing over and above, the obtaining of these facts. And the claim has exactly analogous implications in respect of each mental state-ment and each mental fact. This means, of course, that, in its opposition to mental reductionism, the claim is doubly strong. For not only does it exclude *both* forms of reductionism, but it excludes both forms in respect of *each* aspect of mentality for which the issue might be raised. It claims that no mental statement is amenable to a non-mentalistic analysis and that no mental fact is non-mentally constituted. The only sense in which the claim is not wholly anti-reductionist is that it leaves open the possibility of conceptual analysis and metaphysical stratification within the framework of the mental realm.[6] Thus it claims that all mental statements are irreducibly mentalistic, but leaves room for the conceptual reduction of some to others. Likewise, it claims that no mental fact is wholly con-stituted by non-mental facts, but does not insist that all mental facts are metaphysically basic.

Having dealt with claims [1] and [2], I can afford to be brief about claims [3] and [4]. For the latter are to be interpreted, in respect of the physical realm, in exactly the same way as the former have been interpreted in respect of the mental. Thus [3] asserts the existence of a physical realm (a realm of physical space and its occupants), though without any specific commitments as to its extent and composition, and [4] excludes any kind of analytical or metaphysical reduc-tion of the physical to something else.

Finally, we have claim [5], which asserts that the mental and the physical realms are ontologically separate. Roughly, what this means is that the entities which feature in the one realm are entirely different from those which feature in the other – that the class of mental-realm entities and the class of physical-realm entities do not overlap. However, there are two qualifica-tions.

In the first place, in holding the mental and physical realms to be ontologically separate, the dualist is not denying that they share the same time-dimension – that mental and physical events stand to one another in temporal relations. And since he may also be willing to recognize a domain of time-entities (moments, periods, and their aggregates), the interpretation of [5] has to be correspondingly adjusted.

Secondly, claim [5] is only intended to apply at the level of what is conceptually and metaphysically fundamental. Thus suppose that there is a certain class of entities which have both mental and physical properties and which therefore feature, initially, in both realms. If it can be shown that, in at least one of the realms, these entities do not feature in any facts which are metaphysically basic (not constituted by other facts), or that they do not feature in any such facts when the latter are expressed in their conceptually fundamental (fully analysed) form, then their presence in both realms, as initially characterized, does not constitute a counter-example to [5]. To obtain a counter-example, we have to find an ontological overlap between the two realms which survives when the realms are viewed in their conceptually and metaphysically fundamental perspective. (This qualification picks up the point that, in characterizing a realm as fundamental, the dualist is leaving room for conceptual analysis and metaphysical stratification within it.)

In claiming that the two realms are ontologically separate in this sense, the dualist is committed to saying that they are, in a corresponding sense, factually separate as well – that, when things are represented in their fundamental perspective, the facts, or states of affairs, which belong to the one realm turn out to be entirely different from those which belong to the other. For facts, or states of affairs, cannot be identical if their ontological ingredients are different. On the other hand, this commitment does not hold in reverse. Someone who accepted the factual separation of the two realms could still hold that they ontologically overlap. For he could allow that (even in the fundamental perspective) mental and physical facts sometimes involve the same entities, but insist that they always differ in the properties they assign to them.

3 THE TWO THESES

As I said at the beginning, the five claims which make up the dualist doctrine are naturally seen as falling into two overlapping groups – [1], [2], and [5] combining to form the dualist's thesis about the mind, and [3], [4], and [5] combining to form his thesis about the physical world. Thus claims [1] and [2], being only concerned with the mental realm, occur exclusively in the first group: they combine to form what we might call the thesis of *mental realism*, in opposition to both *mental nihilism*, which denies the existence of a mental realm altogether, and *mental reductionism*, which claims that mentality is (analytically or metaphysically) reducible to something else. Similarly, claims [3] and [4], being only concerned with the physical realm, occur exclusively in the second group: they combine to form the thesis of *physical realism*, in opposition to both *physical nihilism* and *physical reductionism*. Claim [5], in contrast, being equally concerned with both realms, occurs in both groups: by asserting that the two realms are ontologically separate, it forms both part of the dualist's thesis about the mind (in relation to the physical world) and part of his thesis about the physical world (in relation to the mind).

Although this is the natural way of grouping the claims in their present form, it is also possible to divide claim [5] into two components, in such a way that one component covers that part of [5]'s content which is relevant to the issues of the mind, and the other covers that part of its content which is relevant to the issues of the physical world. And, relative to this division, it becomes more natural to group the first component with claims [1] and [2] to form the dualist's psychological thesis, and the second component with claims [3] and [4] to form his physical thesis. To see how this works out, we must start by dividing the positions which are opposed to claim [5] into three general types.

To begin with, there are those positions which deny the ontological separation of the two realms by, as it were, absorbing the mental ontology (or some portion of it) into the physical world, so that the (relevant) mental entities are not only identified with physical entities, but are represented as purely physical in nature – represented as having no properties over and above those which they possess as physical entities. Positions of this sort may be described as 'mental-ontology assimilative' (MO-assimilative). And what needs to be stressed about them is that, while they offer a radical account of the nature of mental phenomena (or the relevant kinds of mental

10

phenomena), they do not in any way affect our understanding of the nature of the physical world: they simply take for granted our ordinary conception of physical things and provide a physicalistic account of the mental realm within that framework. One obvious example of an MO-assimilative position is the psychophysical type-identity thesis, in its standard form, which takes mental universals (psychological types, properties, and states) to be, in real essence, physical.

Next, and in sharp contrast, there are those positions which deny the ontological separation of the two realms by absorbing the physical ontology (or some portion of it) into the mind – an absorption which represents the (relevant) physical entities as purely mental in nature. Positions of this sort may be described as 'physical-ontology assimilative' (PO-assimilative); and again what needs to be stressed is that, while they offer a radical account of the nature of physical objects (or the relevant kinds of physical object), they do not in any way affect our understanding of the nature of the mind. PO-assimilative positions are nowadays rather unfashionable, but examples from the past would be Leibniz's claim that physical objects are collections of rudimentary minds[7] and Berkeley's claim (taken literally) that they are collections of ideas[8].

Finally, and falling between these extremes, there are those positions which claim an overlap between the mental and the physical ontologies, but without absorption in either direction. Positions of this 'non-assimilative' sort affect our understanding of both the nature of the mind and the nature of the physical world, but, in each case, they affect it less radically than the corresponding assimilative positions. An example would be the position of someone who identified mental with physical particulars, but took their psychological and physical characters to be separate and irreducible.

Now, in recognizing an ontological overlap between the mental and the physical realms, all three types of position are in conflict with claim [5]. But the role of [5], in relation to them, varies, according to whether we consider it as part of the dualist's thesis about the mind or as part of his thesis about the physical world. As part of his thesis about the mind, its role is purely to exclude positions of the first and third types (those which are either MO-assimilative or non-assimilative): its exclusion of positions of the second type (the

PO-assimilative) is here irrelevant, since these positions do not conflict with dualism on the issues of the mind. Conversely, as part of his thesis about the physical world, the role of [5] is purely to exclude positions of the second and third types (those which are either PO-assimilative or non-assimilative): here, what is irrelevant is its exclusion of positions of the first type (the MO-assimilative), since these positions do not conflict with dualism on the issues of the physical world. In consequence, we can divide claim [5] into two component claims:

[5a]   Apart from the possibility of PO-assimilation, the two realms are ontologically separate

[5b]   Apart from the possibility of MO-assimilation, the two realms are ontologically separate

where [5a] exactly captures the role of [5] in the dualist's thesis about the mind and [5b] exactly captures its role in his thesis about the physical world. And we can then more precisely formulate the first thesis as the conjunction of claims [1], [2], and [5a], and the second as the conjunction of [3], [4], and [5b].

Although dualism comprises these two theses, I am going to focus almost exclusively on the thesis about the mind. In this, I am following the pattern of most modern discussions, though for rather different reasons. Most modern philosophers focus on this part of the dualist doctrine because they regard the other part as uncontroversial: they take the existence, irreducibility, and *sui generis* character of the physical world for granted – as things on which all 'right-minded' people can agree – and then think of dualism as a controversial thesis about the mind, set in the framework of these uncontroversial assumptions. My own approach to the topic of the physical world is quite different. Far from considering the dualist's position on this topic uncontroversial, I hold a view which is directly contrary. For, in opposition to claim [4], I accept a form of phenomenalistic idealism, taking the existence of the physical world to be wholly constituted by the regularities in, and law-like constraints on, human sense-experience. My reason for focusing almost entirely on the mind-relevant part of the dualist doctrine is simply that I could not do justice to both parts in the space of a single book; and, having already discussed the issues of the physical world at some length elsewhere, I want to concentrate on the issues of the mind here.[9]

It goes without saying that, on these issues, my aim will be to defend the dualist view, since it is precisely at this point that dualism and idealism coincide. It is also obvious why, despite my idealist convictions, I shall have to adopt physical realism as a framework for the discussion. Nothing else would allow me to focus on the issues of the mind without entanglement in the issues of the physical world. Nor, indeed, would it allow me to take seriously the anti-dualist positions and arguments which feature in the modern debate.

4 DEGREES OF DUALISTIC COMMITMENT

There is one final point before we embark on the main discussion. I have represented dualism as a definite doctrine, comprising a set of precise claims, so that a position qualifies as dualist if it fully endorses these claims and as non-dualist if it does not. But I am conscious that this is an oversimplification. In reality, the division between dualist and non-dualist positions is not a sharp one, any more than the division between bald and non-bald people is sharp. Thus some positions which do not accept the relevant claims in full come sufficiently close to them to count as dualist in some decent sense. And conversely, some positions which accept these claims in full fall short of what dualism involves in its most full-blooded form. In short, dualism should really be thought of as an approach, which positions can exemplify to varying degrees, rather than as a definite doctrine with precise truth-conditions. And this applies, in particular, to dualism about the mind, on which our discussion will focus.

The reason why we should think of dualism about the mind as an approach, admitting of degrees, rather than as a definite doctrine or thesis, is that we can envisage positions which give a dualist account of certain categories of mental phenomena and a non-dualist account of others; and such positions cannot be naturally classified as straightforwardly dualist or as straightforwardly non-dualist. How this works out in the case of claims [2] and [5a] is clear enough. These claims respectively assert irreducibility and (with the relevant qualifications) ontological separation in respect of *all* categories of mental phenomena. But, in each case, we can envisage positions which, while fully dualist in other ways, endorse the implications of the relevant claim for only a certain subset of categories. For example, we can envisage a position which, while fully dualist in other ways, accepts a behaviourist account of (say) propositional attitudes, contrary to the full implications of claim [2]; likewise, we can envisage a position which, while fully dualist in other ways, accepts the identity of (say) sensations with brain processes, contrary to the full implications of claim [5a]. Because such positions are fully dualist in their account of certain categories of mental phenomena, it would be unnatural to classify them as simply non-dualist solely in virtue of their rejection of the relevant claim. It would be much more natural to think of them as exemplifying the dualist approach to a certain degree. And if the degree of exemplification were sufficiently high, it would be natural to think of them as predominantly dualist positions, but with certain anti-dualist concessions.

How the point works out in the case of claim [1] is more complicated. Unlike [2] and [5a], [1] is a very weak claim: it asserts the existence of a mental realm, but sets no minimum requirements on its size and richness. Thus, as we noted earlier, the mere existence of a single mind, or the mere occurrence of a single mental event, would suffice for its truth. Presumably, then, if it is possible to think of the dualist view in this area as admitting of degrees, it is because one position can count as more dualist than another by virtue of its commitment to a more extensive mental realm. At the same time, we clearly cannot say that positions *always* count as more dualist, the more extensive they take the mental realm to be. For example, we cannot say that someone who is dualist in other respects can increase the degree of his dualistic commitment by accepting the existence of angelic minds, in addition to those of humans and animals, or by insisting that people are *always* conscious, even during periods of asleep. Nor, conversely, can we say that Descartes was less than fully dualist because he took non-human animals to be mindless automata, or that someone would be making an anti-dualist concession if he claimed that there were no minds apart from his own. In all these cases, the issue over the extent of the mental realm has no bearing at all on the issue of dualism. And indeed, it was precisely this consideration which prompted us to give the dualist's existential claim its maximally weak form.

None the less, there *are* cases in which a stronger existential position can be properly construed as involving a stronger dualistic commitment. These cases are all ones in which what is at issue is not the abundance or scarcity of minds, nor the size of their mental biographies, but whether some particular form (or set of forms) of mentality, normally regarded as part of the standard human repertoire, should be recognized at all. And they are also ones in which the refusal to accord recognition to this form of mentality can be seen as a concession to, or step in the direction of, total mental nihilism – seen as expressing an attitude which, if carried to its extreme, would reject the mental realm altogether. The point would then be that, with respect to the issue of dualism, such a concession to nihilism would have the same kind of significance as the corresponding concession to reductionism: the refusal to acknowledge the existence of this form of mentality would be as much a departure from the full-blooded dualist position as the admission that the relevant psychological concepts were non-mentalistically analysable or that the relevant mental facts were non-mentally constituted. And, set in this context (i.e. seen as in opposition to this partial mental nihilism), the recognition of this form of mentality, in addition to the forms already accepted, could be legitimately thought of as exhibiting a further degree of dualistic commitment.

In all these ways, then, we should think of dualism about the mind as an approach which can be exemplified in varying degrees, rather than as a definite thesis with a precise content. It will still be convenient to take the formulated thesis as the starting-point for our discussion. But, in so doing, we must bear in mind that the underlying issues are not confined to a choice between the acceptance and rejection of its claims. We must bear in mind that, for each claim, there is a spectrum of positions which vary in the degree of their dualistic commitment relative to the factor which the claim concerns, so that each claim is merely one among a range of options to which, in so far as they are strong, the dualist might aspire, or for which, in so far as they are weak, he might settle.

2

NIHILISM AND ANALYTICAL BEHAVIOURISM

1 THE PROJECT

I have represented the dualist doctrine as the conjunction of five claims:

[1] There is a mental realm.
[2] The mental realm is fundamental.
[3] There is a physical realm.
[4] The physical realm is fundamental.
[5] The two realms are ontologically separate.

Claim [5], in turn, divides into two components:

[5a] Apart from the possibility of PO-assimilation, the two realms are ontologically separate.
[5b] Apart from the possibility of MO-assimilation, the two realms are ontologically separate.

where PO-assimilation is the absorption of the physical ontology, or some portion of it, into the mind, and MO-assimilation is the absorption of the mental ontology, or some portion of it, into the physical world. Given this division, claims [1], [2], and [5a] make up the dualist's thesis about the mind, while claims [3], [4], and [5b] make up his thesis about the physical world. As I have explained, it is on the thesis about the mind that I want to focus, and from now on I shall simply refer to it as the *dualist thesis*.

The discussion which now follows divides into two parts. In the first and much longer part (it extends to the end of 7.2), I try to establish the truth of the dualist thesis. My method here will be to consider and argue against the various theories

16

opposed to this thesis – theories which either deny the reality of the mental realm, or seek to reduce it (in whole or in part) to something else, or seek to absorb its ontology (in whole or in part) into the physical world. Thus among the theories I try to refute are mental nihilism, analytical behaviourism, analytical functionalism, metaphysical reductionism, and the two (type and token) theses of psychophysical identity. In the second part, I develop and defend a Cartesian account of the self. This presupposes the dualist thesis already established, but represents the various concrete instances of mentality (sensations, sense-experiences, thoughts, beliefs, emotions, etc.) as the states or activities of non-physical 'basic' subjects.[1] The contrast here is with the Humean form of dualism, which rejects the Cartesian ontology of basic subjects and represents the mind as just a collection of discrete mental items which stand to one another in certain unifying relations.

As might be expected, the first part of the discussion will largely focus on claims [2] and [5a], which are concerned with the clearly controversial issues of reducibility and ontological separation. But since these claims presuppose the existence of a mental realm, it will be appropriate to start with a consideration of claim [1], even if it is hard to see how the dualist's position could be seriously challenged at this point.

2 THE REALITY OF THE MENTAL REALM

Philosophers who reject the dualist thesis – and nowadays they constitute the vast majority – almost always do so in response to, or as a way of trying to establish, some kind of materialism. Materialism has two basic forms, a weaker and a stronger. In its stronger (qualitative) form, it becomes the thesis of total physicalism. This asserts that concrete reality is, at least at the fundamental level, purely physical – that every contingent fact, or state of affairs, is either physical or physically constituted. In its weaker (ontological) form, it merely claims that all concrete entities, or at least all that figure in the fundamental reality, are physical. Anti-dualist positions can almost always be seen as ways of adjusting our understanding of mentality to suit one of these views. I say 'adjusting' because, even in its weaker form, it is clear that materialism runs counter to the outlook of 'common sense'. Thus, even though we are happy to ascribe physical properties to the subjects in whose minds mental phenomena occur (in particular, we assume that human subjects of consciousness are members of a certain animal species), we ordinarily think of the phenomena themselves as, and as irreducibly, non-physical.

The common-sense view clashes with materialism because it accepts the reality of mental phenomena, while denying that they are amenable to a materialist account. Accordingly, there are two quite different ways in which a materialist can seek to adjust our understanding of mentality to suit his restrictive metaphysic. On the one hand, he can try to show that, after all, mental phenomena *are* amenable to a materialist treatment – that, by developing an appropriate account of their nature or status, we can preserve their reality within the materialist framework. It is this kind of adjustment which (in the case of the strong form of materialism) is involved in such positions as the type-identity thesis and the various species of mental reductionism; and it is this kind too which (in the case of the weaker form of materialism) is involved in the thesis of token-identity. On the other hand, the materialist can simply reject the existence of minds and mental phenomena altogether: he can concede that mentality would resist materialist treatment, but insist that there is no mentality to be treated. This is the position of mental nihilism, which stands in opposition to the dualist's claim [1]. Based, as it is, on a materialist metaphysic, this nihilist position is also known (and indeed more commonly known) as 'eliminative materialism'.

The majority of materialists have adopted the first (mind-preserving) approach – though the form of materialism espoused and the way of trying to reconcile it with the recognition of mental phenomena have varied from case to case. The preference for this approach is hardly surprising, since, on the face of it, the idea of denying the reality of mental phenomena altogether is just absurd. Even so, I think it would be wrong to dismiss the eliminative approach without further consideration. This is not just because nihilism has received the backing of at least some distinguished philosophers.[2] It is also, and more importantly, that, from a materialist standpoint, the position does have a rationale. The point is that there are prima facie objections to all the various ways in which, by reduction or assimilation, one might try to accommodate mentality within a materialist framework. So, provided he can offer an adequate case for materialism, and one which is available to him prior to decisions about the reality of the mental realm, the nihilist can defend his position simply by invoking these objections. In other words, he can argue: 'Materialism is true. There is no adequate account of mental phenomena in materialist terms. Therefore, there are no mental phenomena.'

Given the prima facie absurdity of nihilism, our natural inclination, of course, is to stand this argument on its head – to insist that since there clearly *are* mental phenomena (this being something we can know prior to any investigation into the issue of materialism or into the nature and status of the mind), either materialism must be false or there must be some way of developing a satisfactory materialist psychology. In my view, this is indeed the right response. But, at the same time, it is clear that something more has to be said in its defence. For if we are to reject the nihilist view *out of hand* – as something we can know to be false without even considering the arguments which might be adduced in its favour – then at least we need to spell out the reasons why the situation is so clear-cut. It is not enough to point out that nihilism is obviously false: we need to explain what makes it so.

There are in fact a number of reasons why the nihilist position seems clearly untenable and why claim [1] of the dualist thesis seems correspondingly secure. Let me start by setting out the points which I regard as most crucial:

(i) In even raising the issue of whether there is a mental realm, as indeed in raising any issue, we are surely presupposing our capacity to think, and hence presupposing our own mentality. For how could we coherently pose the question, but deny that we are able to consider or even understand it? A closely related point is that the assertion of nihilism seems self-defeating. For how can the nihilist deny that there are mental phenomena without representing this denial as an expression of his own *view* of the matter, and hence as an expression of something which pertains to his mental condition? How can he assert the nihilist position without thereby implying that it is something which he himself *believes* to be true and hence *mentally accepts*?

(ii) Even if the nihilist is prepared to deny that he thinks or has any views, he does not deny that, in company with others, he uses language and that the expressions of language have meaning. Now there is room for disagreement over the exact nature of meaning and the factors from which it ultimately derives. But it is surely clear that, whatever the philosophical details, language-meaning is only possible because language-users have understanding. How, for example, could the term 'cat' have the meaning it does have unless English-speakers knew what a cat was (i.e. possessed a cat-concept) and used the term to signify that sort of thing (thus conceived)?

(iii) In this connection, the nihilist faces a special problem over the meanings of *psychological* terms. In the case of something like 'cat', he might try to meet the objection in (ii) by saying that what gives the term its meaning is our practice of applying it to things of a certain sort – a practice which is purely behavioural and not sustained by any guiding concept of the sort in question. And, with suitable refinements, to allow for such things as definitional complexity and semantic holism, he might try to extend this account to physical (i.e. physical-world concerning) terms in general. Such an account is not, to my mind, at all plausible: I still do not see how we can have genuine meaning without user-understanding. But the point I want to stress is that (plausible or not) the account is simply not available to the nihilist in the case of psychological terms. For if nihilism were true, there would be no psychological objects or situations for these terms to apply to, and hence no application-practices from which the terms could draw the meanings which they actually have. But if the nihilist cannot appeal to such practices, then the original problem returns with a vengence. For the very lack of psychological items for the terms to apply to just serves to emphasize the need for psychological elements (concepts, understanding, intentions, etc.) in the factors which create their meaning.

(iv) Anyone who is in a position to consider the issue of claim [1] is directly conscious of his own current mental states and activities (or at least of some subset of them) in a way which makes it, in the context of that consciousness, impossible for him to doubt their existence. Thus I am now directly conscious of having a certain kind of visual experience – one as of sitting at my desk with a piece of paper in front of me. And while I can envisage ways in which this experience might turn out to misrepresent my physical environment (after all, it might turn out to be an illusion or a hallucination), I cannot envisage how it might turn out to be, qua experience, unreal. Likewise, I have for some time been directly conscious of thinking about a particular philosophical issue (that of mental nihilism); and whatever doubts I may feel about the adequacy of these thoughts, I cannot avoid the certainty that I am thinking them. I do not, of course, have the same direct access to the mental states of others; and, by achieving a suitable level of philosophical detachment, I can acknowledge the possibility that the creatures which I have always assumed to be other persons like myself do not have minds at all. But, with respect to the issue of [1], it is enough for my purposes if I can establish *my own* mentality from *my own* viewpoint – leaving other persons (if there are any) to do the analogous thing from theirs.

(v) Finally, it is worth noting that point (iv) is protected by two fail-safe devices. First, it would be idle for the nihilist to argue that our apparent consciousness of our own mentality is illusory – that things are not as they introspectively seem. For, veridical or not, the introspective experience is itself something mental. Second, any mental procedure by which someone might try to undermine the certainty of his own mentality would only serve to reinforce it, since he would become conscious of the very procedure. Thus if I manage to doubt that I am a mental subject, I become conscious of doubting and hence conscious of engaging in a mental activity. (Along with (iv) itself, these two considerations, of course, featured prominently in Descartes's famous argument in the Second Meditation.)

These points clearly pose very powerful objections to the nihilist position, and, as far as I can see, there is only one way in which the nihilist could try to meet them. This would be by likening our situation to that of an artificial-intelligence (AI) machine. Such a machine, we can plausibly assume, does not have a genuine mind: it is just a complex physical gadget with no more claim to mentality than a washing-machine or a car.

But, unlike these latter gadgets, it does possess, if I may put it thus, the *functional analogue* of a mind, in that it does things which it is normally the distinctive function of mentality to do. For example, a chess-playing machine, though not literally endowed with intelligence, performs operations which functionally simulate some of the thought-processes of a chess-player – processes such as evaluating the merits of a position, calculating the consequences of taking a piece, and looking for a way of avoiding checkmate. Or again, a robot whose behavioural output is appropriately sensitive to its photic input may, though without the aid of perceptual experiences, functionally simulate some of the aspects of pattern-recognition in us. The functional simulation in such cases can be so striking that, when we observe the machines in action, it requires some effort not to think of them as mentally endowed. Thus while I am playing chess against my computer, I tend to think of it as a real opponent, which is pitting its chess wits against mine – though, of course, such thoughts evaporate as soon as I start to reflect on the situation in a more detached way.

Now the nihilist might argue that, in general terms, our situation is like that of these machines: what we possess are not genuine minds, but their functional analogues – analogues which are so elaborate and so perfect as to make our ordinary assent to the mentalistic theory almost inevitable. He could then try to defuse the specific objections we brought against his position by insisting that, in each case, all that the considerations establish is something for which our endowment with this analogue-mentality would be sufficient. Thus, in response to point (i), he could say that, in raising the issue of nihilism (or any other issue), what we presuppose is not that we have a genuine capacity for thought, but that we have a capacity to perform 'information-processing' operations which (whether genuinely intellectual or not) exemplify the functional character of thought. And, in response to points (ii) and (iii), he could likewise insist that what language-meaning requires in the language-user is not genuine understanding, but something which will play the same functional role. He could even pursue this line in response to points (iv) and (v), by arguing that what I have represented as our direct consciousness of our own mentality is no different in general character from the capacity of certain AI machines to monitor and report on their mind-simulative states and processes. The only twist here would be that we have become conditioned to 'misinterpret' (i.e. to do the functional analogue of misinterpreting) our own self-monitoring operations as the genuinely mental monitoring of genuinely mental states – though that too, if the nihilist is right, could in principle be built into a machine.

This, it seems to me, is the only way in which the nihilist could try to defend his position against the objections. But a little reflection shows that it is unsuccessful. In so far as there is any plausibility in the suggestion that our situation is like that of the AI machines, this stems from the fact that, to capture their functional significance in a form that is both succinct and, in relation to our interests, salient, we tend to describe their states and processes in psychological terms. Thus we speak of the machines as processing information, as making calculations, as drawing inferences, as analysing positions, as monitoring their own states, and so on – all descriptions which imply mentality. But, of course, from the standpoint of the nihilist, as indeed from that of common sense, these psychological descriptions are merely metaphorical: a literal specification of what is going on would have to be couched in purely functional or physical terms, without any hint of the presence of mentality or anything akin to it. But when we describe the machines in these terms, with the understanding that anything else would be merely figurative, the suggestion that the nihilist could diffuse the objections in the way envisaged is seen to be clearly misconceived. Thus there is no temptation to think that what we are presupposing, by raising the issue of nihilism (or any other issue), is merely our capacity to perform the relevant functional operations, without any real thought. Nor is there any temptation to suppose that what we ordinarily take to be the direct consciousness of our own mental states is nothing more than the functional self-monitoring capacity of a biological machine, without any real mentality as the monitored input or any real awareness as the output. In effect, then, the nihilist's line of defence is exposed as fraudulent. In trying to persuade us that we are like the machines, he is tacitly exploiting our tendency to describe their states and processes in psychological terms – our tendency, as it were, to project our own psychology on to them. But his purpose in pressing this comparison is to try to establish that, like them, we are wholly mindless. Clearly, the nihilist cannot have it both ways.

It seems to me, then, that the nihilist has no adequate defence against the objections posed, and from now on I shall assume that his position has been refuted and that claim [1] of the dualist thesis is correct. However, there are three further (and quasi-concessionary) points which need to be made in connection with this.

First, in rejecting mental nihilism, we are not excluding the possibility of applying the nihilist approach to some specific category (or set of categories) of mental phenomena, in the way envisaged earlier.[3] Thus the recognition of a mental realm would still leave us free to deny the existence of (say) visual experiences, or desires, or decisions. Admittedly, given our reasons for rejecting the full-blooded nihilist position, the prospects for some kind of concession towards it seem rather poor. Points (i) and (ii) presumably establish the reality of intellectual states and activities, such as thoughts, beliefs, and judgments; and, once these have been accepted, it would be hard to withhold recognition from other forms of propositional (or quasi-propositional) attitude and act, like desires, intentions, and decisions. On the other hand, if the nihilism is directed onto the sensory aspects of mentality, the conflict with our introspective consciousness becomes particularly acute. How, for example, could I take seriously the suggestion that I do not really have sensations of pain or visual experiences and that my apparent consciousness of so doing is an illusion? However, at this stage, it is not necessary to reach a final verdict on these points. We can work on the provisional assumption that we should acknowledge the full range of mental phenomena, without ruling out the possibility that some subsequent argument may show the need to modify this position.

Second, in assuming the reality of the mental realm, we are not assuming its status as something conceptually and metaphysically fundamental. We are not ruling out the possibility that mentality may be reducible to something else – that the conceptually basic description of how things stand in the metaphysically basic reality may be wholly non-mentalistic. This, of course, could have a crucial bearing on how we view our situation in relation to the AI machines. In the discussion above, we rejected the nihilist's comparison and insisted that those states and activities in ourselves which we ordinarily characterize as mental are quite different in character from the functionally similar states and processes which we find in the machines. But, in this context, we were taking it for granted (in company with the nihilist) that the machines do not have minds and that the relevant states and processes which occur in them are not genuinely mental. If we could accept a reductive account of mentality, and in particular a functionalist account, the situation would be quite different. For we could then acknowledge our similarity to the machines without having to abandon our own claims to mentality. We could accept that both we and they are mental subjects, and that, in each case, a subject's mental endowments are wholly the product of his functional organization as a physical system. I am not suggesting that this would be a plausible view. My point is only that, along with other reductive accounts of mentality, it is not something which our rejection of nihilism has excluded.

Third, in assuming the reality of mental phenomena, we are not assuming that our ordinary conception of their psychological nature and our ordinary beliefs about the principles of their organization (both in relation to one another and in relation to the physical world) are entirely correct. In particular, we are leaving room for some degree of conceptual and theoretical development from 'folk-psychology' to 'cognitive science'. Curiously, this point is not always recognized. For the impression is sometimes given that one can make significant progress towards the nihilist position merely by pointing out respects in which, allegedly, folk-psychology is unsatisfactory – for example, respects in which it generates irresolvable conflicts over how certain types of mental situation are to be described, or respects in which it leaves the psychological facts to some degree indeterminate.[4] But, of course, these putative deficiencies in folk-psychology do nothing to impugn the reality of the mental realm which it is trying to characterize. To suppose that they do is as crazy as supposing that, by exposing the faults of classical mechanics, modern science has brought us nearer to a nihilist view of the physical world. This is not to say that a belief in the mental realm could survive a *total* abandonment of our ordinary ways of characterizing it – the term 'mental' would obviously lose all meaning if we *entirely* severed it from our existing theories. But the sort of (alleged) deficiencies which here concern us (deficiencies which show up within the perspective of folk-psychology itself) do not, and never could, call for a total abandonment of our common-sense outlook. At most they call for some revision within a conceptual and theoretical frame-work whose broad structure remains intact.

To be fair to him, this is not the main line of argument by which the nihilist tries to establish his position. His main point, as we envisaged at the outset, is that nihilism is the logical consequence of his materialist metaphysic (which he thinks can be independently vindicated), together with the impossibility (as he sees it) of giving an adequate account of mentality in materialist terms. As yet, I have not tried to deal with this line of argument *directly*. I have been content to refute the conclusion, leaving it for subsequent investigation to reveal where the premises have gone astray. Needless to say (since my aim is to establish the dualist position), my own arguments here will be directed against the materialist thesis and the various ways in which its advocates have sought to defend it.

3 THE NATURE OF ANALYTICAL REDUCTIONISM

Having established the reality of the mental realm, we must now turn our attention to the dualist's second claim, which characterizes this realm as fundamental and which stands in opposition to mental reductionism. The issues here will require a much longer discussion than those concerned with nihilism, partly because there are several importantly different reduc-tionist theories to be considered.

As we have seen, mental reductionism comes in two forms, and both are excluded by claim [2]. On the one hand, there is an *analytical* form, which applies at the level of concepts and meaning. Here the reductionist asserts that the content of statements about the mind turns out, on conceptual analysis, to be non-mentalistic. On the other hand, there is a *metaphysical* form, which applies at the level of facts or states of affairs. Here the reductionist concedes that psychological concepts and statements are irreducibly mentalistic, but insists that mental facts are wholly constituted by non-mental facts. For the time being, I am going to focus exclusively on mental reductionism in its analytical form. I shall also, for the present, ignore the possibility of a reductionism which is *scope-restricted*, only covering statements about *certain kinds* of mental phenomena. I shall assume that the reductionist wants to apply his reductive analysis to *all* psychological concepts, in a way that eliminates the mentalistic content of *all* psychological statements.

We must start by trying to get clearer about the nature of the analytical reductionist's thesis. What exactly does the reductionist mean when he says that the content of statements about the mind turns out, on conceptual analysis, to be non-mentalistic? In what sense does he think that such statements are amenable to a non-mentalistic analysis? It would be natural to represent him as making two claims. The first is that, given any psychological statement *S*, formulated in ordinary mentalistic terms, there is a way of reformulating *S* by a sentence which does not contain any psychological vocabulary, or in any other way presuppose our possession of psychological concepts. The second is that, in each such case, this non-mentalistic reformulation reveals the true propositional content of *S* – makes clear what *S* is really stating, shows us how *S* is to be ultimately construed – in the same way in which, for example, though in these cases quite trivially, 'John is an unmarried (and never previously married) male human adult' makes clear the propositional content of 'John is a bachelor', and 'Henry is the father of a parent' makes clear the propositional content of 'Henry is a grandfather'. In other words, it would be natural to represent the reductionist as proposing, or envisaging the provision of, a method of systematically translating psychological into non-psychological sentences, whereby each proposition expressed by a psychological sentence gets re-expressed, and expressed more perspicuously, by the non-psychological sentence which translates it. The availability of these translations would have the effect of making the psychological language, and the conceptual scheme which it embodies, descriptively redundant: the language could still be usefully retained for the purposes of concision and emphasis, but everything we can say by means of it we would be equipped to say, and say more overtly, in a non-mentalistic way.[5]

I have said that it would be natural to construe the reduction-ist's thesis in this way; and perhaps on the *strictest* inter-pretation of the notion of reductive analysis, this is how we are forced to construe it. However, I want to interpret this notion in a slightly looser fashion, to give the reductionist a little more flexibility in the way he develops his position. The point of allowing him this greater flexibility is that we can envisage circumstances in which it would be legitimate to think of the content of psychological statements as ultimately non-mentalistic, even though there was no way, or at least no relevantly perspicuous way, of exactly reformulating them in non-psychological terms. There are two aspects to this, which I shall consider in turn.

When I speak of the 'reformulation' of a psychological statement in non-psychological terms, I mean, of course, a reformulation of finite length – something which could in principle be fully written out, a sentence with a beginning and an end and a finite internal complexity. I am also assuming this finiteness to be, as it were, *genuine* – i.e. not something which is achieved merely by trivial abbreviation, where what is in effect an infinite expression occurs in stenographic disguise. Now it may be that we cannot describe something as a *sentence* unless it is finite in this way. But let us use the term 'sentential complex' to cover any series of words or symbols which is either a sentence or is something which only fails to be a sentence through its lack of finiteness. For example, even if it does not count as a sentence, an infinite conjunction or disjunction of sentences will qualify as a sentential complex in this sense. Now envisage the following situation:

1 S is a statement about the mind formulated in the psycho-logical language by the finite sentence A. (For example, S might be the statement that Bill is in pain at time t, and A the sentence 'Bill is in pain at time t'.)
2 Outside the psychological language, there is no (genuine-ly) finite sentence which expresses the same proposition as A and which could thus be used to reformulate S in non-psychological terms.
3 There is, however, in some appropriate non-psychological language, an infinite sentential complex B which expresses the same proposition as A.

4 Despite its non-finiteness, it is *B* which expresses the relevant proposition in its fully analysed form and which reveals how *S* itself is to be construed.[6]

If such a situation obtained, there would be a perfectly good sense in which, though not finitely expressible in any but mentalistic terms, the content of *S* would turn out, on conceptual analysis, to be non-mentalistic. So, in this respect, it is appropriate to allow the analytical reductionist a greater flexibility than we initially envisaged. It is appropriate to allow him the option of saying that, in the case of at least some (and perhaps all) psychological statements, the linguistic items which make explicit their ultimately non-mentalistic content are of infinite length, thus showing that the content itself, in its fully analysed form, is of infinite complexity.

The second respect in which we ought to give the reductionist greater flexibility concerns the phenomenon of vagueness. It often happens, quite independently of any issue of reduction, that the content of an ordinary-language statement is vague in relation to the factors on which its truth or falsity ultimately depends. For example, if I say that Smith is bald, the truth or falsity of my statement depends entirely on the amount of hair on Smith's head; but there is no exact amount which constitutes the definite maximum which Smith could possess while qualifying as bald, nor an exact amount which constitutes the definite minimum he could possess while qualifying as non-bald. In other words, between the definite cases of baldness and the definite cases of non-baldness, there is a range of 'borderline' cases whose classification is indeterminate – cases which would make my statement both arguably (but not definitely) true and arguably (but not definitely) false. Other examples of the same phenomenon are the statement that Smith is *tall* (which is vague in respect of height), the statement that *many* people witnessed the accident (which is vague in respect of number), and the statement that the figure is *roughly circular* (which is vague in respect of shape).

Now all these are cases of what we might call *overt* vagueness – vagueness which is apparent in the manifest content of the statements prior to any deep analysis. And, of course, we can construct such cases for any kind of subject-matter simply by employing the appropriately vague terms. However, the relevant point for our present discussion is that, from the standpoint of the analytical reductionist, psychological statements could turn out to have an additional and *covert* vagueness in relation to the non-mentalistic factors which they ultimately concern. That is, it might turn out that, in the case of certain psychological statements which are precise in their own mentalistic framework, we can, for each, envisage a range of non-mentalistically specified situations which, while including all the factors on which its truth-value conceptually depends, do not render the statement either definitely true or definitely false. And if things do turn out this way, there may be no method of exactly reformulating the relevant statements in non-psychological terms. I only say that there *may* be no method, because the fact of covert vagueness would not *automatically* preclude exact reformulation. After all, it may be possible to find non-mentalistic equivalents which exhibit the same vagueness overtly. But the point I want to stress is that we cannot presume that this will be so. We cannot presume that, if psychological statements are vague in relation to the relevant non-mentalistic factors, there will be a way of exactly reproducing this vagueness in a non-mentalistic form.

Here too, then, we should allow the analytical reductionist the appropriate room for manoeuvre. In claiming that the content of psychological statements turns out, on analysis, to be non-mentalistic, the reductionist is committed to claiming that their truth or falsity entirely depends on the relevant non-mentalistically specifiable facts and that each statement is to be ultimately construed in terms of the details of this dependence relative to the whole range of possible non-mentalistically specified situations. But we should allow him the freedom to say that there are possible situations for which a given and not overtly-vague psychological statement has no definite truth-value – situations for which it would be both arguably true and arguably false – and that this covert vagueness prevents the statement's reformulation by any sentence in the non-mentalistic language.

In both these ways, then, I shall allow the reductionist the option of developing his reductive analysis in a non-translational fashion – the option of saying that, because the analysis brings to light either an infinite complexity or a vagueness in the content of (certain) psychological statements, there is no full and exact reformulation of them in non-psychological terms. Of course, if, for either reason, the reductionist avails himself of this option, there is a sense in which his position will be reductively weaker than the translational position we first envisaged. For it will involve acknowledging that the psychological language has a descriptive role which cannot be taken over by anything else – that there are things which we can say by means of it which we cannot say in any other way. In other words, although a form of analytical reductionism, his position will involve conceding to the psychological language, and the system of mentalistic concepts expressible in it, a certain sort of transcendence relative to the rest of our conceptual scheme.

There is one final preliminary point to be made before we begin our evolution of analytical reductionism. We have just seen that, even in its most comprehensive form, where it covers the totality of psychological statements, a non-mentalistic analysis can be thought of as more strongly or more weakly reductive, depending on whether or not it is translational. However, quite independently of this distinction, there is a further respect in which a proposed reduction can be thought of as weaker or stronger. This further distinction turns on the question of whether the non-mentalistic analysis preserves or alters the ontological perspective of our ordinary mentalistic thought. Where it alters this perspective, or, more precisely, to the extent that it alters it, the analysis can be thought of as more strongly reductive in virtue of being more radical – in virtue of creating a greater disparity or contrast between our initial understanding of psychological statements and the way they are to be ultimately construed. But before we can appreciate exactly what is at issue here, we need to say something about our ordinary mentalistic ontology.

Apart from time-entities (moments and periods), there are two kinds of things which we ordinarily think of as featuring in the ontology of the mental realm. On the one hand, there are those entities which form the concrete ingredients of the mind, the particular episodes and instances of mentality; in other words, such things as sensations, perceptual experiences, episodes of thought, decisions, instances of belief or desire, and surges of emotion. I shall call all these, generically, 'mental items'. On the other hand, there are those entities in whose minds these mental items occur – the things which can be said to have experiences, to engage in thought, to take decisions, to hold beliefs, to undergo emotions, and so on. I shall call these entities 'mental subjects'. Corresponding to this distinction, there is also, of course, an analogous distinction between two categories of mental properties – between those properties, like *being a pain* and *being a thought of Vienna*, which apply to items, and those properties, like *being in pain* and *thinking about Vienna*, which apply to subjects. If we ever need labels for these, we could refer to them as 'item-properties' and 'subject-properties'.

Now, whatever the theoretical possibilities, it is clear that any remotely plausible reductive analysis of our ordinary mentalistic thought – any analysis which the reductionist might feel tempted to endorse – will preserve, in some appropriately non-mentalistically characterized form, the ontology of mental subjects. Thus, if the reductionist is focusing on (say) the statement that Bill is in pain, he will look for an analysis which, while eliminating (analysing away) the concept of pain, preserves the reference to Bill – though, of course, as something (presumably a certain kind of biological organism) whose whole nature can be specified in non-mentalistic terms. So, assuming that the analysis is translational, the statement will get reformulated by some sentence of the form 'Bill (this non-mentalistically specifiable object) ...', where what fills the blank is some (possibly very complex) non-mentalistic predicate-expression. However, in the case of the ontology of mental items, the reductionist has a choice between two quite different approaches. On the one hand, he can pursue a reductive strategy which preserves this ontology – which leaves these entities as things which we can refer to, and quantify over, in the conceptually fundamental perspective. On the other hand, he can pursue a strategy which analyses this ontology away, so that any mental-item references or quantifications in our ordinary psychological assertions disappear when the content of these assertions is represented in its fully analysed form. When the first approach is adopted, I shall speak of the analysis as 'item-conservative'; and when the second, I shall speak of it as 'item-eliminative'. Here too it must be stressed that, even where the analysis is item-conservative, the ontology is not conserved in a mentalistic form. Thus just as the reductionist will offer a non-mentalistic account of Bill, so likewise, if his analysis conserves it at all, he will take Bill's pain to be something whose mental character is to be ultimately specified in non-psychological terms. In practice, item-conservative reductionists almost invariably identify mental items with items in the brain and take their intrinsic natures to be purely physical.

There is more that one could say, in abstract, about the distinction between the item-conservative and item-eliminative approaches. But it is probably best at this point to start looking at the whole issue of analytical reductionism in a more concrete way – to start considering the specific reductive theories which philosophers have advanced and the ways they can be attacked or defended. The distinction itself will re-emerge very sharply and clearly in this context. For it turns out that the two major reductive theories of this century, behaviourism and function-alism, differ precisely in this respect – the former proposing a reduction which eliminates the ontology of mental items, the latter proposing a reduction which preserves it.

4 ANALYTICAL BEHAVIOURISM

The simplest and most familiar version of analytical reduc-tionism is that advanced by the behaviourist. The thesis here is that statements about the mind are to be ultimately construed in purely behavioural terms; more precisely, that each state-ment which ascribes a mental state or activity to a human or animal subject turns out, on conceptual analysis, to be a statement about that subject's behavioural condition. This doctrine was quite fashionable in the first half of the twentieth century, mainly owing to the influence of logical positivism. Its advocates have included such distinguished philosophers as Rudolf Carnap, Carl Hempel, and Gilbert Ryle.[7] *Analytical* behaviourism is not to be confused with the *methodological* behaviourism espoused by a certain school of empirical psychology.[8] Methodological behaviourists make no claims about how psychological concepts are to be analysed, but insist that animal and human behaviour is best explained in purely stimulus-response terms (i.e. by establishing laws which directly link sensory input with behavioural output, without reference to any internal states which intervene).

At first sight, it might seem just absurd to claim that

statements about a subject's mentality are to be construed as statements about his behavioural condition. For it is surely uncontroversial that someone can be in a certain mental state without behaviourally manifesting it; for example, someone might be thinking about his holiday without doing anything which reveals the content of his thought or which even reveals that he is thinking at all. However, the behaviourist intends the notion of a behavioural condition to be interpreted in a broad sense. In particular, he intends it to cover not only the subject's actual behaviour (for example, the fact that he is uttering certain sounds or moving his limbs in a certain fashion), but also his behavioural dispositions – for example, the fact that he is currently disposed to make a certain kind of utterance or movement in response to a certain (perhaps not currently realized) kind of physical circumstance. So the fact that mental states can occur without being behaviourally manifested does not automatically rule out a behaviourist construal of the statements ascribing them. Moreover, the relevant notion of a behavioural disposition is itself a broad one. It covers not only dispositions to behave in certain ways in certain kinds of circumstance (what we might label 'first-order' dispositions), but also dispositions to acquire behavioural dispositions ('higher-order' dispositions). And, as well as covering dispositions whose operation is conditional on physical cirumstances in the ordinary sense, it also covers ones whose operation is conditional, or partly conditional, on the obtaining of other kinds of behavioural disposition. So in trying to spell out the content of a psychological statement in behavioural terms, there is a great deal that the behaviourist can draw on in addition to claims about the subject's actual behaviour.

Even so, the prospects for a successful behaviourist analysis are likely to strike us as exceedingly poor. For, irrespective of how such an analysis might be developed, it just seems wrong in principle to suppose that what we mean when we ascribe mental states to people or animals (or what our ascriptive statements mean) could be captured in purely behavioural terms. The difficulties for the behaviourist are especially conspicuous in the case of those mental states which involve some form of conscious experience and whose essential natures seem to be wholly or partly revealed to the subject himself through introspective (self-conscious) awareness. How, for example, taking account of what they feel like from the inside, could we seriously suppose that pain or visual experience or surges of anger are reducible to forms of behaviour and behavioural disposition? Maybe in ascribing such states to someone we are implying things about his behavioural condition. But it seems quite clear that this is not all we are implying. It seems quite clear that we are, in addition, and indeed primarily, saying something about the subject's 'internal' condition – a condition which is causally prior to his behaviour and behavioural dispositions, and of which such behaviour and dispositions are merely the overt symptoms. And this also seems to be the right account of our ascriptions of non-experiential mental states, like beliefs and intentions, even if our intuitions against the behaviourist in this area are not quite so strong.

Since analytical behaviourism is intuitively so implausible, it may be wondered how anyone could have come to accept it. What has persuaded certain philosophers to claim, presumably contrary to their own initial intuitions, that psychological statements are to be construed in purely behavioural terms? The answer may vary in detail from one philosopher to another, but almost invariably the behaviourist's position can be seen as resting on two main contentions. The first contention is that psychological statements depend for their significance, or intelligibility, on there being some adequate procedure for establishing their truth or falsity from a third-person standpoint. The second is that such a procedure is only available because the subject-matter of the statements turns out, on analysis, to be purely behavioural. The basic idea behind the first contention is that, given any mental state, the only way in which one can form a conception of what it is for that state to be realized is in terms of the evidential methods which would enable one to determine its presence or absence in someone else. The basic idea behind the second is that unless psychological statements can be ultimately construed in purely behavioural terms, the presence or absence of a mental state in someone else becomes undetectable: a subject's mental condition becomes something epistemologically 'private', of which other subjects, only having access to his *physical* properties and cirumstances, can have no knowledge.

The claim that, without a behaviourist analysis, the mentality of other subjects would become undetectable is likely to strike us as too strong. For even when we reject behaviourism, it is still very natural to suppose that information about a subject's behavioural condition typically provides good evidence about the nature of his mental life. Without a behaviourist analysis, the steps of inference from this evidence to the psychological conclusions will not be deductive: it will not be a matter of knowing *a priori* that whenever such-and-such behavioural facts obtain the subject is in such-and-such a mental state. And it may follow from this that we cannot establish these conclusions with absolute certainty. But it still seems that, partly by extrapolating from what we know about ourselves and partly by seeing what is required for a satisfactory explanation of other people's behaviour, we can accept the conclusions on a rational basis. Thus, on the one hand, it seems that, in default of any evidence to the contrary, each subject can reasonably assume that the kind of psychophysical system which he knows to obtain in his own case also obtains, in broad outline, in the case of other organisms with substantially the same biological character and behavioural practices. And, on the other hand, taking account of the fact that, typically, the behaviour of other people is systematically *as if* it were in the control of some complex mentality (and perhaps the best example to focus on here is the case of linguistic behaviour), it seems reasonable to conclude, by way of explanation, that it actually is. Put thus briefly, of course, these points are not decisive: further reflection might reveal that neither analogical reasoning nor inference to the best explanation provides an adequate foundation for third-person psychological ascriptions. But if they are not adequate for this purpose, the case against them needs to be made out.

However, there is a sense in which none of this will have much bearing on the real issue. For even if, considered as it were in isolation, the forms of reasoning we have just envisaged might serve to justify our ascriptions of mental states to others, they could not be offered as a way of securing the intelligibility of psychological statements under the verificationist criterion imposed by the behaviourist's first contention. The reason for this is simply that both the analogical and the explanatory methods of inference presuppose that the psychological conclusions to which they lead can be independently understood. Thus it is only because we already have a conception of what it would be for someone else to be in pain, or to be working out a problem, or to hold a certain belief, that we can even raise the question of whether it is legitimate to ascribe such states or activities to him by either of the envisaged methods. And consequently, we cannot see these ways of trying to justify the ascriptions as supplying the basis of their intelligibility. In short, if the behaviourist is correct in claiming that the intelligibility of psychological statements depends on the availability of a procedure for establishing their truth or falsity from a third-person standpoint, then the relevant procedure (assuming that there is one) must be of a quite different kind – one which could be coherently represented as that on which our very conception of the mental is ultimately founded. And the behaviourist's point would then be that it is the verificational procedure resulting from the behaviourist analysis which, and which uniquely, meets this requirement.

Assuming that this last point is right, it is on the status of the behaviourist's first contention, then, that the issue primarily turns. However, it is just in this area, it seems to me, that his argument is at its most vulnerable. It is vulnerable in two respects, as I shall now explain.

The behaviourist is claiming that the intelligibility of psychological statements depends on the availability of a procedure for establishing their truth or falsity from a third-person standpoint – a procedure by which, in favourable cirumstances, one subject can determine whether another subject is or is not in a certain mental state. Moreover, since he is offering this as a vindication of his behaviourist analysis, he must be claiming that psychological statements derive their *whole* significance from this source – that our ability to understand such statements is *entirely* derived from a grasp of the verificational procedures governing the ascription of mental states to others. Now one difficulty with this is that there seems to be no reason to restrict the basis of our understanding to what is available to us in a *third-person perspective*. For why should we not be able to derive this understanding, at least in part, from what we know of the nature of mentality 'from the inside' – from the direct, introspective awareness of our own mental condition? And why should we not be able to use what is revealed to us in this first-person perspective as a route to the understanding of third-person ascriptions, independently of their method of verification? Here again, the point against the behaviourist is especially clear in the case of the *experiential* mental states. Take, for example, the case of pain. It is surely very plausible to say that my basic conception of pain is derived from my introspective knowledge of what it is like to be in pain myself, and that this introspective conception gives me a way of grasping what it would be for someone else to be in pain, irrespective of whether I have any adequate verificational procedure for third-person pain-ascriptions. Admittedly, in learning that this type of sensation is called 'pain', and maybe even in becoming adept at distinguishing it from other types of sensation, I have been assisted by the other-ascriptive practice – by the fact that others have pronounced me to be in pain when they have observed me exhibiting the appropriate behaviour. But this does not affect the point that, if I want to make clear to myself what pain is, or what I mean by the term 'pain', I always, in the end, fall back on some imaginative rehearsal of what it feels like to have this sensation, rather than on the behavioural criteria for its ascription. Wittgenstein, of course, has argued that such imaginative rehearsals are idle, since, with no public checks on the accuracy of my memory, I cannot tell whether the type of sensation which I now refer to as 'pain' is the same as that which I have previously used the term to signify.[9] But the fact that I can show my memory to be reliable in other (publicly testable) areas surely gives me good reason to trust it in the sphere of my own experience too. And even if my usage of the term *has* changed, this does not alter the fact that my present conception of pain is what it is and seems to be introspectively framed in the way envisaged.

As I have said, this difficulty in the behaviourist's argument is especially clear in the case of the experiential states, of which pain is one example. The reason why it is less clear in the case of other mental states, for example states like belief and intention, is that these seem much less amenable to an introspective conception. It is true that someone who holds a belief or has an intention can be directly aware of this aspect of his mental condition: he does not need the behavioural evidence which another person would need in ascribing the state to him. But it is much less plausible to claim, in analogy with the case of the experiential states, that he can derive his conception of the nature of belief and intention from (or partly from) what this introspective awareness reveals. Rather, it seems that this awareness is no more than the conscious exercise of a special kind of non-inferential factual knowledge – a knowledge which is only available because the subject already has, independently, a conception of the mental state whose presence it records. And if this is so, then the behaviourist could still insist that it is from something discernible in third-person perspective that this conception is derived.

However, and this is the second respect in which the behaviourist's argument is vulnerable, even if our conception of such states as belief and intention is formed in a third-person perspective, there is still no reason to claim that it is formed, whether explicitly or implicitly, in a verificationist way. It may well be that our conception of these states does depend, in part, on some a priori recognition of the difference which their realization makes to how it is rationally appropriate for the subject to behave – for example, the recognition that a subject's intention to achieve a certain goal, together with his belief that he can only achieve it by performing a certain action, makes it rational for him to perform that action. And if this is so, then, in so far as the realization of these states requires a framework of rationality, our conception of them implicitly involves an a priori recognition of their likely influence on the subject's behaviour, assuming that he is equipped with a behavioural system and has the capacity to adjust its output in response to his mental condition. But none of this lends any support to the verificationist approach of the behaviourist. It provides no reason for supposing that we derive our conception of such states from a grasp of the method by which we can determine their presence or absence in another subject. Indeed, since the most it yields, epistemologically, is a method of inference from psychological premises to behavioural conclusions (and then only on the assumption that the subject has the appropriate behavioural endowments), it leaves each of us free to be wholly sceptical about our capacity for third-person verification: it leaves each of us free to say that other human beings do not have minds at all, despite the fact that they systematically behave in ways which are amenable to psychological interpretation. The only way that the behaviourist could try to justify his verificationist approach in this area would be by appealing to some quite general verificationist doctrine of meaning – a doctrine which requires the meaning of any factual statement to consist in its method of verification. But I know of no good argument in favour of such a doctrine; and its consequences (not only in the area of mind) are very implausible. These are matters which I have dealt with in detail elsewhere, and, rather than go over the same points again, I simply refer the reader to that discussion.[10]

5 THE PROBLEM OF CONTEXT-DEPENDENCE

We have seen that analytical behaviourism is intuitively implausible: intuitively, it seems clear that when we ascribe a mental state to someone, we are not saying, or at least not just saying, something about his behaviour and behavioural dispositions, but are rather, or additionally, saying something about an 'internal' and causally prior condition, of which his behaviour and behavioural dispositions are merely the overt symptoms. I want now to raise a second problem for the behaviourist. This further problem is more complicated than the first: its formulation will require us to look much more closely at the mechanics of behaviouristic analysis. But in one respect the two problems are intimately connected: both, in their different ways, draw attention to a basic fault in the behaviourist's approach, which the analytical reductionist will need to correct if he is to have any chance of producing a viable account. But more on this later.

Whatever we ultimately take mental states to be, there is no denying that typically, for a given state, the way in which its realization affects the subject's behavioural condition depends, in part, on the larger mental context in which it is embedded. Take the case of desire. If someone wants something, then, other things being equal, he will try to achieve it. But whether other things are relevantly equal will depend on other aspects of his mental condition – for example, on whether he has other desires which demand more immediate attention. And more importantly, even assuming that the subject is trying to implement the desire, what actions he takes will depend crucially on his relevant beliefs: if he wants food, for example, then what he does to obtain it will depend on such things as where he thinks it is available, how he can get there, whether he will need money, and so on. The dependence of the behavioural consequences on the larger mental context is even more conspicuous in the case of belief. Clearly, a subject's beliefs affect his behaviour and behavioural dispositions; but each belief has the potential to affect the behavioural condition in an infinite number of ways according to the other beliefs and motivational states with which it is conjoined. Thus the belief that it is 5 o'clock can prompt someone to stop working, to start working, to put on the kettle, to make a phone call, to alter his watch, to say 'It's 5 o'clock', to say 'It's 6 o'clock', or to do any of an infinity of other things, depending on his desires and other beliefs. Now all this creates a problem for the analytical behaviourist. He is claiming that each statement about the mind is to be ultimately construed in purely behavioural, and *a fortiori* wholly non-mentalistic, terms – construed as a statement exclusively about the subject's behavioural condition and in a form not involving any psychological concepts. But how can the behaviourist achieve such a construal if the behavioural consequences of a mental state depend on the mental context in which it is embedded? How can he avoid the use of psychological concepts, if any specification of the behavioural significance of a given mental state has to take account of the way in which its behavioural role is affected by the presence or absence of other mental states? It seems that any attempt at a behavioural analysis will get vitiated by a kind of regress or circularity, whereby the behaviourist can only deal with one mental state by taking a range of others (those which figure in the specification of its context-dependence) for granted. Let us refer to this as the 'problem of context-dependence'.[11]

The problem can be illustrated by a simple example. Suppose that Smith, who is out walking, wants to head due north. How can the behaviourist construe this situation, or, more precisely, construe the relevant want-descriptive statement, in purely behavioural terms? The construal cannot be of the form:

(1) For that direction D which is due north from Smith, Smith is disposed to walk D-wards

for this takes no account of the way in which Smith's behavioural response to his want is affected by his beliefs about how it can be fulfilled. Thus statement (1) would turn out to be false if Smith were mistaken about which direction was north or had not yet reached a conclusion about the matter. Presumably, then, the behaviourist will have to start with some construal which makes explicit allowance for the dependence of the behavioural outcome on the wider mental context. For example, he might start with something along the lines of:

(2) For any direction D from Smith, if Smith were to believe that D (demonstatively identified) was due north, he would be disposed to walk D-wards.[12]

Or perhaps he would start with (2), together with some additional clause to indicate that Smith would try to identify the northerly direction if he were uncertain as to which it was. But, of course, nothing along these lines could serve as the behaviourist's ultimate construal, since it employs psychological concepts. At best, it would be merely a step towards the ultimate construal, to be supplemented by a further stage of analysis in which the mentalistic clause or clauses were themselves re-expressed in purely behavioural terms.

Let us see, then, how the behaviourist might try to handle this further stage. For simplicity, we shall assume that he has adopted (2) as his provisional construal, so that he is now looking for a way of spelling out in behavioural terms what is meant by saying, of any given direction, that it is the one which Smith believes to be due north. But clearly the problem which beset the first stage recurs here, and in exacerbated form. For just as the behavioural consequences of the want vary with relevant variations in the subject's accompanying beliefs, so also, and more extensively, the behavioural consequences of any of the relevant beliefs vary with variations in the subject's wants and other beliefs. And so, in trying to spell out the meaning of 'Smith believes D to be due north', he will find himself falling back on sentences of the form:

(3) If Smith were to have, additionally, such and such other mental states, he would be behaviourally disposed in such and such ways

and thus he will find himself relying on a further range of

psychological concepts whose behavioural analyses have still to be supplied. But now it is clear that, if it is structured in this way, the analytical process will be unending, and indeed, until it starts to turn back on itself, ever-widening. The behaviourist will never be able to reach an ultimate construal of the original want-statement, since each time he turns his attention to a given mental state which he has so far taken for granted, he is forced to take other mental states for granted in specifying its behavioural significance.

There is only one way in which the behaviourist could try to avoid this problem. When I spoke of 'mental states' in the discussion above, I was primarily thinking of relatively simple states, like having a certain kind of sensation, holding a certain belief, and wanting to achieve a certain goal. Now if he is to have any chance of avoiding the problem of context-dependence, the behaviourist must start by focusing his attention on mental states of a quite different sort – states which I shall refer to as 'total mental conditions'. By a 'total mental condition' I mean something which, necessarily, whenever it is realized, is realized as the complete psychological state of a particular subject at a particular time – a state which includes every aspect of that subject's mentality at that time. Typically, such total conditions will be much more complex than the mental states we were considering earlier; indeed, most of the latter states *could only* be realized in conjunction with other states. But the crucial point is that, whatever its degree of complexity, each total condition is, by definition, incapable of occurring in any larger mental context: each is associated with a set of mental states in such a way that someone qualifies as being in that condition if and only if he is in those states *alone*.

It is this which might offer the behaviourist a way of escape. For if total mental conditions cannot occur in larger mental contexts, then he could hope to spell out the behavioural significance of each without reference to other mental states. And once he had construed the total conditions in purely behavioural terms, he could then provide a purely behavioural construal of each simple mental state by representing it as the disjunction of the total conditions in which it features. Thus, for the example above, we can envisage the behaviourist offering, as the final construal of Smith's want state, something of the form:

43

(4) Either Smith is behaviourally disposed B_1-wise or Smith is behaviourally disposed B_2-wise or Smith is behaviourally disposed B_3-wise or ...

where each disjunct provides the behavioural specification of one of the total mental conditions in which a want of the relevant kind (wanting to walk due north) could occur. Since there are infinitely many total conditions containing such a want (both because there are infinitely many types of mental state and because there is no limit on the complexity of total conditions), (4) will contain infinitely many disjuncts. But, for reasons which we have already made clear (in section 3), this infinite complexity does not as such vitiate the analysis.

Even so, the proposal is unsatisfactory. For while it avoids the problem of context-dependence, it does so by, as it were, sweeping this problem under the carpet, rather than by dealing with the factors from which it arose. It offers a construal of mentality in purely behavioural terms, but only by ignoring the phenomenon of mental complexity in terms of which the problem was formulated. The point is that the behavioural specifications of the total mental conditions treat them as if they were, in their own mentalistic framework, *unitary* states, with no compositional complexity. Of course, these specifications are presumably very complex: they will presumably represent each total condition as a vast cluster of behavioural factors. But this behavioural complexity will do nothing to preserve the structure of the mental complexity of what is supposedly specified: it is just for this reason that each simple mental state can only be behaviourally specified by disjoining the specifications of the total conditions in which it features, rather than by finding some single behavioural factor, or set of factors, which is common to the subject-matter of each. What prevents a preservation of the structure of the mental complexity, or anything approaching it, is, of course, the ubiquitous problem of context-dependence: the ingredients of a total mental condition cannot be matched with the ingredients of its behavioural correlate, because each mental ingredient varies in its behavioural role as it features in different conditions. The upshot is that the proposed method of analysis only succeeds in avoiding the problem by discarding all information about the internal complexity of a subject's state of mind at a time: it does not offer, at the behavioural level, anything which reveals what is genuinely common to all the different occasions on which, in varying mental contexts, the same simple mental state is realized. Conceivably, this might not matter in a theory which was intended to correct our ordinary modes of thought – a theory which deliberately revised the content of our ordinary psychological statements to fit the philosophically identified truth.[13] But it is wholly unacceptable in a theory, like analytical behaviourism, which claims to reveal what these statements really mean – a theory which purports to set out what our ordinary psychological concepts ultimately amount to. It is clearly essential to our actual concept of a want, for example, that where the same (i.e. same type of) want occurs on different occasions or in different subjects (sameness being here determined by coincidence of psychological specification), there are in substance, and not just nominally, different realizations of a common state.

This objection on its own is decisive. But it also brings to light a further respect in which the proposal is unsatisfactory. In adopting the proposal, the behaviourist has to assume that, although the psychological complexity of a total mental condition is not explicitly reflected in its behavioural specification, different conditions always receive different specifications; otherwise he will have no chance of providing even the right truth-conditions of psychological statements in behavioural terms. But though it is required for his theory, this assumption is unwarranted. For if the specification of a total condition merely records its behavioural significance *as a whole*, without characterizing the separate contributions which its components make to the total outcome, then there is simply no reason to assume that different conditions will always get different specifications – no reason to rule out the possibility of cases in which different combinations of mental states have the same overall behavioural outcome. Moreover, it seems that we can actually envisage cases of this kind. Thus suppose that someone is deeply ashamed of having a certain desire and is utterly determined never to allow it any kind of behavioural expression, even in secret. It is surely conceivable that this determination so dominates his motivational system that his overall behavioural condition (at least in so far as it is relevant to the attempted specification of his mental condition) is exactly as it would have been if, with everything else held constant, he had not had this desire, or if he had had a different but equally unpalatable desire which had prompted the same kind of behaviour-suppressing response. If so, then there are different total mental conditions which are not distinguishable by the kind of behavioural specifications they would receive under the proposal at issue. To distinguish such conditions behaviourally, one would need to take explicit account of their compositional complexity and focus on other mental contexts in which the relevant desire, or desires, occurred without the suppression of their normal behavioural influence.

In both these respects, then, the suggested method of avoiding the problem of context-dependence fails. And since there is no other way in which the behaviourist could try to avoid the problem, we must conclude that analytical behaviourism is mistaken. The behaviourist has no way of analysing the content of psychological statements in purely behavioural terms, since he cannot spell out the behavioural significance of one mental state without taking others (those relevant to its context-dependence) for granted. This refutation of his position, of course, is quite independent of the intuitive objection we considered earlier.

3

ANALYTICAL FUNCTIONALISM

1 INTRODUCTION

We have looked at two objections to analytical behaviourism: first, that it just seems intuitively wrong to construe statements about the mind in purely behavioural terms; second, that the behaviourist cannot adequately handle the phenomenon of context-dependence, whereby the behavioural consequences of a mental state depend on, and vary with, the larger mental context. These are by no means the only objections. But they suffice to show that, if the behaviourist approach has any merit at all, it will have to be modified in a crucial respect. Thus modified, analytical behaviourism turns into analytical functionalism, and it is this more promising, and indeed currently more popular, reductionist theory that I want now to explain and evaluate. In case it is felt that I have been too swift with analytical behaviourism, I should point out that all the objections I shall be bringing against this functionalist form of reductionism apply with equal force against the behaviourist.

The position which I am about to explore, and to which I give the title 'analytical functionalism', must be distinguished from two other positions which also qualify as functionalist in a broad sense. In the first place, it must be distinguished from what I would call *metaphysical* (i.e. the metaphysically reductive form of) functionalism.[1] This latter position rejects the possibility of a functionalist, or any other kind of reductive, analysis of psychological concepts, but still insists that psychological facts are wholly constituted by functional facts. The general distinction between the analytical and metaphysical forms of reductionism has already been outlined (in 1.2, pp. 2–7), and I shall be pursuing the case of metaphysical reductionism in detail in Chapter 5. Secondly, analytical functionalism, in the sense I intend, must be distinguished from the position (separately) advocated by both David Armstrong and David Lewis.[2] These philosophers offer a functionalist analysis of psychological concepts, but one which, unlike the position which I am calling analytical functionalism, involves giving a non-functionalist account of the mental universals (i.e. the types of mental state and activity) which these concepts identify. The Armstrong–Lewis approach, and the way it differs from analytical functionalism 'proper', are topics I shall fully explore in the next chapter. Analytical functionalism must also be distinguished from what Ned Block has called 'psychofunctionalism', which advances a functionalist account of mentality as an empirical hypothesis rather than as something to be established by conceptual analysis.[3] But unless it involves some other kind of reductive analysis of psychological concepts (and it is hard to see what this might be), such a position becomes just a special case of the metaphysical functionalism mentioned above.

There are a large number of philosophers who have some sympathy with analytical functionalism in the relevant sense or who apply it to specific areas of the mind. Perhaps the clearest example of someone who is *fully* committed to the position is Sydney Shoemaker,[4] though, in what follows, I shall tend to focus on the abstract issues rather than on the views of any particular functionalist author.

2 THE NEW ONTOLOGICAL APPROACH

To understand the nature of analytical functionalism, and to bring out its crucial difference from analytical behaviourism, we must begin by reminding ourselves of a distinction drawn earlier – between those forms of non-mentalistic analysis which are 'item-conservative' and those which are 'item-eliminative'. Where the analysis is item-conservative, it preserves the ontology of mental items within the conceptually fundamental perspective: it leaves sensations, perceptual experiences, episodes of thought, and all the other concrete ingredients of the mind as entities which can continue to feature in the subject-matter of psychological statements, when this subject-matter is represented in its fully analysed form. Where the analysis is item-eliminative, it discards this ontology: it excludes mental items from the conceptually fundamental perspective and confines them to the subject-matter of our ordinary mentalistic discourse in its pre-analysed form.

Now it is clear that, in terms of this distinction, analytical behaviourism is to be classified as item-eliminative. The behaviourist accepts that there are mental facts, and, in so far as these facts are ordinarily expressed in ways which assert or imply the existence of mental items, he acknowledges the existence of such items. But he sees this whole ontology as merely a by-product of, and something inseparably tied to, a whole system of thought and discourse which entirely disappears when the facts are presented in their fully (i.e. behaviourally) analysed form. Thus while he is happy to acknowledge the truth of psychological statements, given the appropriate behavioural facts, and hence happy to acknowledge the existence of such things as sensations and episodes of thought, he does not identify these things with any entities which feature in his proposed analysis. Rather, he thinks of them as getting analysed away, along with the whole system of mentalistic concepts in whose framework we ordinarily conceive of them. He regards our references to them as just a *façon de parler*, only available within the larger *façon de parler* furnished by the whole mentalistic language. In this respect, the behaviourist's attitude to the ingredients of the mind is exactly like that of the phenomenalist to the ingredients of the physical world.

The move from analytical behaviourism to analytical functionalism is precisely the move from a form of analysis which is item-eliminative to one that is item-conservative. Like the behaviourist, the functionalist claims that statements about the mind are to be ultimately construed in wholly non-mentalistic terms – that the content of each statement is to be ultimately represented in a form which does not involve any psychological concepts. And, again like the behaviourist, he construes such statements in a way which implies an intimate logical connection between the character of a subject's mental states and the character of his behavioural dispositions. Where he crucially differs from the behaviourist is in offering a type of construal which preserves the ontology of mental items – one which allows us to go on referring to, and quantifying over, such items from within the conceptually fundamental framework which it introduces. The reason he is able to preserve this ontology, while keeping the construal non-mentalistic, is that he provides a non-mentalistic account of the psychological properties belonging to such items – an account which represents these properties as, on analysis, purely 'functional'. More precisely, he holds that to say of a given mental item m that it has a certain psychological character (for example, that it is an episode of pain, or a visual experience of a certain kind, or an instance of a certain kind of belief) is, on analysis, to say that things of m's intrinsic type characteristically play a certain role, or cluster of roles, in the complex causal system which links the subject's sensory input (and the environmental factors which give rise to it) with his behavioural output (and the environmental factors which it affects).[5] And this enables the functionalist to retain mental items within the conceptually fundamental perspective, while ultimately characterizing them in wholly non-mentalistic terms.

To make the nature of the functionalist's position clear, let us focus on a particular case. Suppose that Smith has a certain kind of visual experience at a time t. Let us call this experience, i.e. the concrete experiential particular which uniquely occurs in Smith at t, E. Now the analytical functionalist accepts the existence of E. And, unlike the behaviourist, he recognizes it as something which retains its ontological status in the perspective of his non-mentalistic account. He also, of course, accepts that E has a certain psychological character – a character which might get specified in the mentalistic language by some such locution as: 'E is an experience as of seeing a physical scene of such-and-such a sensible type.' But, crucially, he does not take E's psychological character to be, or to be an aspect of, its intrinsic nature – an aspect of what E is like in itself. Rather, he thinks that what gives E this character, what entitles it to be described as a certain sort of visual experience, is the characteristic functional role which events of E's intrinsic type (or of E's intrinsic type and bodily/system-theoretic location) play in a certain causal system – that system, realized in Smith at t, by which light from the environment, along with other forms of sensory input, gets informationally processed and, as the need arises, channelled into some appropriate behavioural response. In other words, he thinks that E's psychological character consists in the fact that, in the framework of the relevant causal laws, Smith's makeup at t is such as to ensure a certain set of functional regularities associated, directly or indirectly, with events of E's intrinsic type (type and location) – such regularities as: that events of this type (type and location), occurring in Smith, tend to be produced by certain kinds of photic input to the eyes (or, perhaps more relevantly, produced by ocular exposure to certain kinds of physical environment); that such events, in turn, though in ways which vary according to what Smith already believes, tend to produce certain kinds of environmental belief; and that such environmental beliefs, in combination with (and in ways which vary according to the character of) Smith's other beliefs and motivational states, tend to produce certain kinds of behavioural response. Moreover, as an *analytical* functionalist, he thinks that this functional account of E's psychological character is to be achieved through conceptual analysis. He thinks that it is in such functional terms that the relevant mentalistic description of E is to be ultimately construed – that this description is just a concise and idiomatic way of specifying the characteristic role of E-type events in the relevant (Smith-at-t) causal system.

Generalizing this account to cover all mental items, we can now see how the analytical functionalist intends to construe our ordinary mentalistic assertions. In most of these assertions, we do not refer to some particular mental item and specify its psychological character. Rather, we ascribe some psychological attribute to a mental subject: we say, for example, that Smith is having a certain kind of visual experience, or that Mary is in pain, or that Henry expects to win the race. But given his account of the psychological character of mental items, it is clear how such assertions will get construed. Thus an assertion of the form:

F1: Subject S is psychologically thus-and-thus at time t

will first get transformed into:

F2: Something with such-and-such a psychological character exists/occurs in S at t

and then the relevant mentalistic description of this psychological character will get construed in functional terms in the way already indicated. So the final construal will have some such form as:

F3: For some intrinsic kind K (or some intrinsic kind K and bodily/system-theoretic location L):
(i) a K-thing exists/occurs in S at t (in S at t at L) and
(ii) K ($K+L$) has, for S at t, such-and-such a functional character

where the *functional character* of a kind (a kind plus a location) for subject at a time is defined by the characteristic functional role, or roles, which things of that kind (kind and location) are equipped to play in the relevant (for-that-subject-at-that-time) causal system. The catch-all expression 'a K-thing exists/ occurs', which is designed to cover any ontological type of momentary mental item, would, of course, get replaced by something more specific (for example, 'a K-event occurs' or 'an instance of a K-state occurs') in each particular case. It should also be noted that, instead of F1, the original mentalistic assertion might be of a form which characterizes the subject's mental condition over a *period* of time, rather than at a moment, and this too would require appropriate adjustments in the style of the functionalist construal.

As we have seen, the functionalist draws a sharp distinction between the intrinsic nature of a mental item (what that item is like in itself) and its psychological character (the characteristic role of items of that intrinsic type in the relevant causal system). But we have not yet said what kind of intrinsic nature he takes such items to have. This omission is quite deliberate. For any claims about the nature of mental items, other than their formal categorization (for example as events or as instances of states), lie outside the scope of the functionalist's analysis. The analysis tells us, for each mentalistically specified item, what kind of functional role things of its intrinsic type (or type and location) characteristically play in the relevant system. But it does not tell us what this intrinsic type is – what the item is like in itself. Indeed, it does not even indicate whether the item is physical or non-physical (or perhaps something which a mixture of the two). This explains why, in my parenthetical references to item-*location*, I have used the bet-hedging expression 'bodily/system-theoretic'. For I wanted the relevant notion of location to be neutral between the case in which, being physical, mental items are located within the subject's body and the case in which, being non-physical, they only have location within the relevant causal system. It must not, of course, be thought that, in leaving open the possibility that mental items are non-physical, analytical functionalism becomes compatible with dualism, as I have defined it. For, as well as requiring the mental and physical realms to be ontologically separate, dualism, thus defined, requires the mental realm to be conceptually and metaphysically fundamental; and this precludes any analysis of psychological concepts in wholly non-mentalistic terms, irrespective of whether the analysis implies that mental items are physical.

Although the functionalist analysis leaves open the possibility that mental items are non-physical, there is a sense in which it facilitates a physicalist account. The main reason why we ordinarily feel some reluctance to accept such an account is that we think of mental items as things whose intrinsic natures are to be specified in psychological terms and thus as things whose distinctive psychological natures set them apart from things in the physical world. The functionalist analysis removes this obstacle. By construing the psychological specification of a mental item in functional terms, it ensures that, whatever the item's intrinsic nature, this nature is to be specified in some other way: it ensures that this nature is, whatever else, non-psychological. And this, of course, while not entailing, at least prepares the way for the conclusion that such items are intrinsically physical. Moreover, once this conclusion has been made available, it becomes, for a number of reasons, hard to resist. To begin with, there is bound to be a presumption that, unless the facts of human (and animal) psychology tell against it (which they do not on the functionalist account), the physical processes that take place in human (and animal) bodies are fully explicable in terms of ordinary physical laws – the same laws that govern the rest of the physical world. And if this presumption is correct, then (barring a rather peculiar form of overdetermination[6]) mental items would have to be physical to have the causal influence on behaviour which functionalism ascribes to them. Further, we already know that human (and animal) bodies contain an internal structure –

the brain – which has the right kind of organizational complexity, the right sort of connections with sense-receptors and
muscles, and an appropriately intimate involvement with the
subject's mental life, to make it seem adequately equipped,
without the need for any non-physical structures, to embody
the relevant causal system – or more precisely, to embody that
central portion of it (between sensory input and behavioural
output) whose purely physical nature is not already presup-
posed by the functionalist analysis. And in any case, once we
have agreed that the psychological properties of mental items
are to be construed in functional terms, the suggestion that
such items are non-physical in nature seems to become the
merest of fancies. For not only is there nothing which we can
cite in its support, but we can form no positive conception of
what such non-physical natures might be.[7] For these and
various other reasons, almost all functionalists assume that the
functional mind is realized by the structure, organization, and
operations of something purely physical, namely the human
or animal organism, or this organism together with its physical
environment. And, in particular, they assume that the mental
items which make up the concrete ingredients of the mind are
to be identified with items (events, state-instances, structures,
or whatever) in the brain.

In identifying mental items with brain-items, the functionalist
is not, of course, endorsing the *type*-identity thesis, which
additionally equates the psychological character of a mental
item with some aspect of its neurophysiological character; for
this would be inconsistent with the functionalist analysis. Nor
is he even committed to saying that psychological and neurophysiological types are uniformly correlated. There is nothing
to prevent him from supposing that the same sort of neural
item has different functional (= different psychological) properties in different species, or in different members of the same
species, or even in the same creature at different phases of its
history. Nor, likewise, is there anything to prevent him from
supposing that, for different species, creatures, or phases,
different sorts of neural item have the same functional (= the
same psychological) properties. This flexibility in functionalism, in contrast with the rigidity of the type-identity thesis, is
usually seen as one of its chief virtues[8] – though, extended

beyond the biological realm, it also (as we shall see in section 5) has its drawbacks.

3 COMPLICATIONS AND REFINEMENTS

In introducing analytical functionalism, I implied that it could be viewed as a kind of modification or refinement of analytical behaviourism, adopted in response to the two objections we mentioned to which the behaviourist's position is vulnerable. Now that we have seen, in broad outline, what this modification amounts to, we must consider how it stands in relation to these objections.

The first objection to analytical behaviourism was a purely intuitive one: it just seemed wrong, in principle, to suppose that the content of our ordinary statements about the mind could be wholly captured in behavioural terms. This objection, as we shall see, has more than one aspect. But the point we focused on was that in ascribing a mental state to someone, we seem to be saying something which is ultimately concerned with the subject's 'internal' condition – a condition which causally affects, and is expressed through, his behaviour and behavioural dispositions, but is not reducible to them. Now it is clear that, at least in this respect, the functionalist is not open to criticism. For although it provides a reductive account of their psychological properties, his analysis preserves the ontology of mental items, and explicitly represents them as the internal causal agents which generate the subject's behavioural responses and sustain his behavioural dispositions. Thus, whatever his other failings, there is no doubt that the functionalist construes statements about the mind as statements about the subject's internal condition in the relevant sense.

What is much less clear is how analytical functionalism is supposed to avoid the problem of context-dependence. There is no getting away from the fact that, for each specific type of mental item (with the possible exception of certain rather basic volitional activities[9]), the behavioural consequences of the instantiation of that type depend on, and vary with, the wider mental context. And since the functional specification of the type will involve, in part, a specification of its functional role with respect to behaviour, it looks as if, like the behaviourist, the functionalist will be unable to provide an analysis of one psychological concept without taking some range of further psychological concepts as primitive. Indeed, as well as the original problem of context-dependence, there are three further respects in which the functionalist is liable to find himself relying on mentalistic concepts. First, there is a further form of context-dependence in the causal influence of sensory input on the occurrence of mental items. For example, the exact character of the visual experience induced by a certain type of photic input will depend, to some extent, on the subject's conceptual scheme and beliefs.[10] Second, in the case of most types of mental item, their relevant functional character will be at least partly a matter of how their instantiation tends to affect and to be affected by the instantiation of other types. For example, in the case of sense-experiences, it will be partly a matter of what kinds of belief they tend to induce; and in the case of beliefs, it will be largely a matter of what kinds of sense-experience and beliefs tend to induce them, and how they tend to affect the formation of wants, intentions, and other beliefs. Third, this functional role of mental items with respect to each other will itself exhibit additional forms of context-dependence. For example, the character of the beliefs induced by a certain type of visual experience will depend on the subject's other beliefs, and the influence of a certain type of belief on the formation of wants will depend on the subject's other wants. All in all, then, there is a multiplicity of ways in which, in trying to provide a functional specification of one type of mental item, the functionalist could find himself having to take others, mentalistically conceived, for granted.

However, while all this certainly generates complications for the functionalist, I do not think it creates an insuperable problem. Given any set s of specific types of mental item, let us say that s is *functionally complete* if and only if, for any type x which it contains, it also contains all types which are relevant to the functional specification of x, in so far as this specification directly bears on the psychological character of x from the functionalist's standpoint. For example, if x is a certain type of belief, and if it is part of the relevant functional character of x that (i) in a certain context of other beliefs, experiences of a certain type tend to induce an instantiation of x, and (ii) in a certain context of other beliefs and wants, instances of x tend to induce the formation of a certain type of intention, then a functionally complete set will contain x only if it also contains the relevant types of experience and intention, together with all the item-types which feature in the relevant contexts. Now suppose M is a specific item-type – say, the belief that cows eat grass – and suppose A is the smallest functionally complete set which contains M. Thus to construct A, we would have to start by finding those types which directly feature in the functional specification of M, then add those further types which directly feature in the functional specifications of these M-relevant types, then add those further types which directly feature in the functional specifications of these additional types, and so on. It is almost certain that A will turn out to be infinitely large, but, for simplicity, let us assume (pretend) that it is finite. Now let P be the total pattern of psychologically relevant ways in which, whether individually or in combinations, A-members are functionally related to types of sensory input, to types of behaviour, and to one another. And let us express A's instantiation of P by the sentence '$F(M, M_1, ..., M_n)$', where '$M, M_1, ..., M_n$' is an exhaustive list of A-members. Because A is functionally complete (because, for each type it contains, it contains all those types which are relevant to the functional specification of that type), the functionalist can say that the psychological character (i.e. the identity) of each member is fixed by its place in the pattern of relationships thus expressed. And this means that, in specifying the character (identity) of any given member, he need only identify the other members which are relevant to this specification by their distinctive places in the pattern. Thus he can specify M as that type x such that, for some series of types $x_1...x_n$, $F(x, x_1, ..., x_n)$ – and likewise for each A-member. This procedure avoids the need for taking certain types, mentalistically conceived, for granted. Each type will get specified partly in terms of its functional relationships with other types, but these types will themselves be identified only by their functional character. The point is that, if functionalism is correct, then the characters (identities) of all the A-types are fixed *en bloc*, or holistically, by the total pattern of functional relationships in which they feature.[11]

Now, of course, this way of presenting the situation is only provisional in relation to the functionalist's account. For obviously the functionalist does not want to develop his analysis in the framework of an ontology of psychological types. But the way to adapt the solution to the requirements of the functionalist's actual ontology is clear. Let us go back to the original schema for construing mentalistic assertions in functional terms, as set out in the previous section. An assertion of the form:

F1: Subject *S* is psychologically thus-and-thus at time *t*

is initially transformed into:

F2: Something with such-and-such a psychological character exists/occurs in *S* at *t*

and this in turn, (though, for simplicity, I here omit the parenthetical references to location), is construed as:

F3: For some intrinsic kind *K*,
     (i) a *K*-thing exists/occurs in *S* at *t*
     and
     (ii) *K* has, for *S* at *t*, such-and-such a functional character.

Now suppose the original mentalistic assertion is:

(1) Smith believes at *t* that cows eat grass

thus ascribing to Smith a belief of type *M*, as discussed above. *M*, as we have seen, is one of a set of psychological types whose characters (identities) are fixed holistically by the total pattern of functional relationships (with sensory input, with behaviour, and with one another) in which they feature. So, in order for an intrinsic kind *K* to have the relevant (*M*-appropriate) functional character for Smith at *t*, *K* itself must be the corresponding member of a corresponding set of intrinsic kinds which collectively display an exactly similar pattern of functional relationships relative to Smith's causal system at *t*. When we feed this into the original schema, we can see that the functionalist's construal of (1) will acquire some such form as:

(2) For some intrinsic kind *K*,
     (i) a *K*-thing exists/occurs in Smith at *t*
     and

    (ii) for some series of intrinsic kinds $K_1...K_n$,
        it is true of Smith's causal system at t that
        $F(K, K_1, ..., K_n)$.

Or put more concisely:

  (3) For some series of intrinsic kinds $K, K_1, ..., K_n$,
      (i) a K-thing exists/occurs in Smith at t
      and
      (ii) F-[Smith, t]$(K, K_1, ..., K_n)$.

Here, the quantification is not over psychological types, but over the intrinsic kinds (whatever they happen to be) by which the types are functionally embodied in a given subject at a given time.

There remain a number of minor complications which are worth mentioning, if only briefly. (The reader who wishes to avoid these could pass straight on to section 4.)

First, psychological ascriptions are not always specific with respect to the mental state or activity ascribed. For example, I might say that Mary is in pain, without thereby specifying the exact psychological character of the pain, or that Smith has a belief about the eating-habits of cows, without thereby specifying the exact content of the belief. Such cases will not require any change to the original construal-schema F3. But in spelling out the relevant functional character, allowance will have to be made for the generic (i.e. less than fully specific) content of the mentalistic description, and this will require some deviation from the example elaborated above. The details of this need not detain us, though it is clear that the specification of the functional character will have to be itself appropriately generic and possibly explicitly disjunctive.

The second complication is more interesting. We have been assuming that where a psychological type is fully specific (determinate) in the perspective of its ordinary mentalistic description, it will be accorded a similar specificity by the functional analysis. But this is something which the functionalist will reject. He will insist that what qualifies in the mentalistic framework as a specific type can assume a variety of different (and psychologically relevantly different) forms in different subjects, or in the same subject at different times, according to the precise nature of the functional system in which it features. For example, given the differences in their cognitive and motivational capacities, he will not think that the belief that cows eat grass (though fully specific in its own mentalistic terms) has exactly the same functional character in a child of four and in an adult zoologist. Since these differences in the functional form of a given type are, from the functionalist's standpoint, relevant to its psychological classification, the functionalist is, in effect, committed to graining the psychological quality-space more finely than the mentalistic language can express. This might prompt him to enrich the mentalistic language – to speak, for example, of the belief$_1$ that cows eat grass, the belief$_2$ that cows eat grass, and so on. But in so far as he is attempting to analyse our mentalistic concepts as they stand, he will have to construe our ordinary mentalistically specific psychological assertions as implicitly disjunctive. Thus in the case of (1), the form of the construal will get revised to:

(4) For some intrinsic kind K,
   (i) a K-thing exists/occurs in Smith at t
   and
   (ii) either
      (a) for some series S_1 of intrinsic kinds,
         F_1-[Smith, t] (K, S_1)
      or
      (b) for some series S_2 of intrinsic kinds,
         F_2-[Smith, t] (K, S_2)
      or ...

Strictly speaking, I should say that the form of the construal will get revised to (4) *or to some non-disjunctive equivalent.* For unless our ordinary system of psychological classifications is not only functionalistically crude, but positively cockeyed, there will be something which the relevant disjuncts have in common – something which will allow us to see the specific functional forms of the belief as variants of a single functional theme. And it is conceivable that, by finding a suitably unitary specification of this generic theme, the functionalist will be able to formulate the construal in a non-disjunctive way.

The third complication is, in effect, a corollary of the second. Since the functionalist insists that each mentalistically specific psychological type can assume a variety of relevantly different functional forms, he is almost certain to insist, additionally, that there is no definite answer to the question of exactly which forms it can assume and which it cannot. The reason is that he will see this question as turning, in part, on distinctions of *degree*: the issue of whether a given intrinsic kind qualifies for a certain psychological description relative to a certain subject at a certain time will turn partly on whether its functional character, for that subject at that time, achieves sufficiently high values along certain functional dimensions. And, of course, any sharp distinction between sufficiency and insufficiency in this respect is almost bound to be arbitrary, in a way for which our ordinary mentalistic concepts make no allowance. This is the phenomenon of covert vagueness we discussed earlier (2.3, pp. 29–30) and it is likely to prevent any exact translation of our ordinary psychological assertions into the functional language. But it does not prevent, in the relevant sense, their construal in functional terms. All the functionalist has to do, in dealing with each psychological type, is to specify that range of functional forms which it definitely can assume and that range which it definitely cannot, and to note that, given the covert vagueness of our ordinary mentalistic concept (its vagueness relative to the functional factors on which its application ultimately depends), the residual range constitutes a class of borderline (irresolvably arguable) cases.

Finally, if the covert vagueness of our ordinary psychological statements is likely to prevent their *exact* reformulation in functional terms, the functionalist may also find that *complete* reformulations get excluded by the infinite complexity of each specimen of functional analysis. We have already seen how, both in dealing with mentalistically generic assertions and in allowing the same mentalistically specific psychological type to assume a variety of functional forms, the functionalist is liable to end up with construals of a disjunctive kind. And there is no guarantee here that the relevant disjunctions will always be finite. Nor are these the only points where he is liable to encounter infinite complexity. For, irrespective of the number of different functional forms which a given psychological type can assume, these forms themselves will tend, individually, to involve infinite clusters of functional factors – each cluster comprising an infinite set of ways in which the type, and the other types which are functionally relevant to its specification in that form, are functionally related to sensory input, to behaviour, and to one another.[12] And while it is conceivable that such infinite complexity can be finitely handled in the functional language, it should not be assumed that it can.

4 THE KNOWLEDGE ARGUMENT

Analytical functionalism is currently the most fashionable version of analytical reductionism. Moreover, as we have seen, it has two important advantages over analytical behaviourism. First, it respects our intuition that, in ascribing a mental state to someone, we are saying something which is irreducibly about his 'internal' condition, of which his behaviour and behavioural dispositions are merely the overt symptoms. Second, it manages to avoid the problem of context-dependence, even if at the cost of certain technical complexities. Both these advantages stem from the fact that, unlike behaviourism, the functionalist analysis is item-conservative: it retains mental items as ingredients of the conceptually fundamental ontology.

Even so, analytical functionalism is open to a number of objections. The most obvious one is that, like behaviourism, it conspicuously fails to do justice to the nature of conscious experience. Consider, for example the case of pain. According to the functionalist, to say that someone is in pain is to say that he is in some (unspecified) state which has a certain (specified) functional character – a state which plays a certain characteristic role, or cluster of roles, in the relevant causal system. This account of pain is, in the two respects mentioned, superior to that of the behaviourist. But it still seems utterly misconceived. For it seems to come nowhere near capturing the full psychological character of pain, as introspection reveals it and as our ordinary pain-assertions record it. The point is that pain is an *experiential* state: in saying that someone is in pain, we are describing how things *feel to him*; we are characterizing some aspect of his *subjective* condition. The trouble with the functionalist's account, or at least the prima facie trouble, is that the functional description of pain seems wholly unequipped to specify its character as an experience, or even to imply that it has an experiential character at all. Moreover, this apparent deficiency in the functionalist's account of pain is repeated for every kind of sensory experience, and indeed for every kind of mental state or

activity which, by essentially including some element of conscious awareness, has an experiential (subjective) character in
the relevant sense. Thus just as the functionalist account seems
unable to capture the experiential character of pain, so,
likewise, it seems unable to capture the experiential (subjective) aspects of visual perception, perceptual recall, imagination, emotion, and conscious thought. In each case, it seems
that the experiential facts, which are introspectively revealed
to the subject, lie beyond the reach of any functional specification and that the experiential statements which record them
are not amenable to any functionalist analysis.

There are a number of ways of developing this general
objection – ways of trying to bring out, with greater clarity and
detail, the problems for any functionalist account of experience. One familiar way is by arguing for the conceivability of a
case (and to provide a refutation of *analytical* functionalism,
conceivability is enough) in which two subjects are in the same
functional condition but have different experiences. The standard case chosen here is that of the inverted colour-spectrum,
in which we envisage two subjects who are relevantly alike in
their functional organization, but experience complementary
colour-qualia in response to the same photic input.[13] Another
familiar line of argument is that we can conceive of something
(for example, a robot) which satisfies all the functional requirements for a human-like mentality, without having any consciousness at all.[14] (In the next section, I shall develop an argument
of this sort myself, though without restricting the issue to the
case of *experience*.) However, I think the most effective way of
developing the objection is by employing what has come to be
known as the 'knowledge argument'. In this line of argument,
we focus on the case of someone who, owing to a systematic
deficiency in his psychological repertoire, does not, for a
certain category of mental states, have any introspective data
from which he can derive a knowledge of their experiential
character. We then claim that, contrary to the implications of
analytical functionalism, the subject cannot acquire the relevant experiential knowledge from information about the functional roles of these states in the causal systems of those who
have them. Prominent among recent defenders of the knowledge argument have been Frank Jackson and Howard
Robinson.[15] Both these philosopher, however, see the

argument as constituting an objection not just to analytical functionalism, but also to any full-blooded form of physicalism. This raises some important issues which I shall deal with in the Postscript at the end of the section.

The knowledge argument can assume a variety of different forms, according the nature of the psychological deficiency envisaged and the reasons why it obtains. Like Robinson, I shall here focus on a case of someone who is congenitally devoid of a particular sense-realm.[16]

Suppose that Smith is congenitally blind. He has been blind from birth, indeed from conception. Not only this, but he has never even had any (non-perceptive) visual sensations or framed any visual images. Nor, in his present cerebral condition, does he have the capacity to have such sensations or images. In short, he is, in every respect, totally deprived of the visual sense-realm. Being in other respects normal, and having grown up in a normal (predominantly sighted) society, he has long since come to realise that other people have a perceptual capacity which he lacks. Thus he knows that there is a range of region-pervading physical qualities called 'colours'. He knows that, by the use of their eyes, other people are able, in suitable circumstances, to perceive portions of the colour-arrangement in their environment. And he knows that this type of perception, which is called 'visual perception' or 'seeing', involves a distinctive kind of sensory experience – a kind which is different from, but of the same genus as, the kinds of sensory experience which occur in other forms of sense-perception. At this stage, however, he has no idea what this distinctive kind of sensory experience is, qua experience, like. Or at least, he has no idea of what it is like, beyond, perhaps, a knowledge of certain aspects of its formal structure – for example, a knowledge of the formal geometry of the visual field and the formal structure of the sensory colour-spectrum. In this respect, there is something which he does not know about the psychological character of visual experience but which sighted people do know – something which sighted people know through their direct introspective access to the experiences themselves. And this additional thing, which they know through introspection, is similar to the additional things which he himself knows in the case of other forms of sense-perception, where his sensory capacities are not impaired.

Is there, then, some way in which, while retaining his sensory deficiency, Smith could acquire the knowledge which he currently lacks? Well, if analytical functionalism were true, it seems that there would be. For according to analytical functionalism, to specify the full psychological character of any mental state, we only have to specify its functional character; and there seems to be no reason why Smith's sensory deficiency should prevent him from having access to information about visual experience set out in purely functional terms. In other words, if analytical functionalism were true, it seems that Smith could come to know the full psychological character of visual experience, and hence come to know all that the sighted know through introspection, simply by discovering the characteristic role of such experience in the causal system which the sighted instantiate. Such a discovery could come about in either of two ways. On the one hand, a sighted person, who was additionally adept at conceptual analysis, might simply communicate to him in functional terms the knowledge which he himself had gained introspectively. On the other hand, assuming that the 'hardware' of the causal system is purely physical (as the functionalist is almost certain to accept), Smith might acquire the relevant functional information by gaining a detailed scientific knowledge of how the visual system of sighted people works in neurophysiological terms. But it is surely clear that Smith could *not* acquire the experiential knowledge which he currently lacks in either of these ways – that information about the functional character of visual experience, from whichever source it was obtained, would not suffice to impart a knowledge of its experiential character, as introspection reveals it. In the respect in which, in his initial position, he would say: 'I don't know what it's like, experientially, to see', he would surely acknowledge the same ignorance after the receipt of the functional information. On the face of it, then, the example constitutes a decisive objection to analytical functionalism. It seems to provide a clear case in which the functional specification of a certain category of mental states fails to cover a crucial aspect of their psychological character.

Now of course this is only one case. Even if we are right in supposing that analytical functionalism fails to provide an adequate account of visual experience, it does not automatically follow that it fails in any other case, much less that it fails for mentality in general. None the less, it is clear, on reflection, that the example does pose a threat to the functionalist's position on a broader front. In the first place, exactly the same argument could be developed with respect to each sense-realm: thus we could envisage someone who is, say, congenitally deaf or congenitally incapable of (sensory) pain, and make exactly the same points as we made in the case of Smith.[17] And secondly, even if they are only *explicitly* concerned with some form of sensory experience, such arguments have implications for experience in general. For they serve to confirm our initial intuition that the experiential aspects of mentality lie beyond the reach of any functional specification. Thus once it has been established, from cases like that of Smith, that what introspection reveals about the character of sensory experience cannot be captured in functional terms, there is no way of avoiding the conclusion that, in the case of any kind of mental item with an experiential character, the functionalist cannot provide an adequate account of the exper-iential facts as introspection reveals them. Admittedly, this would still leave the possibility of a purely functionalist account of the *non*-experiential aspects of mentality. But, for the moment, it is only the case of experience which concerns us.

So far, I have only presented the case of Smith as affording an objection to analytical functionalism which is *prima facie* decisive: I have not claimed that the functionalist's position has been definitely refuted. The reason for this caution is that there are a number of things which the functionalist could say in reply. Before we reach a final verdict, therefore, we must look carefully at these possible responses. Some of them, admittedly, are hardly worthy of serious consideration. But, as the issue is an important one, I shall try to cover every conceivable form of counter-argument, however naive or im-plausible. I think we can divide the possibilities into four basic options, though some of these can be developed in slightly different ways.

The first thing which, conceivably, the functionalist might say is that what prevents Smith from deriving a knowledge of the experiential character of seeing from the relevant func-tional information is simply that, being deprived of the visual sense-realm, he is not conceptually equipped to grasp the experiential proposition, or propositions, in question. It is not that the functional premises are deductively inadequate – that there are aspects of the experiential facts which they fail to cover. It is rather that, having no visual experience and even lacking the capacity to form visual images, Smith does not possess the experiential concepts required for an under-standing (for, as it were, a mental formulation) of the experien-tial conclusions which these premises entail. So, although the case of Smith is as we described it, it does not constitute a counter-example to the functionalist thesis: Smith's incapacity to acquire the relevant experiential knowledge reflects the peculiarity of his own situation rather than any inadequacy in the functionalist's account.

This reply is clearly hopeless, and it would only be in a moment of aberration that the functionalist could come to offer it. If analytical functionalism were correct, then all the experiential concepts required for a grasp of the relevant propositions could be analysed in functional terms, and so would be in principle available to Smith, despite his sensory deficiency. The presumption that his deficiency prevents him from acquiring them is already a tacit acknowledgement that such an analysis is impossible, and that there is something about the psychological character of visual experience which can only be grasped introspectively. So in offering the envis-aged reply, the functionalist would be implicitly conceding defeat.

A second reply, and on similar lines, would be that what prevents Smith from acquiring the relevant experiential knowl-edge is that he is not conceptually equipped to understand the functional premises – that, while the psychological charac-ter of visual experience can be fully specified in functional terms, he is not able, as we initially supposed, to take in this specification. The point would be that some of the functional information he would need to possess, in order to discover the experiential character of seeing, concerns the ways in which the visual system of the sighted equips them to detect, and to respond appropriately to, *physical colour*. For example, it would concern such facts as that (given their knowledge of the Highway Code and their desire to drive correctly) sighted motorists are disposed to stop when the traffic lights are red and to start again when they turn green. This sort of information, it would be alleged, is not accessible to Smith, because his blindness precludes his having an adequate conception of physical colour: he does not fully know what is meant by saying that the lights are *red*, or that the lights are *green*, or anything else of a similar kind.

This reply is hardly any better than the first. It is, of course, perfectly legitimate (and I have no doubt expedient) for the functionalist to insist that the causal system relative to which visual experience possesses its functionally defined psychological character includes the physical environment from which the sighted receive their photic input. (In other words, he does not have to embrace what Hilary Putnam has called 'the assumption of methodological solipsism'.[18]) And, in this connection, the detection of, and response to, the environmental arrangement of colour is indeed likely to be of crucial importance. But in so far as physical colour is described scientifically, i.e. in terms of wavelengths and intensities of light and in terms of the reflective properties of pigment, there is nothing to prevent Smith from acquiring an adequate conception of it. What he lacks, and apparently cannot acquire, is merely a conception of how physical colours *look to the sighted*, and this deficiency is just one aspect of his not knowing what it is like, experientially, for the sighted person to see. Thus the only respect in which he fails to grasp what is meant by saying that the traffic lights are red, or green, is that he does not know what sort of experience the sighted person has when, exposed to the lights, his eyes receive photic stimulation of the relevant wavelengths and intensities. But, of course, this knowledge is precisely what, if analytical functionalism were true, he would be able to derive from some appropriate functional specification. So in the only respect in which he is unable to form an adequate conception of physical colour, this inability merely reflects the deficiencies of the functionalist's account. It just shows that, to grasp the full psychological character of visual experience, one needs to know more than its functional role in the causal system. Once again, then, the functionalist's reply is tacitly an admission of defeat.

In these first two replies. the functionalist concedes that Smith cannot derive a knowledge of the experiential character of seeing from the relevant functional information, but sees this as reflecting the conceptual deficiencies of Smith rather than some deficiency in the information as such. In his third reply, the functionalist adopts a quite different approach. Not only does he insist that the functional information is complete, but he also insists that Smith can in fact derive from it a full knowledge of the experiential facts. What he thinks that Smith cannot do is, as it were, to mentally-formulate that knowledge in the conceptual perspective available to the sighted through introspection; and it is this incapacity which creates the false impression that the functional information itself is deficient. In other words, the functionalist insists that there is no restriction on the *amount* of knowledge available to Smith, since the full psychological character of visual experience can be revealed to him in functional terms. But he claims that, being blind, and lacking even the capacity to visualize (to form visual images in his mind's eye), Smith cannot conceptually focus on this psychological character in the *way* that the sighted can. The blind subject knows, or can come to know, exactly what it is like, experientially, for the sighted to see. What he cannot do, even in his imagination, is to achieve their introspective viewpoint: he cannot imagine himself, from the inside, as a subject of visual experience.[19]

There is no denying that this reply is more promising than the first two. At the very least, the distinction which it invokes, between knowing the psychological character of a certain type of experience and knowing this character in the perspective afforded by introspection, is sound. To take a different example, there are some pitches which are too high for me to hear or even to capture by an auditory image. Suppose, then, that P is the highest pitch in my (sensory and imaginative) auditory range. If we define P' as the pitch which is one tone higher than P, there is a perfectly good sense in which I fully know what it is like, experientially, to hear P'. For I am familiar with the generic character of auditory experience and can exactly locate the position of a P'-experience in the auditory spectrum. All I lack is the *kind* of knowledge available to someone who is either having the experience or can imaginatively achieve the viewpoint of one who is having it – the kind of knowledge which someone would mentally formulate by saying to himself: 'A P'-experience is that of hearing "..." ' (where I use the quotational designator, or designative schema, ' "..." ' to represent the subject's identification of P' by means of an auditory image or image-like concept[20]). If so, why should we not say, analogously, that Smith has, or can acquire, a full knowledge of the experiential character of seeing, but not in the introspective (i.e. visualizing) manner?

However, a little reflection reveals that the two cases are not analogous and that the distinction which applies to the one does not apply to the other. In the auditory example, what enables me to know the full psychological character of the relevant type of experience is that, while I cannot directly grasp it in the introspective manner, I can define it in terms of other types of experience and experiential relations whose character I *can* grasp in that manner. For there are lower pitches which I can identify by auditory images and from which I can abstract the general notion of the tonal interval; and, by reference to these pitches and by use of this notion, I can then identify, and know the full qualitative nature of, the higher pitches which lie beyond my imaginative range. Indeed, although I cannot form an image of P' and thus cannot achieve an introspective conception of the nature of a P'-experience, my knowledge of the qualitative nature of P' (together with my general faculty of imagination) at least equips me *to try* to do these things: it sets up a definite target for my imaginative efforts, and may even delude me into supposing that, with a little more exertion or concentration, I could reach it. The case of Smith is quite different, since he has no introspective reference-points by which he can break into the sense-realm in question. His knowledge of the psychological character of seeing is limited to what he can gather from his functional information – information which he acquires without the benefit of any introspective grasp of the nature of visual experience. It is surely quite clear that the knowledge thus obtained will be not only different in its conceptual perspective from that afforded to the sighted, but fundamentally incomplete – that it will simply not reveal the experiential facts which introspection reveals. It is not just a case of his not knowing something in the way in which the sighted know it, but of his not knowing what they know in any way at all.

Admittedly, there is one trivial way in which we can represent Smith and the sighted as knowing the same thing in different ways. For if we introduce the name 'V' as a purely referential designator of the generic experiential character of seeing, and define the 1-place predicate 'F' to mean *instantiates V*, then both Smith and the sighted can be said to know that seeing is F – the former identifying V by its functional properties (i.e. identifying it as that experiential character whose instances have a certain characteristic role, or cluster of roles, in the causal system of the sighted), the latter identifying it introspectively. Likewise, of course, for any particular visual experience E, if we introduce a name of its specific experiential character and the corresponding predicate signifying the instantiation of that character, we can represent a suitably informed Smith as knowing, in company with the relevant sighted subject, that E has this character. But obviously these are not really cases of Smith knowing, in a non-introspective way, the facts which are known to the sighted through introspection. To suggest that they are, would be like suggesting that we know the identity of the Victorian mass-murderer by knowing that it was Jack the Ripper – or worse, like suggesting that we are all omniscient, and hence know all that God knows, simply by knowing that the Actual World obtains. (Curiously, as applied to the experiential case, this strange suggestion seems to be just what Michael Tye is relying on in his recent attempt to rebut the knowledge argument.[21])

At this point, the functionalist might try to develop his third reply in a quite different way. So far, we have represented him as conceding that the sighted have a special way of knowing about the character of their visual experiences through introspection, but as claiming that, by unpacking his functional information, Smith is, after all, able to acquire a different type of knowledge of the very same facts. But in the face of the difficulties with this approach, he might be tempted to opt for something more radical. Thus instead of claiming that Smith can come to know in functional terms what the sighted know introspectively, he might simply deny that introspection yields that sort of knowledge at all. More specifically, he might say that what we would ordinarily describe as the sighted person's knowing, from the inside, what it is like to see, is not factual knowledge at all, but just a special cluster of skills – at best a kind of knowing-*how* rather than a knowing-*that*. And this would enable him to say that the functional information, available to Smith and the sighted alike, does suffice for a full knowledge of the psychological character of visual experience. This, in effect, is the position of David Lewis (except that Lewis is not strictly speaking a functionalist in my sense[22]): 'knowing what it's like is not the possession of information at all .... Rather [it] is the possession of abilities: abilities to recognize, abilities to imagine, abilities to predict one's behaviour by means of imaginative experiments.'[23]

Despite Lewis's advocacy of it, it is difficult to take this position seriously. Of course, in the functionalist's system, the mental component of any sort of knowledge will be given a functionalist analysis, and this might, quite generally, involve construing the possession of knowledge (including factual knowledge) as a kind of ability. But, whatever, its ultimate nature, I do not see how we can avoid taking the relevant knowing-what-it's-like to be genuinely factual. Suppose that, as a result of an operation, Smith himself gains the power of sight, thus coming to know, in his own case, what it is like to see. Whatever it amounts to, this new knowledge surely enables Smith to raise the question of whether other sighted subjects have experiences of that sort. And, since the question is clearly a factual one, this surely shows that the knowledge which underlies it is factual too. I suppose the functionalist might retort that, in so far as it transcends what can be answered on the basis of functional information alone, the factual question is merely whether Smith and the others have experiences *of the same sort* – a question which Smith can raise without having special knowledge of the particular sort (perhaps to be specified neurophysiologically) involved in his own case. But it is just obvious that this is not so. It is just obvious that, once he has become familiar with seeing in his own case, the question Smith raises is exclusively aimed at dispelling his ignorance about *others*. Knowing how things are experientially for himself, what he now wants to know is whether they are like *that* for others too.

It seems to me, then, that, in whatever form it is developed, the functionalist's third reply fails, and that we cannot avoid the conclusion that there are genuine experiential facts which the sighted know through introspection, but which Smith cannot deduce from the functional facts available to him in his original (congenitally blind) condition.

There is still one final way in which the functionalist might try to meet the objection. For he might concede that the functional specification of an experiential state does not cover all that introspection reveals, but insist that what it fails to cover is also beyond the reach of any *mentalistic* specification, and so does not feature in the content of the psychological statements which he is trying to analyse. His point would be that even the mentalistic terms we employ in characterizing experience must have meanings which are intersubjectively communicable (that when one subject describes an experience as, say, *a pain* or as *a surge of anger* or as *a presentation of a red flash*, it must be, in principle, possible for other subjects to understand him and to know that they do), and that, consequently, since each subject has introspective access to his own experiences alone, it is only those aspects of experience which can be grasped non-introspectively (and without even the help of introspective reference-points) that are accessible to mentalistic description. Thus, in the example we have been considering, the functionalist might concede that there is something about the experiential character of seeing – a purely 'subjective' aspect – which the sighted know through introspection and which Smith cannot deduce from his functional information; and he might also concede that the reason why Smith cannot make the deduction is simply that the information does not cover this aspect. But he might claim that what Smith cannot deduce is something which even the sighted cannot linguistically record. They may say such things as 'I seem to see a tree' or 'there is a tree-like shape in my visual field' or 'such-and-such a colour-array is visually presented to me'; but all such assertions are (he might claim) to be taken as entirely neutral with respect to the purely subjective facts and thus as fully comprehensible to someone with no introspective knowledge of the visual realm. On this basis, the functionalist might accept the case of Smith as we described it, but – at least with respect to the domain of what is linguistically expressible – see it as posing no threat to his analytical claims. He might acknowledge that there are psychological aspects of visual experience which cannot be functionally specified, but still insist that all psychological *descriptions* and *statements* can be fully construed in functional terms.

Whether this reply is better thought of as a way of trying to *defend* the original functionalist position, or as an attempt to *salvage* something from it, is a moot point. Certainly it was not part of the original plan that the subjective aspects of experience should lie beyond the scope of the functionalist analysis, and I doubt if those who were sympathetic to functionalism as it was initially conceived would find the new version very attractive. Still, the main question is whether the version is tenable. And, for more than one reason, I think it is not.

Let me begin with a point which is more of a challenge than a decisive objection. Even if the functionalist is right in insisting that the only mentalistic terms available for describing experience are ones whose meanings are intersubjectively communicable, it is far from clear why this should put the purely subjective aspects of experience beyond the reach of mentalistic description. The argument seems to be that, because each subject has introspective access to his own experiences alone, each subject can only detect the purely subjective aspects of experience as they occur in his own case; and because each subject can only detect these aspects in his own case, there is no way in which different subjects could establish that they were using the same term to signify the same aspect. But this argument is clearly not adequate as it stands. For, although it is uncontroversial that each subject only has introspective access to his own experiences, it might still be true that what is introspectively accessible to one subject is epistemologically accessible to others in a different way; and if this were so in the case of the purely subjective aspects of experience, there would be nothing to prevent their being covered by terms whose meanings are intersubjectively communicable. At the very least, then, the functionalist will need to reinforce his argument at this point. He will need to substantiate his assumption that the purely subjective aspects of someone's experience are epistemologically private – aspects of which the subject is immediately conscious, but which no one else can detect in any way at all.

Well, for the sake of argument, let us suppose that this has been done – that the functionalist has established the absolute privacy of experience in its purely subjective aspects. On the face of it, he then has a watertight case for concluding that such aspects cannot be covered by terms whose meanings are intersubjectively communicable; and, from this, together with the premise that the meaning of any mentalistic term has to be intersubjectively communicable, it would follow that such aspects are beyond the reach of mentalistic description altogether. But the crucial question now becomes: why should we accept this semantic premise? After all, if the subject can introspectively identify these aspects as they occur in his own case, it must surely be possible for him to describe them in terms which *he* can understand. If he can introspectively identify some experiential feature, and can thus form an introspective conception of it, what could prevent him from giving it a descriptive label – from stipulating that, in his own private usage, a certain term is to signify this feature and have a meaning which exactly matches this introspective conception? Nor, in fact, does it have to be a case of stipulation, in which the subject deliberately endows a certain term with a certain meaning. For it could also be, and in practice is more likely to be, a case in which the subject is simply conditioned to interpret a certain term, which he has picked up from others, in a certain (private) way. For example, he may be taught to say 'I am in pain' on occasions when he has injured himself and is exhibiting what others take to be signs of distress; and, because his experiences on these occasions resemble one another in a certain purely subjective respect (the respect of how it *feels* to him), he may then come to interpret the word 'pain' as signifying this common subjective feature and employ it in this sense in his ascriptions of pain to himself and others.

Now it might be said that all this is begging the question. There are, after all, some familiar arguments (ones found in or inspired by the writings of the later Wittgenstein[24]) designed to show that meaning has to be intersubjectively communicable and that there is no possibility of an *essentially* private language, or private vocabulary, whose terms are necessarily comprehensible to only one subject. If we are willing to suppose that the subjective aspects of experience are epistemologically private, and if we grant that this puts them beyond the reach of terms with intersubjectively communicable meanings, surely we need to evaluate these arguments before we can come to any conclusion on the issue at hand. But the point is that, whatever their merits (and I find none of them convincing), these arguments cannot be of any assistance to the functionalist in the present context. The functionalist is claiming that there are aspects of experience which the subject can introspectively identify but not descriptively label, facts which he can know through introspection but not linguistically record. But in all these standard arguments, purporting to show that meaning must be intersubjectively communicable, there is a clear commitment to the view that the subject's cognitive and linguistic capacities cannot be prised apart; that any essential limitations on what the subject is capable of *saying* are equally limitations on what he is capable of *knowing*. Indeed, in so far as these arguments are successful, the conclusion to which they lead is not only that there can be no essentially private meaning, but that experience itself does not have an essentially private component, and that the theory of knowledge which could prompt one to postulate such a component – the theory which credits each subject with an epistemologically privileged access to his own experiences – is mistaken. Nor are there any other arguments which the functionalist could call on in the present context. For there is no getting round the point that if a subject does have an introspective knowledge of the purely subjective features of his experience, and if he already has mastery of the public language, then he must possess the resources to give linguistic expression to this knowledge, even if in terms which only he can understand. In short, once the functionalist has conceded that the aspects of experience which resist functional specification are introspectively revealed to the subject, he cannot coherently deny that they are available for mentalistic description, whether or not the descriptive terms involved have meanings which are intersubjectively communicable.

As a last resort, I suppose the functionalist might just settle for a restriction of his analysis to those concepts which are expressible in the public language – expressible by terms with intersubjectively comprehensible meanings. In other words, he might make a double concession – acknowledging both that each experience has a subjective aspect which is not functionally specifiable and that what cannot be functionally specified can (in its way) be mentalistically specified – but still insist (i) that such mentalistic specification is never in a form which is intersubjectively comprehensible and (ii) that any psychological statement which is intersubjectively comprehensible can be construed in purely functional terms.

However, even this weaker position would be untenable. And here the most crucial point is not that the functionalist still has to produce some argument in support of claim (i) – or more precisely, in support of the assumption of epistemological privacy which underlies it. It is rather that, even if we concede that the subjective aspects of experience cannot be mentalistically specified in intersubjectively comprehensible terms, there is no denying that we can formulate intersubjectively comprehensible statements *about them.* And the very admission that the aspects cannot be functionally specified would then prevent a construal of such statements in purely functional terms. Thus if there can be no purely functional specification of the subjective character of a visual experience, then there can be no purely functionalist construal of such intersubjectively comprehensible statements as that John and Mary are having visual experiences of *exactly the same subjective type,* or that John's visual experiences are *subjectively different* from their functional counterparts in Mary. Indeed, it is hard to see how the functionalist could even hope to handle *ordinary* experiential statements, such as that John is in pain or that Mary seems to see a cat. For once it has been acknowledged that experience has a purely subjective aspect, it is very hard to deny that such statements *carry the implication* that such aspects are present in the experiences they describe. And if the aspects themselves resist functional specification, there is no way in which a purely functionalist account of the statements could capture that implication.

I think we have now considered all the possible, or at least remotely feasible, ways in which the analytical functionalist could try to defend himself against the original objection, and since each line of defence has proved ineffective, we must conclude that the objection is correct. There *is* something which Smith cannot deduce from his functional information, but which he would able to deduce if analytical functionalism were true. So, at least in this area, analytical functionalism is false.

Postscript on Jackson

It might be thought that, as well as refuting analytical functionalism, the case of Smith would equally serve as a decisive objection to any full-blooded *physicalistic* account of experience. After all, suppose that, in addition to his functional information, Smith were to have (at least in so far as it was relevant to vision) complete physical information about the sighted and their relationship with the rest of the physical world. This additional information would still not allow Smith to gain a knowledge of the experiential character of seeing. And from this it might seem to follow that any physicalistic account of the situation fails to cover all the facts. This was essentially Frank Jackson's point in his much-discussed version of the knowledge argument.[25] Thus focusing on the case of a scientist (Mary) who, though hitherto confined to an entirely black-and-white environment, has managed to aquire complete knowledge of the physics and neurophysiology of colour-vision, Jackson asks: 'What will happen when Mary is released from her black and white room .... Will she *learn* anything or not?'[26] His answer is:

> It seems just obvious that she will learn something about the world and our visual experience of it. But then it is inescapable that her previous knowledge was incomplete. But she had *all* the physical information. *Ergo*, there is more to have than that, and Physicalism is false

But we must be careful here. Jackson defines *Physicalism* as the thesis that 'all (correct) information is physical information'. [27] If we follow this definition, and combine it, plausibly, with a sufficiently intensionalist construal of information (so that the information that p includes the information that q only if there is a valid deductive route from the proposition that p to the proposition that q), then no doubt cases like that of (my) Smith and (Jackson's) Mary do refute Physicalism. But these cases do not, at least immediately, refute all positions which would normally be thought of as physicalist, nor even those that would be thought of as physicalist in the strongest sense. And by calling what they refute 'Physicalism', Jackson gives the impression that they do.

The point is that some positions which by any ordinary standards qualify as physicalist in the strongest sense do not, as such, imply the deducibility of mental truths from physical truths. And, in the case of a physicalist position of this sort, the fact that the subject is unable to derive the relevant experiential knowledge from his physical information does not constitute an immediate objection. Two positions in particular remain, at present, unscathed. The first is the type-identity thesis. This claims that the psychological character of a mental item is an aspect of its physical character, but it is not committed to claiming that the psychological description of a mental item can be deduced from its physical description. The second is the thesis of physicalistic metaphysical reductionism. This claims that mental facts are wholly constituted by physical facts, but it is not committed to claiming that statements recording mental facts can be deduced from statements recording the relevantly constitutive physical facts. Because these positions are not committed to the relevant deducibility claims, they cannot be refuted merely by appealing to the fact that someone with all the relevant physical information would not be able to extract the psychological information from it. In the case of the type-identity thesis, admittedly, the knowledge argument is liable to bite at another point. For even though the thesis itself does not entail the deducibility of mental truths from physical truths, its defence may well turn out to require the acceptance of a reductive analysis of psychological concepts in terms which show how the relevant psychophysical identities are possible. And, of course, any such reductive analysis is likely to fall foul of the Smith and Mary cases in just the same way as analytical functionalism. But even if it becomes vulnerable to the knowledge argument at some point, the fact remains that the identity-thesis is not immediately refuted by the argument as such.

These points, of course, are ones which we shall be dealing with more fully over the next two chapters, when the topics of type-identity and metaphysical reductionism come up for detailed consideration. I mention them now to avoid a possible source of confusion. Whether Jackson himself was confused is not entirely clear; for, as I have conceded, the knowledge argument does succeed in refuting 'Physicalism' as he defines it. But certainly many of his critics[28] have taken him to be implying that any position which deserves to be thought of as physicalistic in a strong sense (in effect, anything amounting to what I have described as 'strong materialism' (see 2.2, pp. 17–18)) is eliminated.

5 FUNCTION WITHOUT MIND

The case of the blind subject has shown that the analytical functionalist cannot provide an adequate account of visual experience, and this serves to confirm our initial intuition that, quite generally, the experiential aspects of mentality – those aspects which, in some way or another, directly concern the existence or character of the subject's conscious awareness – resist specification in functional terms. However, it does not follow from this that analytical functionalism has to be entirely abandoned. For the functionalist could still claim that he can deal adequately with the *non*-experiential aspects of the mind – that he can successfully apply his analysis to (for example) statements about propositional attitudes, like beliefs and desires, and statements about personality and character traits, like friendliness and vanity. Of course, in so far as they can become objects of introspective awareness, even these kinds of mental item can make a difference to the subject's experiential condition. But the point is that they are not themselves states of awareness; nor, since they can be present at times (as in sleep) when the subject is unconscious, are they even *essentially* objects of awareness. And, for this reason, the functionalist could still hope that their psychological character will turn out to be fully specifiable in purely functional terms. It is to this further issue that we must now turn.

We must start by making it clear exactly what the issue is – exactly what form of functionalist position we are trying to evaluate. We saw earlier (section 3) how, given any type of mental item, the functional character of this type (that is, the functional character which the functionalist takes to be definitive of its identity) is not confined to its direct and self-contained causal links with forms of sensory input and behavioural output (or with the external physical factors to which sensory input is responsive or which behavioural output affects), but involves a large cluster of functional relationships with other types of mental item – both those with which it has relevant causal links and those which contribute to the mental contexts on which its causal role depends. Now if someone endorses analytical functionalism in its fully comprehensive form, where it is claimed that every item-type is definable in purely functional terms, he has to find some way of handling these functional relationships among types without recourse to any primitive mentalistic concepts – so that, for example, if he counts it as partly definitive of type M_1 that, in a given kind C of mental context, it tends to produce a realization of type M_2, then he needs to find some way of replacing the mentalistic identifications of C and M_2 by ones which are purely functional. In other words, in endorsing analytical functionalism with respect to *all* item-types, he is committed to providing, for each type, an account which is *fully reductive* – an account which defines that type in terms which are wholly non-mentalistic. And indeed we have seen, in broad outline, what sort of procedure he would here have to adopt. However, the functionalist position which we are now considering is not fully comprehensive in this way. For it is the position of someone who concedes that the experiential aspects of mentality cannot be specified in functional terms and only claims that functionalism works for the other aspects. But just because he is making this concession with respect to the experiential aspects, and is thus content to leave the latter as things to be ultimately conceived of in a purely mentalistic way, the proponent of this modified functionalist position has a choice between two analytical projects with respect to the non-experiential item-types that he wants his account to cover. On the one hand, he could aim to deal with these types in a way which is fully reductive – to define them by their functional character and specify this character in terms which are wholly non-mentalistic. On the other hand, in specifying their functional character, he could allow himself the option of making irreducibly mentalistic references to the experiential item-types which his account is not intended to cover. The point of this option would be to equip him to deal with cases, if there are any, in which a non-experiential type derives some of its psychologically relevant functional character from its relationships with experiential types.

Now what needs to be stressed at the outset is that the functionalist project which presently concerns us is of the first and fully reductive kind. It is true that, as we are now envisaging it, this project is restricted in its scope: it is only aiming to provide a functionalist account of the non-experiential aspects of mentality. But, if it is to be relevant to our present concerns, it must aim at an account of these aspects which is wholly non-mentalistic: it must not allow itself the option of employing those experiential mentalistic concepts which it is not attempting to analyse. The reason for this is simple. Whatever flexibility we build into analytical functionalism, we want it, in the present context, to be something which stands in opposition to dualism. The trouble with allowing it to become not only scope-restricted, but also non-reductive, is that it would lose its anti-dualist character: it would no longer come into conflict with, or set limitations on the scope of, the dualist's claim that mentality is conceptually fundamental. After all, even a fully committed dualist might be prepared to divide types of mental item into two groups: a primary group, whose members are to be ultimately conceived of in a purely mentalistic way, and a secondary group, whose members are to be defined by their functional character in relation to the primary group (or perhaps in relation to the primary group together with the repertoires of sensory input and behaviour). The only kinds of analytical functionalism which the dualist is obliged to deny are those which claim that certain item-types can be functionally defined in terms that are entirely non-mentalistic.

Granted, then, that the modified functionalist position which we are now considering is, within the scope of its own concern, fully reductive, what are we to make of it? Is a (reductive) functionalist account of the non-experiential aspects of mentality any easier to defend than a functionalist account of experience? Well, there is no denying that, from the standpoint of our initial intuitions, it is not so manifestly implausible. And here the point is not just that the non-experiential states can occur without consciousness; it is also that, even when the subject is conscious, they do not reveal themselves to the subject's introspective awareness in the same concrete way as the elements of experience. It is true, of course, that when he addresses himself to the question of (say) what he believes or desires, he (at least typically) comes up with the answers. But it is far from clear that introspection reveals some psychological content in these states over and above what the functionalist is willing to assign to them. There is not, in these cases, the presentation of some intrinsic mental 'quale', as there is, or seems to be, when one introspectively focuses on (for example) one's pains or visual experiences. It is because of this, as I mentioned earlier (2.4, pp. 38–9), that it is much less plausible here, than in the experiential cases, to suppose that the subject can derive his conception of the relevant states from what his introspection reveals. Indeed, on the face of it, it seems that the subject's introspective access to these states depends on his already having a conception of them – a conception which equips him to receive the factual data (i.e. about their occurrence) which introspection supplies. And the functionalist will say that it is precisely because the states are definable in functional terms that such a prior conception is available.

Admittedly, it may still be wondered whether the functionalist can give the subject's introspective access to these states the right kind of epistemic status. We normally assume that when someone addresses himself to the question of what he believes or desires, the facts are directly evident to him in a way which both makes his introspective judgments immune from error (or at least from the kinds of error which can arise in ordinary areas of empirical investigation) and entitles him to be, in a distinctively strong and scepticism-proof sense, certain that he has reached the truth. And it is hard to see how this infallibility (or quasi-infallibility) and right to certainty can be preserved within the framework of the functionalist account. But to the extent that he cannot accommodate our ordinary assumptions about introspection, I think that the functionalist would be happy to reject them. I think he would be content to represent our introspective access to our own attitudinal states as simply a further aspect of our functional organization, whereby the internal items which functionally qualify as beliefs and desires causally equip us to make, in the verbally succinct form afforded by the mentalistic language, correct judgments about the relevant aspects of our functional condition. And he would see this self-monitoring capacity as no different in general character or epistemic status from the sort of self-monitoring capacity which we could build into (say) a chess-playing computer by giving it the resources to 'report on' its internal states and activities from a chess-playing standpoint. If this does not give the subject the kind of immunity from error and right to certainty that we ordinarily assume him to have, so much the worse for our ordinary assumptions.

Even so, the modified functionalist position is still very hard to accept. The most obvious objection to it is that, for any kind of causal system which the functionalist might take as sufficing for certain forms of non-experiential mentality, it seems we can envisage something which instantiates that system without having any mental capacities at all. Thus let C be the causal system which obtains in a certain (normal) human adult at a particular time. Since (apart from its two-way links with the environment) C is defined in a purely abstract way, without any specification of the 'hardware' in which it is realized, it would be possible, at least in principle, to construct a machine (a non-biological machine) which instantiated it. Moreover, while it may be, for technical reasons, absurd to try to do it in this way, it would be in principle possible to construct a C-instantiating machine which was, in the manner of Leibniz's mill,[29] *crudely* mechanical (if I may put it thus), so that, instead of involving the silicon chips and electronic circuitry of modern computers, it worked entirely by such things as cogs, levers, pulleys, and springs. Or at least, it would be possible to construct it in this fashion apart from those components which were designed to receive the various forms of 'sensory' input[30] and adapt them to the causal needs of the rest of the system. Suppose, then, we have constructed such a machine. Even with his modified position, the analytical functionalist is obliged to say that this object's causal organization guarantees it the same non-experiential mental capacities as the human subject on which it is modelled. Indeed, he must hold it to be a conceptual truth that anything with that organization has those capacities. But, far from accepting that these capacities are guaranteed, we would surely deny that the machine has any mentality at all. Even the suggestion that it *might* have a mind strikes us as just absurd.

It might be wondered why, in presenting this example, I have insisted that the hypothetical machine be *crudely* mechanical, rather then allowing it the benefit of modern technology. Could not the same point be made in the case of an *electronic* machine – something whose central component consisted of a modern-style computer? Well, no doubt it could, so long as we were clear-headed. But the danger of focusing on a modern computer is that there are factors here which, quite independently of the relevance of functional organization, could make us more inclined, or less disinclined, to credit the machine with mentality. For, in the first place, the processes which occur in the human brain – processes which we ordinarily think of as in some way sustaining mental activity – have a much closer resemblance to the processes which occur in a modern computer than to such things as the movements of cogs and levers: at the very least, the cerebral and computer processes are alike electrical. And secondly, the fact that electricity itself is imperceptible and, as it were, ethereal, in contrast with the visible and tangible processes of something crudely mechanical, may make it seem a more plausible candidate for the role of the stuff of mentality. The point of focusing on a crudely mechanical machine is that it enables us, without any extra effort, to exclude these irrelevant considerations and attend exclusively to the issue of what can be deduced from the functional facts alone. And when we do this, our intuitions are unequivocally against the functionalist. We would think of the machine as merely functionally *simulating*, not as functionally *reproducing*, the mental endowments of its human counterpart. And this applies to all aspects of mentality – as much to the non-experiential states, like propositional attitudes and personality-traits, as to conscious experience.

Ned Block has devised a different but equally striking way of illustrating the same general point.[31] In his example, what instantiates the relevant causal system, or more precisely the system's central component, is a vast population of human beings, who are organized, by a combination of communication-technology and conditioning, into a sort of collective brain – each individual playing, as it were, the role of a single neuron. So as to gain the right sort of links with the environment, this 'brain' is connected, at the appropriate points, to a robot-body, which is equipped with devices to provide repertoires of sensory inputs and motor outputs to match those of a normal human being. Most of the individuals involved, like most neurons in a real human brain, have the job of receiving messages from other members of the team and passing them on. But some – those which play the role of sensory nerves – have the job of monitoring, and passing on messages about, sensory input (though we do not need to suppose that they recognize the information they are handling *as* sensory). And others – those which play the role of motor-neurons – have the job of pressing output-controlling keys in response to messages they receive (though again we do not need to suppose that they know what effects these key-pressing responses have). Assuming that each individual is fully conditioned to perform automatically the minimal tasks assigned to him and that their collective organization (perhaps by mirroring that of a human brain) is of the requisite functional type, the functionalist is committed to crediting the whole system with the relevant forms of functionally sustained mentality. But, here again, this commitment is plainly contrary to our ordinary intuitions. We have no inclination at all to suppose that, in addition to the individual minds of its human components, there is a further mind – perhaps only a non-experiential mind – which is created by their collective organization. Indeed, as in the case of the crudely mechanical machine, the suggestion that there might be such a mind strikes us as absurd.

These two cases, of the crudely mechanical machine and the collective brain, are being offered as counter-examples to the modified functionalist thesis, which restricts the functionalist analysis to the non-experiential aspects of mentality. However, it should not be thought that our intuitions about these cases are entirely independent of our unwillingness to accept a functionalist account of experience. For our refusal to credit these objects with any sort of mentality – even with such non-experiential states as propositional attitudes and personality-traits – derives at least in part from two other factors. The first is our unwillingness to credit them with any form of consciousness, or potential for consciousness. The second is our unwillingness to ascribe any sort of mentality to something which has never possessed either consciousness or the potential for it. This second factor, of course, in no way conflicts with our readiness to ascribe non-experiential mental states to those who are asleep or under a general anaesthetic. And it even allows us to ascribe them to those (for example, in an irreversible coma) who have not only lost consciousness, but are incapable of ever regaining it, though in this latter case we may well be disinclined to do so. The reason for this disinclination is that, while we accept that such states can be present during periods of unconsciousness, we find it much harder to suppose that they could be present without having the potential to affect the subject's conscious activities – in particular, his conscious judgments and decisions – in appropriate ways.

At any rate, for whatever reasons, we intuitively feel it to be wrong, and indeed absurd, to ascribe any sort of mentality to the crudely mechanical machine or collective brain. And since these objects could satisfy all the functional requirements for the possession of mentality, and, in particular, for the possession of a repertoire of non-experiential mental states, we are led to view these cases as refuting even the modified functionalist position. Of course, the functionalist might simply dig his heels in and say that our intuitions are mistaken. Thus, on the one hand, he might insist that, although the envisaged objects are incapable of consciousness, we are wrong in thinking that they lack mentality altogether. Or on the other, he might insist that, although they could not possess mentality without some capacity for consciousness, we are wrong to think that they lack this capacity. But without the backing of arguments to substantiate the functionalist view, such dismissals of our intuitions would be merely idle gestures. And so far we have come up with nothing in favour of analytical functionalism, other than its superiority to the behaviourist position out of which it developed.

Finally, it is worth noting that this intuitive case against the functionalist position would not be strengthened by the addition of John Searle's 'Chinese room' argument.[32] It is not just that this argument only directly bears on a narrow form of functionalism – a form which treats mentality as a kind of (installed) computer program. It is also, and more crucially, that the argument is clearly fallacious.

Searle wants to prove that genuine thought and understanding involve more than just the implementation of a computer program. He argues in the following way. Suppose someone has devised a very clever program which enables a computer to simulate the understanding of Chinese to the requirements of the 'Turing test' (so that, behaviourally, its linguistic performance would not be distinguishable from that of a genuine speaker of the language). Even so, the computer is not thereby equipped with a real understanding of Chinese, since it is only sensitive to the 'syntactic' (= physical) features of the language, not to its semantics.[33] To help see this point, we are to envisage a situation in which the program is, in effect, run through an ordinary person. Thus suppose someone with no understanding of Chinese is placed in a room containing baskets of Chinese characters. He has a rule book, written in his own language, which refers to the characters by their physical features and tells him what to do with them on any given occasion. In particular, the arrangements permit Chinese speakers outside the room to pass in sequences of characters, which they intend as questions or messages, and the rules enable the subject to pass back sequences which those outside can interpret as appropriate verbal responses. Let us assume that the subject's manipulation of the characters in accordance with the instructions in his book exactly mirrors the running of the original program through a computer. Searle's point is then this. We know, from how we have set up the case, that the person in the room has no understanding of Chinese. But his activities in the room, together with the input and output systems, constitute an implementation of the original program. So the implementation of the program does not as such suffice for the relevant form of mentality. It would be as misconceived to ascribe an intellectual mastery of Chinese to the computer, purely on the basis of its execution of the program, as it would be to ascribe such mastery to the person in the room. Both the computer and the person are merely responding to the syntactic (physical) features of the symbols, without attaching any meaning to them.

At first sight, Searle's argument seems very plausible. It seems uncontroversial that the person in the room does not know the meanings of the symbols he manipulates, since that is how the example was constructed. So, granted that the rules of manipulation exactly match the computer program, Searle's conclusion seems unavoidable. However, there is something of crucial importance which Searle has overlooked. For although it is, in a sense, uncontroversial that the person in the room does not know the meanings of the Chinese characters, this ignorance pertains to a quite different mental life from that to which the defender of program-functionalism would want to attribute understanding. Thus while the program functionalist, if he is to be consistent, will have to ascribe an understanding of Chinese to this person, qua human organism – or at any rate, ascribe it either to this person (organism) or to some larger physical system (e.g. room + organism) of which this person is a part – this putative understanding stands to the person's ordinary mental life in exactly the same relation as the mind which the ordinary functionalist is obliged to ascribe to Block's collective brain stands to the separate minds of its human components. Thus just as these latter minds are only relevant to the existence of the putative collective mind in so far as they form, in the first instance, part of the hardware in which the relevant functional system is realized (and I say 'in the first instance' because, of course, the functionalist will offer a functionalist account of this mentality too), so too the ordinary mental life of the person in the room is only relevant to the mentality which his manipulation of the symbols supposedly creates in so far as it is, in the first instance, causally involved in such manipulation. Indeed, in both cases, it would be just as good from the functionalist's standpoint if the human or humans involved were replaced by machines which performed the same operations. So although there is no denying that, in respect of his ordinary mental life, the person in the room does not have, or come to acquire, any understanding of Chinese, Searle was wrong to conclude, on that basis, that no such understanding (whether to be ascribed to the human organism or to some larger system) is logically created by the special way in which, partly by means of that ordinary life, the subject functions in the envisaged situation.

I am not, of course, saying that Searle is wrong in his conclusions. Indeed, it seems to me quite clear that neither the functions of the person in the room nor the running of the computer program would create any genuine understanding of Chinese, and that they would not do so even if the relevant input and output systems had (what might count from the functionalist standpoint as) more appropriate causal links with the environment. My point is simply that, to reach these conclusions, we have to rely on the same kind of intuitions as we brought to bear in the cases of the crudely mechanical machine and the collective brain. We cannot use our independent knowledge of the ordinary mental life of the person in the room to establish the conclusions in a more rigorous way.

Curiously, if Searle's argument did go through, it would prove too much from his own standpoint. For although he assumes the human brain to be capable of real thought and understanding, and draws a sharp distinction between 'the formal symbol manipulation that is done by the computer' (= the handling of 'syntax') and 'the mental contents biologically produced by the brain' (= the grasp of semantics),[34] he also accepts that, at a sufficiently fundamental level, the workings of the brain are to be ultimately described in purely physical terms,[35] which would represent it as (in his special sense) a 'syntactic' rather than a 'semantic' machine. Hence, by Searle's own argument, the Chinese themselves would have no better understanding of their language than the person in the room.

6 MIND WITHOUT BEHAVIOURAL FUNCTION

It may be a case of overkill, but I want to round off the present discussion by attacking analytical functionalism from a quite different direction. So far, the objections which we have brought against the functionalist position have all, in one way or another, turned on the claim that functional facts, or their specifications, do not have the requisite psychological implications. In contrast, the objection which I now want to develop turns on the claim that psychological facts, or specifications, do not have the requisite functional implications. Since this raises a completely new issue, it will be appropriate to return to the functionalist's position in its original, unrestricted form, though my arguments apply to both forms in exactly the same way.

According to analytical functionalism, as we have so far characterized it, the psychological character of a mental item is conceptually fixed by the characteristic functional role which things of its intrinsic kind play in the relevant causal system, where the *relevant* causal system is the one which is realized in the *relevant subject* (the subject in whose mind the item occurs) at the *relevant time* (the time at which the item occurs). But, quite apart from the problems which we have already discussed, such a position seems clearly untenable. For it seems we can envisage situations in which the subject has a repertoire of mental capacities without instantiating a causal system of the requisite type. There are a number of different cases we could take here. The simplest, and it is on these that I shall mainly focus, are those in which the causal system lacks any behavioural component.

Suppose someone contracts a disease which causes the wholesale decay of his motor-neurons, and, as a result, becomes totally paralysed. Assuming that his physical system is not impaired in other respects, we can surely envisage his mental life continuing. Thus we can surely suppose that he sees the hospital ward where he is being cared for and hears the nurses talking to him; that he retains his former beliefs, and acquires new ones on the basis of what he sees and hears; that he spends long periods brooding on his current plight or recalling earlier experiences; that he yearns to regain his former powers, and sometimes makes desperate mental efforts to move his limbs or speak. But relative to the causal system which he currently instantiates, none of this mentality has any functional role with respect to behaviour; for the system no longer contains a behavioural component. And presumably this means that his mental states and activities do not meet the require-ments which the functionalist position, as we have so far characterized it, imposes on them. For presumably anyone accepting this position will have to accept, as a consequence, that a crucial part of what determines the psychological charac-ter of any mental item is the characteristic role which, in the relevant causal system, items of that intrinsic kind have (either directly or via their effects on the occurrence of other mental items) in influencing behaviour.

I have said that *presumably* anyone accepting the functionalist position will have to accept this consequence. But it is just conceivable that someone might claim that, in cases like the one we have envisaged – cases where the relevant causal system lacks a behavioural component – the mental items in question draw their whole psychological character from their functional role with respect to sensory input (and its environmental causes) and one another. After all, this claim would not imply that, in *normal* cases, the behavioural component was psycho-logically irrelevant. Nor would it even imply that, in normal cases, the behavioural component was irrelevant with respect to those types of mental item which, as we mentalistically describe them, feature in the repertoire of the paralysed subject; for, as we noted earlier (pp. 59–60), the functionalist is already insisting that what qualifies in the mentalistic framework as a specific psychological item-type can assume a variety of different (and psychologically relevantly different) functional forms in different subjects or in the same subject at different times. However, even if the claim is formally available to the functionalist, and even if it can be reconciled with the approach he wants to adopt in normal cases, it is (even from his own ideological standpoint) clearly unacceptable. For given that his account has to be fully reductive, and so cannot fall back on primitive mentalistic concepts in specifying the functional relations between different types of mental item, there is no way in which he could hope to capture the psychological character of the paralysed subject's mental states and activities purely in terms of their functional role with respect to sensory input and one another. This applies to all the various types of states and activities, but is especially clear in the case of those of a motivational or volitional character, such as the subject's desire to regain his motor powers and his unsuccessful attempts to speak.

Given, then, that the relevant mental items do not derive their full psychological character from their functional role in the diminished causal system, the case of the paralysed subject, as we have envisaged it, stands as a counter-example to the functionalist position in its present form. Of course, it would still be possible for the functionalist to deny that such a case could arise. For he could insist that, contrary to what we ordinarily suppose, the paralysed subject *would* lose all his mental capacities, and that this is implicit in our very concept of the mental. But I take it that such a response would be manifestly absurd. In whatever other respects it might be appropriate for the functionalist to challenge our ordinary intuitions, it is obvious that he cannot afford to dismiss the envisaged case in this way.

It follows that the only way in which the functionalist could hope to meet the objection would be by modifying his position, so that it no longer required mental items to derive their full psychological character from their role in the causal system in which they actually feature. The modification which first suggests itself would be to say that, in the case of someone who is paralysed, the psychological character of each of his mental items is determined by the functional role which *would be* characteristic of things of its intrinsic type if his behavioural system were still intact. But while this takes care of the specific case envisaged, it does not cover all the other cases of the same general kind. Thus suppose someone is born without motor-neurons at all, though in other respects he is normal. Such a person could surely have the full range of sense-experiences, other than kinaesthetic ones. And with the right kinds of sensory exposure to the environment and to language, he could surely acquire normal beliefs about the physical world and develop normal capacities for thought. He could also, presumably, have desires and emotions, though these are likely to be very different from those of normal people. Now, in this case too, the subject's mental states and activities do not derive the whole of their psychological character from their functional role in the causal system which actually obtains. But the functionalist cannot here appeal to the functional role which they would have if the subject's behavioural system were still intact, since there never was a system to remain intact.

To deal with this new case, the functionalist will have to accept a further modification. The obvious suggestion would be this: where a subject has never had a behavioural system, the psychological character of his mental states and activities is determined by the functional role which they would have had if, without change to the rest of his causal system, he had been endowed with the behavioural capacities which are normal for members of his species.[36] Admittedly, there may be a slight awkwardness in making the subject's mentality depend on what is normal for his species, rather than exclusively on facts about him. But since what is normal for the species determines what would be, in some sense, *natural for him* – since it shows the respects in which his actual causal system falls short of what, as it were, nature intended it to be – I doubt if we could turn this point into a clear-cut objection.

However, even this additional modification does not equip the functionalist to deal with all conceivable cases in which a mental subject lacks a behavioural system. Thus suppose that, by genetic engineering, we create a new biological species. The members of this new species are like human beings, except that they have no muscles or motor-neurons apart those involved in such processes as blood-circulation and digestion; and let us assume that they are anatomically structured in a way which leaves no room for the insertion of a neuro-muscular system. The creatures only survive because we artificially feed them (for example, through tubes into the stomach); and they also depend on human interference for their reproduction (for example, IVF–pregnancy terminated by Caesarean delivery). But despite all this artificiality, they constitute a separate species, whose members can breed with one another, but cannot breed with us or with the members of any other species. Now assuming that, apart from the motor-neural deficiency, their sense-organs and brains are structured and function just like ours, we can surely suppose that, if they are treated in the same sort of way as the subject in the preceding example (with the same kinds of sensory exposure to language and the environment), these creatures will have mental lives of a similar kind. But, in this case, the functionalist cannot account for their mentality in terms of how things would be if they had the normal capacities of their species, since *ex hypothesi* they do. It is as fundamental to the genetic character of this species that its members have no neuro-muscular system as it is to the character of the human species that its members do not have wings or more than two legs. Nor can the functionalist dismiss the example as a flight of fancy. It may indeed be biologically impossible to create such a species. But the mere fact that it is conceivable means that the functionalist analysis has to take account of it.

The functionalist will now have to say that, in a case where a species lacks a behavioural system, the mentality of its members is to be functionally specified by reference to the larger causal system which would obtain if, perhaps by some suitable change to their genetic makeup, a behavioural system were added. But the trouble is that there are different ways (indeed infinitely many) in which this behavioural system could be designed, and these ways are not all equally good at capturing the mentality which we are supposing the creatures to possess. Thus it would be no use envisaging a system whose only effect was to make the subject's ears twitch whenever he was thinking. Nor would it be any use envisaging a system which (though without disturbing the causal relations in which different types of mental item stand to one another) made the subject's desires and intentions work towards their own frustration. Clearly, the sort of behavioural system which the functionalist needs to envisage must be one which is, in each case,

appropriate to the subject's mentality – a system which is adequately sensitive to the details of the subject's mental condition, and which, in conjunction with the pre-behavioural system
already in place, accords to each type of mental item in the
subject's repertoire a behaviour-affecting role which matches,
or fits, its psychological character. But how, in the framework
of the functionalist's theory, can the appropriate type of system
be selected? Obviously the functionalist cannot gauge the
appropriateness of a system by reference to the character of
the mentality which it is intended to express, since he can only
gauge the character of the mentality by first selecting the right
system. But, once it has been conceded that the subject's
mentality cannot be adequately specified simply in terms of its
functional properties in the pre-behavioural system, I do not
see how appropriateness could be gauged in any other way.

In the present case, admittedly, the functionalist could select
an appropriate system just by specifying it as that which would
come closest to the actual system of the closest species. For, as
we have devised the example, the closest species would be the
human one, and the human behavioural system would be
appropriate to the mentality of the envisaged creatures. But
this procedure would not yield a solution to the general
problem. For it is only contingent that the closest species has a
system which is appropriate to its own mentality. After all, we
might have created *two* species, one (as already envisaged)
with no behavioural system at all, and the other with a system
which was, in relation to its mentality, conspicuously impoverished. The second species could turn out to be the closest to
the first (in particular, closer than the human species in virtue
of its impoverished system), but the addition of its behavioural
system to the causal system of the first would not yield the
right results. What the functionalist needs is a general definition
of appropriateness framed in non-mentalistic terms. And it is
this, as far as I can see, that he cannot achieve.

We can also now see that the functionalist is in trouble in
another respect. So far, in considering the issue of behavioural
deficiency, we have focused on cases in which the subject lacks
a behavioural system altogether. Now in these cases the functionalist at least has a rationale for modifying his position in
the ways envisaged – a rationale, that is, which is more than
just the need to avoid counter-examples. For it is clear that, in

formulating his original position, he was working on the assumption that the whole causal system contains a behavioural component; and so he can plausibly claim that, in invoking a hypothetical behavioural system to deal with the relevant cases, he is merely amending the letter of this position to conform to its spirit – that he is spelling out the implications of his general approach for a range of cases which its original formulation was not designed to cover. But now suppose we focus on a case in which the subject *has* a behavioural system, but one which is not appropriate to his mentality. To make the case particularly sharp, let us assume that the behavioural (i.e. behaviour-affecting functional) roles of certain types of mental states are systematically at variance with their psychological character, so that the way the functionalist would psychologically interpret these states in the framework of his original position would be erroneous. Now here again, the functionalist can only correctly represent the psychological character of the relevant mental states by invoking some type of behavioural system which the subject does not actually possess. But since there is nothing in his general approach which indicates that the original psychological interpretations are mistaken, he has no rationale for moving to a new system at all. It is not just that he has no way of ensuring that he selects a system of the appropriate sort: he does not even have a way of recognizing the case as a counter-example to his original position.

4

THE TYPE-IDENTITY THESIS

1 INTRODUCTION

We have rejected analytical functionalism on three counts. In the first place, we showed that the position does not do justice to the nature of conscious experience. We showed this by elaborating a version of the knowledge argument, in which we focused on the case of a congenitally blind subject, who was unable to derive a knowledge of the experiential character of seeing from his functional information about the sighted. Secondly, we argued that we can envisage objects which meet all the functional requirements of mentality without possessing minds. The cases we focused on here were those of the crudely mechanical machine and the collective brain. Thirdly, and conversely, we argued that we can envisage objects which *do* have minds, but lack the requisite functional organization. Here we focused on cases in which the mental subject lacked a behavioural system. All three objections to analytical functionalism also, of course, apply with equal force against analytical behaviourism – in addition to the objections considered earlier, which apply against the behaviourist alone.

As we shall see, there is still one further form of analytical reductionism to be considered. But it will be best to look at this in the context of another anti-dualist position with which it is intimately associated and for which it provides a rationale. This further position, which is not as such a form of analytical reductionism, is the thesis of psychophysical type-identity, and it is this thesis which will form the main topic of our present discussion.

2 TYPE-IDENTITY AND THE FUNCTIONAL-PROFILE THEORY

The (psychophysical) type-identity thesis asserts that each mental 'type' is identical with a physical 'type'. It is to be distinguished from the weaker *token*-identity thesis, which merely asserts that each mental 'token' is identical with a physical 'token'. The terms 'type' and 'token' mark a distinction between mental or physical universals and the particulars which instantiate them. Thus suppose that, at a certain time *t*, both John and Mary believe that dodos are extinct. Then, on the one hand, there is the single belief-type which John and Mary share: this is a mental universal, capable of occurrence (realization) in any number of minds on any number of occasions. And, on the other hand, there are the two belief-tokens (tokens or instances of this type) which separately occur in John and Mary (i.e. the John-*t* believing that dodos are extinct and the Mary-*t* believing that dodos are extinct): these are mental particulars, each of which is confined to one mind and one time. Exactly the same distinction can be drawn for each category of mental phenomena (desire-types being distinguished from desire-tokens, sensation-types from sensation-tokens, and so on); and, of course, with spatial location replacing mind-location, there is an analogous distinction in the case of physical phenomena. It will be noticed that, as the particular episodes or instances of mentality (the concrete ingredients of the mind), mental tokens are what I have already labelled 'mental items'. So the token-identity thesis can be re-expressed as the claim that mental items are identical with physical items.

I have said that the type-identity thesis is stronger than the token-identity thesis. By this I mean that it entails but is not entailed by it. Thus anyone who claims that each mental type is identical with a physical type is obviously committed to saying that any token of a mental type is also a token of that physical type with which the mental type is identical. But someone who claims that each mental item is identical with a physical item is not committed to saying that the mental type which an item exemplifies is the same as some physical type which it exemplifies. Indeed, his acceptance of the token-identity thesis does not even commit him to saying that mental and physical types are uniformly correlated: there is nothing to prevent him from supposing that items of the same mental type sometimes exemplify quite different physical types and that items of the same physical type sometimes exemplify quite different mental types. It should also be noted that, just as token-identity does not entail type-correlation, so the conjunction of token-identity and type-correlation does not entail type-identity. Thus there is no logical inconsistency in maintaining that a certain mental type and a certain physical type are distinct, while conceding that any instance of the one is an instance of the other. Indeed, one could insist that the types were distinct, while conceding that their uniform correlation was (and in the strongest sense) necessary. What the type-identity thesis claims, over and above token-identity plus type-correlation, is that the psychological character of a mental item is quite literally an aspect of its physical character – that an item's being a pain, or a decision to walk north, or an instance of the belief that dodos are extinct, is quite literally the same as its being an item of a certain physical sort.

The type-identity thesis leaves room for a range of more specific theories, according to the precise nature of the identities which are postulated. On this point, and for reasons which will become apparent, defenders of the thesis tend to leave their options open: they claim that mental types are identical with physical types, without saying exactly *which* physical types are involved. None the less, they almost invariably assume that the relevant types are neural. Thus without specifying its exact physical nature, they almost invariably assume that each type of mental state is identical with some type of brain (or central-nervous) state, and that each type of mental evant is identical with some type of brain (or central-nervous) event. Hence the familiar example, in which the identity-theorist is represented as identifying pain (the mental type) with C-fibre firing (the physical type). It is clear how, in this psycho-neural form, the thesis avoids at least two of the objections we brought against analytical functionalism. Thus, on the one hand, the identity-theorist will not be forced to ascribe mentality to such things as the crudely mechanical machine and the collective brain. For although these objects enjoy all the functional trappings of mentality, the hardware in which the functional organization is realized is not of the relevant physical type. On the other hand, the theorist has no difficulty in ascribing mentality to someone who lacks a behavioural system. For so long as the subject has the right kind of central-nervous hardware, the theorist can take it to sustain a mental life – irrespective of whether the mental states which occur in it have any behavioural outlet.

Despite having these advantages over analytical functionalism, the type-identity thesis might initially strike us as absurd. In claiming that mental types are identical with physical types, the thesis is claiming not only that mental items are physical, but that their mental properties are physical too – that the psychological character of each item is, or is an aspect of, its physical character. But how can this be? We cannot deduce that something is a pain-event from its description as an event of C-fibre firing, nor deduce that something is an event of C-fibre firing from its description as a pain. And, quite generally, from the physical description of a neural item nothing can be deduced about its (supposed) psychological character, conceived in psychological terms, and from the psychological description of a mental item nothing can be deduced about its (supposed) physical character, conceived in physical terms. So how is it possible to think of mental and physical types as identical? If the predicates 'is a pain-event' and 'is an event of C-fibre firing' are not inter-deducible, how can it be thought that they might signify the same property?

However, the type-identity thesis cannot be so simply dismissed. For we can find examples in the physical realm where properties or types can be equated, but where the corresponding predicates, or sortal terms, have quite different implications. A familiar case is the identity of water with H_2O. Assuming that we are using the term 'water' in its ordinary, pre-scientific sense (to express the same water-concept as our ancestors possessed thousands of years before the discoveries of modern chemistry), we clearly cannot deduce that something is an instance of H_2O from its description as an instance of water, nor deduce that something is an instance of water from its description as an instance of H_2O. But given the scientific findings, there can be no denying that water and H_2O are the same substance, and that, in consequence, the predicates 'is an instance of water' and 'is an instance of H_2O' signify the same objective property.[1] What makes these identities possible is that our ordinary concept of water, though not specifying its chemical composition, identifies it in a way which does not purport to reveal its real nature (real essence), and hence leaves this nature (essence) as something which can be scientifically determined. Thus our ordinary concept identifies water by reference to such factors as its sensible appearance, its ordinarily-observable forms and sources, and its ordinarily-observable powers and propensities – factors which do not reveal what water is really like in itself. And then science discovers, by a deeper empirical investigation, that the substance which has these observable properties, and hence qualifies as water under our ordinary concept, is H_2O. Other examples, which work in essentially the same way, are the identity of physical heat with molecular motion, the identity of lightning with a certain kind of electrical discharge, and the identity of gold with the element whose atomic number is 79. In each case, the type-identity is established empirically, not a priori. And, in each case, what makes the empirical equation possible is that our ordinary, pre-scientific concept of the relevant type (a concept which identifies the type as something satisfying certain observational criteria) identifies it only 'opaquely', i.e. in a manner which conceals its real nature, thus leaving room for science to uncover this nature and provide its 'transparent' specification. It must be stressed that, while these identities can only be established empirically, they are none the less objectively necessary. We need scientific evidence to establish that they hold; but given that they do hold, they hold in all possible worlds. This does not prevent our envisaging worlds in which the substance-type which satisfies the observational criteria for water is something other than H_2O, or in which the energy-type which satisfies the observational criteria for heat is something other than molecular motion. But, in describing such worlds, we cannot correctly designate these universals as *water* and *heat*.[2]

Now the proponent of the *psychophysical* type-identity thesis will argue that *his* identities should be viewed in a similar way.[3] Thus he will start by claiming that there is a similar opacity in the way that mental types are identified by our ordinary psychological concepts – that, for each such type, our ordinary, pre-scientific concept of that type (the concept signified by its ordinary psychological description) identifies it as the thing which satisfies certain folk-psychological criteria, but without revealing, or purporting to reveal, its real nature. He will then point out that, being opaque, this ordinary mode of identification leaves open the possibility that mental types are, in their real nature, purely physical – that their transparent specification is to be provided in physical, and presumably neurophysiological, terms. Finally, having thus disposed of any a priori objections to it, he will insist that the hypothesis that mental types are in fact physical is, scientifically, a very plausible one and worthy of provisional acceptance. This conclusion, of course, is rather weaker than the identity-theorist would like. The reason why he cannot claim more is that the issue ultimately depends on the results of a scientific (neurophysiological) investigation which is not yet (and indeed nowhere near) complete. After all, the only way to *establish* that a given mental type is physical would be to discover, empirically, its physical nature – in the same sort of way as water was discovered to be H_2O and heat was discovered to be molecular motion. At present, not even the most ardent supporter of type-identity could claim that such discoveries have been made.

It is the first stage of the theorist's argument, however, which is the most crucial one, and on which I want to focus. The identity-theorist is claiming that our ordinary psychological concepts identify mental types *opaquely* – without revealing their real natures. But clearly this opacity-thesis will have to rest on some more specific (and positive) account of the character of these concepts – an account which explains exactly why they are unrevealing in the relevant way. Formally, there are a large number of possibilities here. But the position now standardly adopted is that our ordinary psychological concepts identify the relevant types by reference to the functional properties ascribed to them by common-sense ('folk') psychology. This is the position vigorously defended (separately) by David Lewis and David Armstrong,[4] and I think it is the only one which the theorist could embrace with any degree of plausibility. In particular, even for the case of sensory experience, it is a clear improvement on the earlier suggestion advanced by J. J. C. Smart that the relevant types are identified exclusively by reference to the external (stimulus) conditions which typically induce their instantiation.[5]

To see what this standard position involves, let us focus on a particular case. There are various things which we ordinarily believe about the functional properties of pain, in relation to sensory input (plus its environmental causes), behavioural output (plus its environmental effects), and other mental types.[6] Thus we believe that, unless a person is unconscious or anaesthetized, certain kinds of bodily injury (e.g. grazing of the skin) will induce a sensation of pain in (i.e. phenomenologically in) the affected region. We believe that, in the normal subject, intense pain tends to induce certain kinds of semi-automatic response, like shrieking and wincing. We believe that normal subjects are strongly motivated to avoid pain, and so tend both to keep clear of (what they take to be) pain-inducing situations and to seek relief for pain they already feel. And of course we could go on, almost indefinitely, adding further items to the list or spelling out the details of those already cited. Now, in the position we are envisaging, the type-identity theorist represents these common-sense beliefs about pain, or some appropriate selection of them, as constitutive of our ordinary, pre-scientific concept. He claims that our ordinary concept of pain identifies it as that state (type-state) which meets the conditions imposed on it by these beliefs – as that state which is functionally related to input, behaviour, and other mental types in the ways that these beliefs specify. In short, he claims that our ordinary concept of pain identifies it by its 'folk-psychological' functional profile. And, of course, he advances an exactly similar claim with respect to each mental type. Let us call this account of our ordinary psychological concepts the 'functional-profile' theory. It is clear how the truth of this theory would suffice to sustain and explain the relevant opacity. For if our ordinary psychological concepts identify mental types exclusively by reference to their functional properties, then there is no question of their disclosing the real type-natures. In each case, the concept identifies the type (merely) as that whose instances have a certain characteristic functional role, or cluster of roles, without revealing what the type is in itself.

There is obviously a close resemblance between the functional-profile theory and analytical functionalism. Both positions are claiming that the content of our ordinary psychological concepts is to be spelt out in functional terms. More specifically, both analyse ordinary psychological concepts in such a way that something's qualifying as a mental item of a psychologically specified type depends entirely on the functional role (or cluster of roles) assigned to things of its intrinsic kind. Thus if P is a particular pain-event occurring in Smith on a certain occasion, both the functionalist and the profile-theorist will say that there is some intrinsic type T such that P is an instance of T and such that P qualifies as a pain-event, and as a pain-event of a specific sort, solely in virtue of the fact that T-events have a characteristic functional role (or cluster of roles) in the relevant (class of) causal system(s). None the less, the two positions are also crucially different. For while functionalism equates an item's psychological character with the functional role assigned to its intrinsic type, the functional-profile theory takes an item's psychological character to be an aspect of its intrinsic character, and sees the relevant functional role (which implicitly features in our ordinary conception of its psychological character) as the means by which this intrinsic aspect is initially (albeit opaquely) identified. Thus while the functionalist will say that for Smith to be in pain is for Smith to be in an intrinsic state with the requisite functional properties, the profile-theorist will say that there is an intrinsic state with the requisite functional properties such that for Smith to be in pain is for Smith to be in that state. In other words, while the analytical functionalist construes mental types as functional types, though ones which are always realized by some aspect of the subject's intrinsic condition, the profile-theorist takes them to be intrinsic types, though ones which our ordinary concepts identify by reference to their functional significance.

This difference is directly reflected in the different meanings which the two positions assign to ordinary psychological statements. Thus consider the statement:

(1) Smith is in pain at t.

The functionalist takes pain to be a functional type, but one which can only be realized by the occurrence of some intrinsic state with the requisite functional properties. So, in accordance with the general pattern specified earlier (3.2, p. 52), he construes (1) as equivalent to:

(2) For some intrinsic state (type-state) S, an instance of S

104

occurs in Smith at t, and S has, for Smith at t, such-and-such a functional character

where 'such-and-such ...' gets replaced by a specific functional description appropriate to the concept of pain. In contrast, the profile-theorist takes pain to be an intrinsic type, though one which our ordinary pain-concept only identifies by its functional significance. So he sees (1) as dividing into two components, one of which makes a functionally-mediated identificatory reference to a certain intrinsic state, and the other of which (presupposing the first) ascribes this state, thus identified, to Smith. In other words, he construes (1) as equivalent to:

(3) Concerning that intrinsic state (type-state) – let us call it S – which has, and is unique in having, such-and-such a functional character: an instance of S occurs in Smith at t.

Thus the two construals employ the same basic materials, but in quite different logical arrangements. The functionalist's construal represents (1) as an ascription of a functional state, intrinsically realized: the profile-theorist's construal represents it as an ascription of an intrinsic state, functionally identified. And this pattern, of course, will be repeated for all other psychological statements of a similar form.

The difference between the two positions becomes even more conspicuous when we consider their application to counterfactual situations. Let us suppose that, in the actual world, the functional role conceptually associated with pain is assigned, and uniquely assigned, to the intrinsic type T (say, the firing of C-fibres). Then both the functionalist and the profile-theorist will then want to say, with respect to the actual world, that something is an instance of pain if and only if it is an instance of T. But the assignment of functional roles to intrinsic types is only contingent. So we can envisage a possible world W (a way things might have been) in which T does not have the relevant (pain-associated) functional role. The question is: focusing on the situation from the viewpoint of the actual world, what will the advocates of the two philosophical positions say about the psychological character of T-instances in W? Well, they will make quite different claims. The functionalist, who construes mental types as functional types, will deny that *T*-instances in *W* are instances of pain. He will say that, in any world, actual or possible, something qualifies as an instance of pain if and only if its intrinsic type has the requisite (pain-associated) functional role, and, consequently, he will say that, because *T* lacks that role in *W*, its instances in *W* lack that psychological character. In contrast, the profile-theorist, who construes mental types as intrinsic types, will say that *T*-instances in *W* are (just like *T*-instances in the actual world) instances of pain. For he will say that, in the actual world, *T*'s functional role ensures its identity with pain, and that (like any genuine identity) this identity will then have to hold constant though all possible worlds. The example, of course, could be developed in further ways. Thus we could envisage a world in which, as well as no longer having the pain-associated functional role, *T* has (and is unique in having) the role conceptually associated with some other mental type. Likewise, we could envisage a world in which, as well as losing its assignment to *T*, the pain-role is assigned (and uniquely assigned) to some other intrinsic type. But whatever case we focus on, the general point is that the functionalist always gauges the psychological character of an intrinsic type in a given world by reference to its functional character *in that world*, while the profile-theorist always gauges this by reference to its functional character *in the actual world*. Of course, for the case where the given world *is* the actual world, these methods of gauging coincide – hence the point of focusing on counterfactual situations to bring out the difference between the two positions.

I have offered this as an account of how the functionalist and the profile-theorist handle counterfactual situations. Strictly speaking, I should offer it as an account of how they *ought* to handle them; for, of course, a philosopher may not always draw out the consequences of his position correctly. And in fact David Lewis errs in just this way. For, contrary to the logic of names and transworld-identity, he accepts the type-identity thesis, backed by the functional-profile theory, but allows the physical nature of a given mental type to vary across possible worlds with the varying functional roles assigned to it:

> On my theory, 'pain' is a *contingent* name – that is, a name
> with different denotations in different possible worlds –

since in any world, 'pain' names whatever state happens in that world to occupy the causal role definitive of pain.[7]

If pain is identical to a certain neural state, the identity is contingent. Whether it holds is one of the things that varies from one possible world to another.[8]

Lewis's error stems from his confusion of two quite different questions. The one question is: what would it be correct to say (i.e. from the standpoint of the new world) if a certain hypothetical situation obtained? The other is: what is it correct to say (i.e. from the standpoint of the actual world) about a certain hypothetical situation? Thus Lewis correctly observes that, on the profile-theory he is defending, 'the concept of pain ... would have applied to some different state if the relevant causal relations had been different'.[9] But he wrongly concludes from this that, in contemplating or describing such a possibility, we should apply the concept of pain to the state to which it would have applied had the possibility been actual, rather than to the state to which it in fact applies in the actual world. Thus the whole passage runs:

> The concept of pain, unlike the concept of that neural state which in fact is pain, would have applied to some different state if the relevant causal relations had been different. Pain might not have been pain. The occupant of the role might have not occupied it. Some other state might have occupied it instead. Something that is not pain might have been pain.

The conclusion should have been: pain is the same neural state in all worlds, but there are possible worlds in which pain (= this neural state) does not play the role conceptually definitive of pain (as it functions in the actual world), and there are possible worlds in which some other neural state (not pain) does play this role.

Of course, one can see why Lewis did not *want* this conclusion. For although it follows from his basic position, it does not seem very plausible to suppose that pain and other mental states are rigid with respect to their physical constitution in this way. But the conclusion cannot be avoided just because the advocate of type-identity finds it unpalatable. If Lewis wants the same mental state to vary in its physical constitution over possible worlds, he should embrace the functionalist position in its pure form (in which mental types are construed as functional types) rather than seek to combine a functionalist approach with an acceptance of type-identity. (Incidentally, I am not at the moment saying anything about the issues of variability/rigidity within the actual world. That will be the topic of our discussion in the next section.)

Although it is crucially different from analytical functionalism, the functional-profile theory is, like the latter, a form of analytical reductionism. For it represents our ordinary psychological concepts, and the statements in which they feature, as ones whose content is, in the last analysis, non-mentalistic. Thus, like the functionalist construal which it replaces, the fully elaborated version of (3) above (which was the profile-construal of the statement the Smith is in pain at *t*) would not contain any psychological terms nor presuppose a prior grasp of psychological concepts. And the same would be true of the profile-construals of all other psychological ascriptions. It is true, of course, that the functional profile of a mental type includes facts about its relations with other mental types – a point which might make it seem that the theorist will have to rely on certain primitive psychological concepts. But I am assuming that the holistic solution which we earlier devised for the functionalist (see pp. 56–9) will be available here too.[10] In other words, I am assuming that the profile-theorist can claim that each mental type is identifiable by its place in the total pattern of functional relationships between types, with the consequence that, in the final analysis, each of these relationships can be specified non-mentalistically.

It was to the functional-profile theory that I was referring at the beginning, when I said that there was a further form of analytical reductionism to be considered. Whether this new form will fare better than the two already considered and rejected remains to be seen, though we have already noted one respect (concerning the physical constitution of mental types across possible worlds) in which its consequences are likely to strike us as implausible.

3 THE PROBLEM OF IDENTIFICATION

One thing is clear. With respect to the experiential aspects of the mind, the functional-profile theory fares no better than the straightforwardly functionalist position it replaces. For the very considerations which led us to reject the functionalist account of experience can be seen to discredit the profile account too. Thus just as it seems intuitively clear that the ascription of an experiential state to someone is more than just the ascription of a functional state, so equally it seems intuitively clear that such an ascription is more than just the ascription of an unspecified intrinsic state functionally identified.[11] And just as the blind subject's inability to derive the relevant experiential knowledge from his functional information counted as a decisive objection to a functionalist analysis of experiential concepts, so also it counts as a decisive objection to a profile analysis. At least it does so if, as I am here assuming, the relevant experiential propositions are couched in the ordinary, pre-scientific terms to which the analysis applies, rather than in the physical terms by which the theorist (assuming he accepts type-identity) would ultimately describe the corresponding states of affairs. Moreover, it is clear, I think, that the considerations which discredit the functionalist and functional-profile accounts of experience, would also preclude *any* analytically reductive account. For, in the light of our previous discussion, it is surely now just obvious that our experiential concepts cannot be analysed in wholly non-mentalistic terms.

The fact that the functional-profile theory fails for experience does not, however, mean that it is wrong altogether. Thus just as we envisaged the functionalist responding to these objections by adopting a more cautious position, in which he confined the scope of his reductive analysis to the non-experiential aspects of the mind, so likewise we can now envisage the profile-theorist accepting a similar restriction and claiming that it is only our concepts of the non-experiential mental types which are to be construed in the relevant way. For this reason, while taking note of the inadequacies of the profile-account of experience, we need to investigate the theory on broader front. Is it only the theory's account of experience which is defective? Or does it encounter some more general objection which precludes its application to *any* area of the mind? I shall argue that it does. My argument will be concerned with the familiar topic of 'variable realization'[12] though I shall approach this topic in a slightly unusual way.

The first point which needs to be stressed is that the profile-theorist owes us some further account of how his theory works. For, as things presently stand, it is quite unclear *how* our ordinary psychological concepts are equipped to identify mental types in the way envisaged. To bring out the problem, let us suppose that M is a certain mental type and that F is the functional role (or role-cluster) by which the theorist thinks that M is identified by our ordinary M-concept. Now it could turn out that F is assigned to different intrinsic types in different contexts. For example it could turn out that the type which plays the F-role in one animal species is different from that which plays it in another. Or it could turn out that, within a single species, the type which plays the F-role in one individual is different from that which plays it in another. It could even turn out that, within the history of a single individual, the type which plays the F-role at one phase is different from that which plays it at another. But now envisage a situation in which one of these possibilities obtains. For such a situation, the description 'F-playing type' is not uniquely-identifying: there is no intrinsic type which qualifies as *the* (uniquely) F-playing one. So how, for such circumstances, does the profile-theorist see our ordinary M-concept as homing in on its target? How does he think that the concept manages to identify a unique intrinsic type in cases where more than one type plays the relevant functional role? Let us refer to this as the 'identification-question'.

Theoretically, of course, the profile-theorist could respond to this question by denying that it arises. For he could insist that if the relevant functional role is assigned to different intrinsic types in different contexts, then our ordinary concept simply fails to identify any particular type, and for this reason turns out to be defective. In other words, he could insist that each of our ordinary psychological concepts carries the presupposition that there is only one type which meets the relevant functional conditions, and that in the event of this presupposition failing, the concept lapses.[13] But although it is theoretically available, I doubt if any profile-theorist would

wish to avail himself of this response. For it is surely just obvious that our ordinary psychological concepts do not make themselves hostages to fortune in this way. Thus, on the assumption that mental states are neurally realized, it is surely quite clear that our ordinary concept of pain allows for the possibility that the neural states which play the pain-role in humans are intrinsically different from those which play this role in (say) cats. And, on the same assumption, it is surely equally clear that our ordinary concept of the belief that dodos are extinct allows for the possibility that the neural state which plays the relevant functional role in John is intrinsically different from that which plays this role in Mary. Still more dramatically, it is also surely clear, at least from the mechanistic standpoint of the profile-theorist, that our ordinary psychological concepts allow for the possibility of constructing a machine which reproduces the functional organization of human mentality in a medium which is not even biological. In this last case, admittedly, we are unlikely to think of the object with the relevant functional organization as having a mind – and certainly we would be unwilling to credit it with a mind if it were, as I earlier put it, 'crudely mechanical'.[14] But this has no bearing on the present issue. In his attempt to dismiss the identification-question, the profile-theorist was claiming that each ordinary psychological concept carries the presupposition that there is only one intrinsic type which meets the relevant functional conditions. If our ordinary concepts allow us to envisage a case in which the functional organization of human mentality is reproduced in a non-biological form, it obviously goes against that claim – irrespective of whether the reproduction of the organization brings the mentality with it too.

Another way in which the profile-theorist might try to defuse the problem of identification would be by claiming that where the relevant functional role is assigned to more than one intrinsic type, the mental type is correspondingly generic. Thus, if it turns out that, for a certain pain-type P, the P-associated functional role is assigned to the neural state (type-state) N_1 in humans and to the quite different neural state (type-state) N_2 in cats, then he might say that P is to be identified with the generic state N^* defined by their disjunction (so that, necessarily, something is an instance of N^* if and only if it is either an instance of N_1 or an instance of N_2), or by

whatever larger disjunction is needed to cover further cases of the same sort. Likewise, if it turns out that the functional role associated with the dodo-belief is assigned to different neural states in John and Mary, he might identify the belief-type with some disjunctively defined generic type which covers these states and any others that are relevant. In general, he might say that, for each mental type, our ordinary psychological concept identifies it as that generic type which disjunctively covers all and only those specific intrinsic types to which, in the actual world, the relevant functional role (or role-cluster) is assigned.

There are two things wrong with this proposal. In the first place, although the idea of identifying (ostensibly determinate) mental types with generic intrinsic types may not itself be absurd, the idea of identifying them with the sorts of generic types here envisaged surely is. The trouble with these latter types is that they do not, except *per accidens*, have any real internal unity: each one is defined by the disjunction of a certain set of intrinsic types, which are not required to have anything in common other than their functional role. Indeed, there is not even a guarantee that the set will be confined to *biological* types, since, as we have noted, the relevant functional organization could in principle be reproduced in a non-biological machine. But, given all this, there is surely no case at all for identifying the mental types with these disjunctive types, rather than with the functional types which determine how the disjunctions are composed. For it is surely a presupposition of our ordinary psychological concepts that, even if the mental types they identify are to be ultimately specified in non-psychological terms, these specifications will represent each type as possessing an internal unity appropriate to its unitary status at the psychological level. (Perhaps this point becomes even clearer when we remind ourselves that any type-identities which we accept for the actual world, we have to accept for all possible worlds as well.)

Secondly, even if we waive our intuitions on this point and suppose that there is no objection to identifying mental types with these disjunctive types, the proposal does not succeed in its own terms. The point of the proposal was to ensure that, in a situation where the relevant functional role (or role-cluster) is assigned to different intrinsic types in different contexts,

our ordinary psychological concept still manages to be type-identificatory. But, of course, if there can be situations in which, in different contexts, the same role is assigned to different types, there can equally be situations in which, in different contexts, different roles are assigned to the same type. For example, we can suppose that the neural state which in humans plays the role associated with a certain type of pain, plays the role associated with a different type of sensation in cats. Or again, we can suppose that the neural state which in John plays the role associated with a certain type of belief, plays the role associated with a different type of belief in Mary. But if such a situation obtained, the proposed method of mental-type identification would clearly fail. Thus suppose that, in John, the neural state N has the role associated with the belief that dodos are extinct, and that, in Mary, this same state (with appropriately different connections with the rest of the system) has the role associated with the belief that dinosaurs are extinct. Let us call these respective belief-types B_1 and B_2. Now the proposal is that each mental type is to be identified with that generic type which disjunctively covers all and only those specific types to which (in the actual world) the relevant functional role is assigned. So, according to the proposal, N counts as a determinate of both belief-types: it counts as a determinate of B_1 in virtue of playing the B_1-associated role in John, and it also counts as a determinate of B_2 in virtue of playing the B_2-associated role in Mary. But this obviously leads to absurdity. It would oblige us to say that any instance of N in John is not only an instance of the belief that *dodos* are extinct, but also (though functionally irrelevant to it in this context) an instance of the belief that *dinosaurs* are extinct. And likewise it would oblige us to say that any instance of N in Mary is not only an instance of the belief that *dinosaurs* are extinct, but also (though functionally irrelevant to it in this context) an instance of the belief that *dodos* are extinct. All this would be manifestly unacceptable even from the profile-theorist's own standpoint. Clearly, the theorist cannot afford to make mental types generic at the cost of blurring the distinctions between them.

One way of modifying the proposal, in an attempt to remedy these defects, would be to relativize mental types to the relevant contexts. Thus, in response to the possibility that the

functional role associated with a certain pain-type P is assigned to different neural types in different species, the profile-theorist could say that, even within its own mentalistic framework (the framework available prior to the discovery of its intrinsic nature), we should think of P as a generic mental type with a distinctive specific form for each species – so that we recognize such specific types as *human P*-pain, conceptually identified as whatever 'human-bound' intrinsic type plays the relevant (P-associated) role in humans, and *feline P*-pain, conceptually identified as whatever 'cat-bound' intrinsic type plays this same role in cats. Similarly, in response to the possibility that the functional role associated with the dodo-belief is assigned to different neural types in different human subjects, he could say that, again within its own mentalistic framework, we should think of this belief as a generic type with a distinctive form for each subject – so that we recognize such specific belief-types as *Johannine* believing that dodos are extinct, conceptually identified as whatever 'John-bound' intrinsic type plays the relevant role in John, and *Marian* believing that dodos are extinct, conceptually identified as whatever 'Mary-bound' intrinsic type plays this same role in Mary. And of course the profile-theorist could apply this same procedure to all other cases. The force of the expressions '...-bound', employed in the above examples, is as follows. Suppose that C is a relevant context (e.g. a subject or species of subjects) and T is a type capable of instantiation in C. We can then define the *C-bound variant of T* as that type T' such that, necessarily, something is an instance of T' if and only if it is an instance of T in C. And we can then say that a type is *C-bound* (*tout court*) if and only if there is a type of which it is the C-bound variant. The point of requiring the relevant intrinsic types to be context-bound in this way is to set appropriate limits on the instantiation-fields of the corresponding mental types. Thus the profile-theorist wants the feline form of P-pain to be something which is confined to cats and the Johannine form of dodo-believing to be something which is confined to John.

This relativization of mental types to contexts is the solution favoured by David Lewis,[15] and it certainly avoids the second of the two defects in the previous proposal. Thus, with the relevant intrinsic types context-bound, there is no danger of the theorist's having to count something both as an instance

of the belief that dodos are extinct (in virtue of instantiating the intrinsic type which plays the relevant role in John) and as an instance of the belief that dinosaurs are extinct (in virtue of instantiating the intrinsic type which plays the relevant role in Mary). Moreover, this new approach might also be thought to help with the first defect. For although the unrelativized mental types of our ordinary conceptual scheme still get identified with disjunctively defined intrinsic types, and although the relevant disjuncts are not required to have anything in common apart from their functional role, this may not seem quite so objectionable if the mental types themselves are construed as disjunctive at the psychological level – if, that is, each of these ordinary types is construed as a class of psychologically distinct, context-relativized types. However, whatever its advantages over the earlier proposal, this new position too must be rejected. For a little reflection reveals that the relativization-manoeuvre does not yield a range of mental types which are psychologically distinct in the required way, as I shall now explain.

There can be no denying that, given an ordinary mental type M, whether specific or generic in its own mentalistic framework, we can define a range of context-specific forms of M. For we can define a range of types which are context-bound variants of M in the sense explained above. Thus, given the ordinary dodo-belief B, we can define (amongst other things) both a Johannine form (as that B^j such that, necessarily, something is an instance of B^j if and only if it is an instance of B in John) and a Marian form (as that B^m such that, necessarily, something is an instance of B^m if and only if it is an instance of B in Mary). All this would be no different from, say, defining an Oxford-specific form of scarlet (as necessarily applying to all and only scarlet things in Oxford) or a Cambridge-specific form of circularity (as necessarily applying to all and only circular things in Cambridge). However, dividing an ordinary mental type into context-specific forms in this sort of way does not ensure that the resulting forms will differ in psychological character. And indeed, unless the original (unrelativized) type is independently generic (generic, that is, independently of its representation as a class of context-specific types), it is certain that they will not. This can be seen very clearly in the case of the dodo-belief. Its Johannine and Marian forms, as defined above, are distinct; indeed, they are so defined that nothing can be an instance of both. But clearly they do not differ in psychological character. For each is just the same psychologically determinate belief-type confined to a distinct context of instantiation. There is no more a case for distinguishing the psychological characters of John's believing that dodos are extinct and Mary's believing that dodos are extinct than there is for distinguishing the colour-characters of Oxford and Cambridge patches of scarlet or the shape-characters of Oxford and Cambridge circles. But this means that, with respect to the problem of identification, the whole relativization-procedure is pointless. For where two context-specific types have the same psychological character, the theorist will have to accord them the same intrinsic character too. Thus, faced with the possibility that the functional role associated with the dodo-belief is assigned to different neural types in different subjects, the theorist gains nothing by dividing this belief into its subject-specific forms. For he still has to find a common intrinsic type to identify with the context-generic, but psychologically specific, mental type which they all exemplify.

As far as I can see, there is only one way left by which the profile-theorist could try to secure type-identification. This would be to say that, although, for each mental type M, it is possible for the functional role which is conceptually associated with M to be assigned to different intrinsic types in different contexts, our ordinary concept selects some context as the one which is uniquely relevant to M, and identifies M as the type which plays the relevant role in *that* context. Thus, in response to the possibility that the functional role associated with pain (or P-pain) is assigned to different neural types in different species, he might say that our ordinary concept of pain (P-pain) identifies it as that intrinsic type, whatever it is, which plays the relevant role in *humans*. And, in response to the possibility that the functional role associated with the dodo-belief is assigned to different neural types in different human subjects, he might take a particular individual to be the 'paradigm' dodo-believer and say that our ordinary concept of this belief identifies it as that intrinsic type, whatever it is, which plays the relevant role in *him*. In fact, of course, even such subject-paradigms would not guarantee uniqueness of identification, since the functional role associated with a given mental type could be assigned to different intrinsic types in the same subject at different phases of his history. Thus to be sure of success in the case of the dodo-belief, the theorist would have to say that our ordinary concept of this belief selects some *subject-moment* as the paradigm context relative to which the relevant intrinsic type is identified.

With sufficiently circumscribed paradigms, this approach would manage to secure type-identification: it would ensure that our ordinary psychological concepts identified unique intrinsic types. However, it would do so in a way which was manifestly unacceptable. In fact, it would be unacceptable in two distinct, though closely related ways, which I shall take in turn.

First, the instantiation-conditions which the proposal yields for mental types in relation to non-paradigmatic contexts (i.e. contexts other than those by reference to which the types are identified) are simply not credible. Once again, the case of the dodo-belief offers a very clear example. Let us suppose that, in response to the possibility that the functional role conceptually associated with this belief is assigned to different intrinsic types in different subjects, the profile-theorist recognizes John as the paradigm; in other words, he claims that our ordinary concept of the dodo-belief identifies it as that intrinsic type (whatever it happens to be) which plays the relevant role in John. And let us further suppose that, as a matter of fact, the functional role associated with this belief is assigned to the neural state (type-state) N_1 in John and to the quite different neural state (type-state) N_2 in Mary. In combination, fact and theory will then yield the result that, not only in John, but also in Mary, something qualifies as an instance of the dodo-belief if and only if it is an instance of N_1. But given that, in Mary, the role which is associated with the belief is assigned to N_2 rather than to N_1, this result is clearly unacceptable. For it is clear that we want to tie the presence of this belief in Mary to whatever intrinsic state plays the relevant belief-role in *her* rather than to whatever plays it in someone else. The theorist could, of course, block part of this unacceptable result by claiming that our ordinary concept of the belief represents it as not only paradigmatically but exclusively John's – in other words, by claiming that our ordinary concept, identifies it as that *John-bound* intrinsic type which plays the relevant role in him. This would mean that, while being an instance of N_1 remained a necessary condition for being an instance of dodo-believing, it was no longer sufficient. But this alteration would hardly count as an improvement. For it would yield the even more peculiar result that no-one but John was capable of holding the dodo-belief at all. Moreover, in even allowing the theorist to settle for a *subject*-paradigm, we are, in a sense, pulling our punches. For, as we noted, in order to ensure its identificatory success, the theorist will ultimately have to represent our belief-concept as making reference to a particular subject-*moment*. And with a subject-moment as the paradigm, the resulting implications of the theory, with respect to non-paradigmatic cases, become even more dramatically absurd.

Second, whatever case there may be for supposing that our ordinary psychological concepts (being *our* concepts) accord a special status to *us* in relation to other species, there is clearly no case at all for supposing that, within the human species, there is a particular subject which they characterize as special in relation to other subjects, or (still worse) a particular subject-moment which they characterize as special in relation to other subject-moments. To distinguish this from the first point, we must put the stress on the peculiarity of the particularistic bias rather than on the implausibility of the instantiation-conditions which it yields. The point that is now being made is that, whatever reason there may be for taking mental types to be intrinsic, and for concluding that, in cases where it gets assigned to different intrinsic types in different subjects (subject-moments), the functional role associated with a given mental type does not have a constant psychological significance in all contexts, there would still be no reason for taking the relevant psychological concept to select one particular subject (subject-moment), in preference to the others, as the standard by which the intrinsic nature of the mental type is to be assessed. The only way in which we could begin to make sense of such a bias would be by supposing that each subject's psychological concepts are biased towards himself (or that each subject's concepts at a time are biased towards himself at that time) – so that, for example, my concept (my concept now) of dodo-believing represents me (me-now) as the paradigm, yours (yours now) represents you (you-now) as the paradigm, and so on. But it is surely clear that, even if our ordinary psychological concepts are speciesist, they are not, in this way, egocentric ('ego-currentist'). How, for example, could I seriously think of myself (or worse my current self) as the paradigm believer that dodos are extinct?

We began this whole discussion, not by explicitly attacking the functional-profile theory, but by asking for clarification. For, given the possibility that the relevant functional roles are assigned to different intrinsic types in different contexts, we wanted the theorist to tell us how our ordinary psychological concepts are assured of identificatory-success. If I am right, it turns out that this question has no satisfactory answer: there are a number of ways in which the theorist can try to deal with the issue, but each of them is either unsuccessful in its own terms or involves an account of our concepts which is clearly mistaken. In short, the identification-*question* has now turned into an identification-*objection*, and one which, as I see it, the theorist is unable to meet. And this objection, of course, will discredit the theory not just as an account of *experience*, but with respect to *every* area of the mind.

4 LOCKWOOD'S HYPOTHESIS

Let us now consider where this leaves the type-identity thesis. We have represented the advocate of this thesis as invoking the functional-profile theory as part of the defence of his position. Thus we have represented him as claiming that what makes it possible that mental types are physical is that, for each such type, our ordinary psychological concept of it (the concept signified by the corresponding psychological term) identifies it *opaquely* – i.e. in a way which does not reveal, or purport to reveal, its real nature. And we have further represented him as basing this opacity-claim on the functional-profile theory – as claiming that what creates the relevant opacity is the fact that our ordinary psychological concepts identify mental types exclusively by reference to their functional properties. Now that we have shown the functional-profile theory to be untenable, must the type-identity thesis be rejected too? Or is there some other and more effective way of defending it?

There are two quite different directions in which the type-identity theorist could look for a new line of defence. On the one hand, he could continue to assume that the possibility of type-identity rests on the identificational opacity of our ordinary psychological concepts, but see whether there is a new way of establishing this opacity. On the other hand, he could abandon the opacity-thesis altogether, along with the functional-profile theory on which it was originally founded, and see whether there is some quite different way of securing the possibility of type-identity. No doubt the theorist will start by trying out the first of these approaches, since it involves a much less radical departure from his original (= the standard) position.

There are two reasons, however, why this first approach can be quickly dismissed. In the first place, there is no remotely feasible alternative to the functional-profile theory as a basis for the supposed opacity. The only possibility which suggests itself would be to claim that our ordinary psychological concepts identify mental types wholly or partly by reference to their introspective appearance – in the same way as, for example, our ordinary concepts of water and physical heat identify these things partly by reference to their *sensible* appearance. The idea would be that, with an appropriate distinction between appearance and reality, we could then represent these introspective identifications as opaque. But, as well as only having application to a limited range of mental phenomena (those which, by their experiential character, have an introspective appearance in the relevant sense), this proposal is patently absurd. For, in the case of mentality (or at least, the experiential mentality to which the proposal applies), the distinction between how things are and how they subjectively seem cannot be drawn, at least in this sharp way. We can make sense of the claim that the way physical heat feels to a percipient conceals its real nature, since its feeling this way is just a matter of its having certain sensory effects on the mind. But we cannot make sense of the suggestion that the way pain feels to its subject conceals its real nature, since pain and this way of feeling are one and the same. Admittedly, we could choose to redefine the term 'pain' so as to signify, not the feeling itself, but whatever physical state causally underlies it, and (assuming for the sake of argument identificatory success) this would create the relevant identificational opacity. But it would also leave us without any reason to classify pain in its new sense as a mental state – let alone as a form of experience. And of course it would still leave the theorist unable to cope with the feeling itself.

The second reason why the first approach must be rejected is that, even if the identity-theorist could find a suitable replacement for the functional-profile theory (i.e. a replacement which was prima facie feasible from his own standpoint), the new account would be bound to fall foul of the same kind of identification-objection as the original. For we can see in advance that, within the limits set by the opacity-thesis, there is no way of assigning content to our ordinary psychological concepts which *both* ensures identificatory success (each concept identifying a unique mental type) *and* yields mental-type instantiation-conditions that are remotely plausible. The point is that, granted the assumption that the intrinsic character of a mental item cannot be, even in part, transparently specified in psychological terms (an assumption to which the defender of the opacity-thesis is committed), it is just obvious that, for any given mental type, our ordinary psychological concept of it leaves room for the possibility of its 'variable realization' – the possibility of its assuming quite different intrinsic (presumably different physical) forms in different contexts. And our earlier discussion already makes it clear why the recognition of such a possibility cannot be satisfactorily combined with a construal of mental types as themselves intrinsic.

What then of the second approach, in which the identity-theorist tries to base his position on something other than the opacity-thesis? Well this too might not, at first sight, look very promising. For granted that psychological and physical descriptions (at least when they are *explicitly* psychological and physical) are not deductively related, it might seem that the only way to make sense of the suggestion that mental types could turn out to be physical would be by supposing that their real natures are not fixed by our conception of them in psychological terms. And this, of course, would be to invoke the discredited opacity-thesis in the way already envisaged. In fact, though, there is another possibility. For conceivably, the identity-theorist might try to reach his goal from the opposite direction. Thus instead of basing his position on the claim that the real natures of the relevant mental types are not revealed by their psychological descriptions, and hence are available for ultimate physical specification, he might base it on the claim that the real natures of the relevant physical types are not revealed by their (ordinary) physical descriptions, and hence are available for ultimate psychological specification. This new strategy is altogether less familiar than the one we have been considering, and before I try to specify more precisely what it involves, I must spend some preliminary time setting the scene.

A claim commonly made by empiricist philosophers – at least by those of a broadly Lockean persuasion – is that we can only acquire knowledge of the *structure* of the physical world, not of its (fundamental) *content*. Now, granted the framework of physical realism, which takes the physical realm to be conceptually and metaphysically fundamental, and confining our attention to knowledge which we acquire, directly or indirectly, through sense-perception, this claim, suitably interpreted, seems to me well-founded. Thus while, from our observations, and from the way these observations support certain kinds of explanatory theory, we can establish that there is an external 'space' with a certain geometrical structure (i.e. one that is three-dimensional, continuous, and (approximately) Euclidean), I would argue that we can never find out what, apart from its structure, this space is fundamentally like in itself – what kind of thing it is which has these geometrical properties and which forms the medium for physical objects and events.[16] Likewise, while, in the same empirical way, we can establish that there are external objects located in this space, and can discover their shape and size, their spatial and spatiotemporal arrangement, their causal powers and sensitivities, and the various ways in which complex objects are composed of simpler ones, I would argue that we can never discover the fundamental nature of their space-filling content, since we can never find out, beyond their spatiotemporal and causal properties, what the simplest objects (the fundamental particles) are like in themselves. Of course, we ordinarily *take* our physical knowledge to be more than merely structural; for, prior to philosophical reflection, we think of physical space and its occupants as being, in their intrinsic natures, as our sense-experiences (especially our visual and tactual experiences) represent them. But while this view is natural enough, and perhaps, for ordinary purposes, unavoidable, it has, as I see it, no rational justification – at least if taken as a view about the fundamental reality. We cannot directly compare our sensory representations with the external items to see if they match, since we only have access to these items through the representations. Nor can we use an inference to the best explanation to justify an ascription of sensible content to the physical world, since it is only the theories about structure which play an explanatory role. The only way we could legitimately credit physical objects with the sensible qualities which characterize their appearance would be by adopting one or other version of the dispositional account discussed earlier, taking their possession of such qualities to be, or to be constituted by, their relevant powers to affect human sense-experience.[17] But such an approach would obviously have no bearing on the issue of *fundamental* intrinsic content.

Let us call this account of our epistemological situation the 'structuralist thesis'. Now obviously this thesis calls for a much more detailed elaboration and defence than I have provided here.[18] But, for the sake of the present discussion, let us assume that it is correct. The crucial point now is that the thesis might be of use to the advocate of type-identity. For if sense-perception, together with all the scientific theorizing which we build on it, only furnishes us with structural knowledge of the physical world, then perhaps we could think of introspection as revealing, in certain special (cerebral) regions, aspects of its fundamental content. It is this ingenious suggestion which has recently been advanced by Michael Lockwood, developing some of the key ideas in Russell's theory of neutral monism.[19]

Let us focus on an example. Suppose that, on a certain occasion, Smith is in pain. Let X be the particular pain-item occurring in Smith's mind on this occasion, and let Y be that neural item (e.g. a particular event of C-fibre firing) which simultaneously occurs in Smith's brain and with which, according to the identity-theorist, X is to be identified. (So far, of course, this is only to envisage a *token*-identity.) Now using only sense-perception and scientific inference, we have no way of discovering the fundamental intrinsic nature of Y beyond a specification of its structural properties. The closest we could come, by such methods, to a knowledge of Y's fundamental nature would be to gain a description of it in the perspective

of particle physics. And while such a description would reveal
Y as an instance of a certain spatial or spatiotemporal configuration of particles, with certain powers and sensitivities, it would
not reveal anything about Y's fundamental intrinsic content: it
would not tell us anything about what the particles are like in
themselves, beyond (if they have any) their shape and size,
nor anything about the nature of the space in which they are
arranged, beyond its geometrical structure. In the face of this,
Lockwood's suggestion is that we should identify X with Y
(assuming that Y is the *right* neural item) and take X's
'phenomenal' character as a pain, i.e. its psychological character as revealed by introspection, to form, or to form an
aspect of, Y's fundamental physical content. In other words,
Lockwood asks us to suppose that, while the physical scientist
who investigates Smith's brain from the outside cannot discover
anything about Y's fundamental physical content, Smith himself
is, from the inside, directly aware of at least some aspect of
this content, simply by feeling the pain. Moreover, he invites
us to reach a similar conclusion with respect to experience in
general. He asks us to suppose that, whenever a human subject
has an experience, the experience is identical with some neural
item in the subject's brain, and that its 'phenomenal' (introspectible) qualities form, or contribute to, its fundamental
physical content.

Lockwood's proposal, as I have said, is ingenious. What is
less clear is whether there is any reason to accept it. Certainly
the structuralist thesis on its own does not seem to provide
much in the way of support. For why should the fact that
fundamental physical content is beyond the scope of sense-
perception and scientific inference give one any reason to
suppose that, in the case of the relevant neural items, it
coincides, wholly or partly, with what is introspectively revealed
to the subject? Admittedly, it can be plausibly argued that the
limitations on the scope of perception-based physical *knowledge* carry over into our very system of physical *concepts*, and
that it would only be in introspective terms (by forming an
introspective conception of it) that we could so much as form
a positive conception of what the fundamental content of a
physical item might be like. But even if this point affords some
grounds for supposing that the intrinsic qualities which
feature in the various forms of fundamental physical content

are the same as, or of the same general sort as, those which feature in human experience (and it is by no means clear that it does), it does not, as such, afford grounds for postulating any special connection between neural items and the experiences of the subjects in whose brains these items occur. It does not, for example, afford any grounds for supposing that Smith's pain-experience is identical with some neural event in his brain and that the introspectible character of the experience forms, or forms an aspect of, this event's fundamental physical nature. In other words, even if our inability to form any positive conception of an alternative counts as a reason for taking the fundamental content of the physical world to be, in some way, mental or mind-like, it cannot possibly, on its own, give us reason to expect some sort of coincidence, at the point of our brains, between the nature of this mental content and human psychology.

However, I take it that Lockwood is not trying to base his hypothesis purely on these points about our epistemic and conceptual situation in relation to the physical world. Of course, these points are crucial in providing the basic framework in which we can begin to make sense of the hypothesis. But, for its positive support, I assume that he is relying on a number of further claims about human mentality, which are quite independent of these limitations on our epistemic and conceptual capacities. There are, in particular, four claims that I think he would want to advance for this purpose: first, that, irrespective of how we go on to deal with mental *types*, there is a strong scientific case for taking mental *items* to be physical, and, in particular, for identifying them with neural items in the subject's brain; second, that the case for taking mental items to be physical is also a case for supposing that it is *as physical* items (i.e. by virtue of their physical properties) that they are able to exert a causal influence on what takes place in the physical world; third, that, irrespective of whether mental items are physical or non-physical, it is clear that introspection reveals aspects of their intrinsic natures – or at least that it does so in cases where the items are experiential; and fourth, that once it has been agreed that mental items have a causal influence on the physical world, it is very hard to deny that their psychological properties, as revealed by introspection, typically contribute to this influence. In combination, these four claims point to precisely the conclusion which Lockwood reaches. The role of the structuralist thesis would then be to show how such a conclusion is possible – to show that our ordinary, perception-based knowledge of the physical world runs out at just the point where the putative introspective form becomes available. And the role of the further thesis, concerning the limits on our powers of conception, would be to show that the conclusion is one which, on reflection, we should not find unnatural or inherently implausible, since the only alternatives which we can concretely envisage are ones of the same general (mentalistic or quasi-mentalistic) kind.

Let us assume, then, that Lockwood is approaching things in this sort of way – that he is relying on an independent argument about mentality to provide the positive support for his hypothesis, and that he is using the theses about physical knowledge and conception only as a way of trying to show that we can follow through the argument without creating problems on another front. Even so, I think that his position is open to a decisive objection. For although our perception-based knowledge only covers the structure of the physical world, not its fundamental content, it seems to me that the character of the structure, as science reveals it, does not permit the content to take the form that Lockwood envisages: the pegs of human experience are not appropriately shaped to fit the holes defined by the structural theories of science.[20]

Let us continue to focus on the case of X and Y. As we have said, physical science would ultimately characterize Y as a spatial or spatiotemporal configuration of particles. The gaps in what science can thereby reveal concern the intrinsic natures of the particles, apart from (if they have any) their shape and size, and the intrinsic nature of physical space, apart from its geometrical structure. But how could Y's being a pain help to fill those gaps? Or how could it be an aspect of what fills them? The basic problem is that, even if we can make sense of the idea of pain as a form of physical content, there seems to be no suitable connection between its supposed occurrence as an introspectible aspect of the neural item and this item's scientifically revealed complexity. To envisage a content for Y, we have to assign content-properties to its component particles and represent the particles as standing in certain content-specific spatial relations. But is very hard to see how such properties and relations, even if psychological in character, could combine to yield the introspectible pain-quality which allegedly attaches to the neural item as a whole.

Lockwood might say, I suppose, that the relationship between Y's introspectible pain-character and the properties of its microstructure is like that between the overall shape of some complex of dots and those detailed facts, about the sizes of the dots and their spatial arrangement, by which its shape is ultimately determined. Consider, for example, the following array:

If we stand at some distance from it, we only detect its overall squareness, not its internal, dot-formed complexity. None the less, it is precisely the details of its dot-formed complexity which give the array its overall shape and allow its visual appearance, as an unbroken outline, to count as a veridical representation in a certain perspective. Perhaps Lockwood could say that, in a similar way, Y's character as a pain is formed out of the properties of its constituent particles and the character of their arrangement, but that Smith's intro-spection just presents the psychologically significant gestalt, without revealing the underlying complexity. However, I cannot see how such a suggestion could be coherently developed. The only way we could begin to make sense of it would be by supposing that Y's constituent particles were themselves minute pains, or perhaps pains with minute phenomenological loca-tions. But this would fail to explain why other types of neural item, though built (in different spatial or spatiotemporal arrangements) out of similar physical components, produced quite different kinds of experience. How, for instance, could a different arrangement of pain-particles yield a visual experi-ence or a surge of anger? In short, the gaps in what science reveals have to be plugged in a consistent manner – so that if a certain type of particle has a pain-content in one context, it has a pain-content in all. But, with such consistency, the suggested approach does not permit a sufficiently diverse range of introspective gestalts, simply because *all* neural items are built out of the same types of fundamental physical ingredient.

The only other thing Lockwood could say would be that, though part of its fundamental (irreducible) physical content, Y's pain-character is something causally 'emergent', and hence something which (though causally depending on them) is logically separate from, and genuinely additional to, the forms of content which permeate Y's microstructure. It would then no longer matter that all types of neural item involve the same types of microstructural content, since Lockwood would not be trying to provide a microstructural explanation of the introspectible quale except in (contingent) causal terms. But this proposal too, it seems to me, makes no sense. For unless the pain-character has a more intimate (logical) connection with the properties of the microstructure, I do not see how it can count as an aspect of Y's *physical* nature. It is not that there is any difficulty as such in the notion of an emergent physical property: we can easily enough envisage a case in which the microstructural properties of a physical item cause it to have a further physical property with an ontological life of its own. But, in any such case, our conception of the relevant property as physical and our understanding of how it characterizes the relevant item are quite independent of the causally emergent role to which we assign it. The trouble in the present case is that our initial conception of the pain-quality does not represent it as physical, and so, in trying to explain the sense in which the quality forms an aspect of Y's physical nature, its causal emergence from Y's microstructural character is the only factor to which we could appeal. But clearly this factor is not enough for that purpose. For the fact that its realization causally results from certain aspects of Y's physical nature does not oblige us to think of the quality itself as physical. It does not even oblige us to think of the quality (whether physical or non-physical) as a quality of Y.

It might be wondered whether Lockwood's theory would fare better in the case of something like *visual* experience, where there seems to be more chance of the introspectible complexity matching that of the neural item. But, for three reasons, such a change would make no difference. In the first place, whatever type of experience we consider, its complexity will be considerably less than that of its neural correlate as specified at the level of particle physics. So, in the last analysis, the situation in the new case will be the same as in the case of pain. Secondly, however complex the experience, its complexity will have a quite different form from that of the neural correlate as specified by particle physics. The point here is simply that, to the extent that there is any mirroring of the experiential structure in the neural structure, this will only show up when the neural item is specified at a much higher level of physical theory – presumably at the level of neurophysiology. Thirdly, and perhaps this is the most crucial point, even if an experience and its neural correlate were relevantly isomorphic, there would still be the problem of how to give the fundamental physical constituents sufficient experiential flexibility. Thus if we are dealing with a visual experience, then presumably we have to assign visual qualities to the constituents of the neural item in order to account for its introspectible character. But these qualities would not be appropriate to the roles of similar physical constituents in neural items correlated with non-visual experiences. There is no getting away from the fact that, at the level of particle-physics, *all* neural items, whatever their experiential character or experiential associations, are built out of the same types of physical ingredient.

It seems to me, then, that, for all its ingenuity, Lockwood's version of the type-identity thesis cannot be coherently developed. There is still, of course, the four-claim argument which I envisaged Lockwood offering in support of his position, and I have yet to deal with this. My response here will be to reject the argument at its first stage – to deny that there is a strong scientific case for taking mental items to be physical. But this is a matter which is best left till later, after we have had an opportunity to look in more detail at the whole issue of token-identity.

Finally, although we cannot take human introspection to be the revealer of physical content in the way that Lockwood suggests, I think that the structuralist thesis *does* allow us to envisage ways in which fundamental physical content could turn out to require a psychological specification. It is just that, to envisage these ways, we would need to alter Lockwood's approach in two crucial respects. Thus, in the first place, we would need to look for an account which, while still physically realist, was *radically* mentalistic – an account which represented the whole physical world as mental through and through. And secondly, we would need to abandon any idea of an overlap, even at the point of the human brain, between the mentality which is constitutive of the physical world and the mentality of human subjects. Exactly how such mentalistic accounts could be developed, and whether they would have any rationale, are matters I have dealt with in detail elsewhere, and I shall not try to go over the same ground here.[21] In any case, such issues lie outside the scope of our present concern. For they are relevant to an enquiry into the nature of the physical world, rather than into the nature and status of the mind.

5

TOKEN-IDENTITY AND METAPHYSICAL REDUCTIONISM

1 INTRODUCTION

As we have seen, the thesis of psychophysical identity comes in two versions. On the one hand, there is the thesis of *token-identity*, which applies to mental particulars. This asserts that each mental item is identical with a physical (neural) item, where the expression 'mental item' is used to cover all the various episodes and instances of mentality – to cover all those particulars, like sensations, sense-experiences, imaginings, and believings, which form the concrete ingredients of the mind. On the other hand, there is the stronger thesis of *type*-identity, which applies to mental universals. This asserts that each mental type (i.e. type of mental item) is identical with a physical (neural) type (i.e. type of physical item). In other words, as well as accepting the identity of mental items with physical items, it asserts that the psychological character of any such item is identical with some aspect of its physical character. We have already examined and rejected the *type* thesis. But we have still to consider the *token* one, and it is to this that I now turn. Doing so will also give me the opportunity of filling a crucial gap in our previous discussion at another point. For the topic of token-identity will immediately lead us into a consideration of metaphysical reductionism – a position we have frequently referred to, but not yet properly discussed.

There is one small preliminary point of terminology. Mental items, and the physical particulars with which the identity-theorist wants to equate them, are of various ontological sorts. But, in what follows, it will be convenient to classify them all as *events*. In doing so, we shall be giving the term 'event' a

131

slightly broader-than-usual sense. We normally only speak of something as an event if it involves some change in the condition of the world at the time, or over the period, of its occurrence. But, as we shall now use the term, any instance (concrete realization) of a state at a time will qualify as an event, whether or not it marks some alteration in how things are. Thus we shall be able to speak of the event of someone's believing something at a certain time (= the instance, or concrete realization, of the relevant belief-state in this subject at that time), without implying that the belief is one which he has just acquired; and we shall be able to speak of the event of someone's being in a certain neural state at a certain time, without implying that the state is one into which he has just come. Although a departure from ordinary usage, this broad use of the term 'event' has become the standard philosophical practice in this area, and it is for this reason that I adopt it in the present discussion.

In adopting this broad use, we must be careful not to confuse an *event* of something's being in a certain state with the corresponding *state of affairs*. States of affairs are individuated more finely than events: if the properties of being F and being G are distinct, then, for any object x and time t, the states of affairs of x's being F at t and x's being G at t must also be distinct. But the corresponding events may be the same. To take a simple example, suppose someone is holding something (e.g. a penny) which is both round and brown. Then the state of affairs of his holding something brown is different from the state of affairs of his holding something round. But there is only one concrete event. This distinction between events and states of affairs is obviously crucial in the present context, where we are formulating the token-identity thesis as a thesis about events. Without it, the *token* thesis would become equivalent to the *type* thesis which we have already rejected.

2 TOKEN-IDENTITY: THE PRIMA FACIE PROBLEM

The token-identity thesis is currently very popular. The main reason for this is that it seems to permit a more plausible account of the causal relations between mind and body than any which is available if the thesis is rejected. There are two related aspects to this. In the first place, if we suppose that mind and body are ontologically separate, so that mental items do not occur within the framework of the physical world, there is the problem of how we can make sense of the claim, which it would be difficult to deny, that there is causal traffic between them. How can we think of the mind and the body as coming into causal contact unless the events which take place in them are located in the same spatiotemporal system? Secondly, the impressive progress of physical science makes it natural to assume that any physical event, to the extent that it can be causally explained at all, can be causally explained in purely physical terms – in terms of prior physical events and conditions and physical laws. And it seems that once this assumption has been made, we would be obliged to identify mental events with physical events in order to allow them the causal efficacy which we believe them to possess. Both these issue are ones which I shall be discussing in detail in the next chapter. I mention them now to give some rough idea of the kinds of consideration on which the token-identity thesis is based.

Whatever arguments the token-identity theorist can develop in support of his position, they will not be effective if the position itself is incoherent. And it is here that we encounter the most fundamental issue. Can we really make sense of the psychophysical identities which the theorist is postulating? Can we understand what it would be for the event of someone's being in pain to be the very same as the event of his neurons firing in a certain way, or for the event of someone's believing that dodos are extinct to be the very same as the event of his brain containing a certain neuronal network? The prima facie problem is obvious. Mental and neural events seem to be events of quite different kinds – events with quite different intrinsic natures, needing to be specified in quite different terms. Are we not obliged to say that the events are different simply because their natures are different – in the way that cabbages are different from kings and lumps of chalk are different from lumps of cheese?

Of course, there is no difficulty as such in the notion of the same concrete event being an instance of different event-types. The event of someone's pressing a switch, for example, may be the same as the event of his turning on the light, and the event of someone's moving a piece of wood from one square on a board to another may be the same as the event of his checkmating his opponent. These cases are unproblematic, because we can see exactly how each of the event-types leaves room for, and combines with, the other. Thus we know that an event of switch-pressing will qualify as an event of turning on the light if it has the appropriate electrical and photic effects. And we know that, in the context of chess, the movement of a piece will qualify as an event of checkmate if it conforms to certain rules and creates a position of a certain kind. The problem in the case of the alleged psychophysical identities is that there seems to be no analogous way of understanding how the event-types fit together – of comprehending how the psychological and physical descriptions home in on the same target. Suppose, for example, we are considering the alleged identity of a pain-event P, occurring in Smith's mind at t, with a neural event N (e.g. some firing of the C-fibres), occurring in Smith's brain at t. Our conception of P in terms of its psychological (introspectively manifest) character seems to offer no clue as to how it could also have a neural character, and our conception of N in terms of its physical (scientifically discoverable) character seems to offer no clue as to how it could also have an experiential character. Nor, on the face of it, does there seem to be any way of combining these different conceptions in the framework of some richer perspective in which the coincidence of their objects is made clear. Thus once we have envisaged something as a pain, we seem to have no way, other than by merely stipulating that it is a neural item, of making it clear to ourselves how this same thing could be available for inspection by a physiologist. And once we have envisaged something as an event of C-fibre firing, we seem to have no way, other than by merely stipulating that it is a mental item, of making it clear to ourselves how this same thing could be accessible to introspection. In short, it seems that we can form no conception of what it would be for the relevant psychological and physical event-types to be coinstantiated other than a purely formal one – the formal grasp of what it means to say that there is something which is an instance of both.

The difficulties for the identity-theorist become even more

manifest when we consider the modal properties of mental and neural events. Let us continue to focus on the example of *P* and *N*. We have a strong initial intuition that, whatever its relations with the physical world, *P* is *essentially* a pain-event – that it would be logically impossible for *P* to occur without possessing its pain-experiential character. At the same time, we have the equally strong intuition that, whatever its relations with *P*, *N* is *not* essentially a pain-event. For we can surely envisage a counterfactual situation in which exactly the same neural event occurs in Smith's brain at *t* (its identity as *N* being fixed by its physical properties, its brain location, and its causal origins), but in which, with a suitable change in psycho-physical law, Smith does not have a pain-experience at *t*. But if we retain both these intuitions, we are forced to conclude that *P* and *N* are numerically distinct. For, between them, the two intuitions entail that there is a property (that of being essentially a pain-event) which is true of *P* but not of *N*. Moreover, it seems that the same considerations will preclude psycho-physical identity in each case. For, given any mental event *x* and neural event *y*, we have the same two initial intuitions that *x*'s psychological character is essential to *x* but not to *y*.

This, in effect, is Kripke's argument against token-identity, as briefly presented in his *Naming and Necessity*.[1] The argument is not, as it stands, conclusive, since the identity-theorist might still be able to find some way of discrediting one of the modal intuitions on which it is based. Thus, in the case of *P* and *N*, he might be able to show that, despite initial appearances, the pain-event does not possess its pain-experiential character esssentially. Or alternatively, he might be able to show that, despite initial appearances, we cannot envisage a counterfactual situation in which the neural event occurs without Smith's being in pain. In the present context, the point of introducing the argument is to bring out the full measure of the prima facie problem which the identity-theorist faces. If the theorist is to retain his position, he must show us how to make sense of the postulated identities; and this means, in particular, showing us how we can discard one of the two modal intuitions which jointly entail that the relevant events are distinct.

One thing which promises to make the theorist's task more difficult is that the two most obvious ways of trying to meet the problem have already been blocked by the results of our previous discussion. Thus:

(i) The theorist might try to make sense of his position by invoking a functionalist analysis of our psychological concepts. Clearly, if it were available, such an analysis would be ideal for his purposes: it would eliminate the prima facie problem at a stroke. Thus if the psychological specification of P were construed as a specification of its functional character (i.e. of the characteristic role of events of P's intrinsic type in the relevant (Smith-at-t) causal system), there would be no difficulty in understanding how P could be identical with N. For, thus construed, the psychological specification of P would be neutral with respect to its intrinsic nature and so leave open the possibility of P's being intrinsically physical. Nor, of course, would there be any problem with the modal intuitions. It may not be entirely clear what functional properties, if any, are essential to N. But once this had been settled, one or other of the two modal intuitions would be discredited. Most likely we would decide that it was logically possible for N to occur without having that functional character required for its qualification as a pain-event, and, on this basis, conclude that P itself (= N) only possesses its pain-experiential character contingently.

(ii) The theorist might try to make sense of his *token*-identity position by invoking the stronger thesis of *type*-identity. Again, if available, this would be ideal for his purposes. If P's psychological type could be equated with a neurophysiological type, there would be no difficulty in understanding how P could be identical with N. For to understand this identity, we would only have to understand how N itself could have the appropriate neurophysiological character. Nor, once the essential physical properties of N had been fixed, would there be any difficulty in discarding one of the modal intuitions. Most likely, the relevant neurophysiological type (i.e. the type with which P's psychological type gets identified) would turn out to be essential to N, with the result that its pain-experiential character would be essential to it as well.

Both analytical functionalism and the type-identity thesis, then, would ideally serve the token-identity theorist's purposes: they would leave us with no difficulty over under-standing how mental and neural events could be identical. The only trouble is that, since each has been refuted in our previous discussion, neither of these positions is now available. Admittedly, in the case of analytical functionalism, the theorist might still be able to salvage something. For, in rejecting the full-blooded functionalist position, I have left room for the adoption of a weaker position, which is both scope-restricted and less-than-fully reductive – a position in which the func-tionalist analysis is both confined to the non-experiential aspects of mentality and makes explicit use of the experiential concepts which it does not attempt to cover. And this weaker form of functionalism could then be used to facilitate token-identity within the area to which it applies, i.e. token-identity with respect to those categories of mental phenomena whose psychological character is being construed in functionalist terms. However, for the time being, I want to confine my attention to a token-identity thesis which is not restricted in this way – a thesis which asserts that *all* mental items are identical with physical (neural) items. And for the defence of this thesis, the weaker form of functionalism would be of no . avail.

Analytical functionalism and the type-identity thesis were the theorist's most obvious options, and the fact that these have been blocked makes his situation much more difficult. In effect, he has to accept that the identity of a mental with a neural item involves the co-instantiation of two quite different intrinsic natures, thus acknowledging the prima facie severity of the problem posed. Even so, there is still one further way in which he could try to make sense of his position. To see how, we need to remind ourselves of a possibility to which I accorded some prominence in my introductory remarks,[2] but which has hardly surfaced in the subsequent discussion.

3 METAPHYSICAL MENTAL REDUCTIONISM

In the first chapter, I drew a distinction between two forms of mental reductionism, which I labelled 'analytical' and 'meta-physical'. The analytical form claims that statements about the mind turn out, on conceptual analysis, to have a content which is wholly non-mentalistic. At its strongest, this becomes the claim that each statement about the mind can be exactly reformulated by a sentence which does not contain psychological terms, or in any other way presuppose a grasp of psychological concepts, and which reveals the statement's true propositional content. The metaphysical form, in contrast, concedes that statements about the mind have an irreducibly mentalistic content, and hence resist non-mentalistic reformulation, but claims that mental facts are wholly constituted by non-mental facts – that, for each mental fact F, there is a non-mental fact or set of facts F', such that F obtains in virtue of F' and such that the obtaining of F is nothing over and above the obtaining of F'. Thus, while the analytical reductionist thinks of mental facts as just a subset of non-mentalistically expressible facts (or, at least, of facts which would be non-mentalistically expressible but for the factors of vagueness and infinite complexity[3]), the metaphysical reductionist regards them as *sui generis* but metaphysically derivative: he acknowledges that such facts can only be expressed or conceived in mentalistic terms, but insists that their obtaining is wholly sustained by a realm of more fundamental facts of a quite different kind.

We have examined and rejected three versions of analytical reductionism – that of the behaviourist, that of the functionalist, and that of the functional-profile theorist. As far as I can see, these are the only versions worth considering. And in any case, I think it is clear that the arguments we have brought against them would, suitably adapted, suffice to refute any other version that might be suggested. From now on, therefore, I shall take it as established that analytical reductionism is false.

What we still have to consider is the possibility of *metaphysical* reductionism. And this further issue is important in two ways. First, it is important in its own right, in as much as metaphysical reductionism is an anti-dualist position which we have not yet refuted. Secondly, it is of crucial relevance to the issue of token-identity. For it is here that the identity-theorist gets his further (and final) chance of trying to make sense of his position. The point is that, while the failure of both analytical reductionism and type-identity forces the theorist to accept that the psychological character of a mental item is something *sui generis* (something which cannot be specified or conceived in any but mentalistic terms), it does not commit him to regarding it as metaphysically fundamental. He is still free to insist that an item's possession of this character is wholly constituted by other (more fundamental) facts about it. And, consequently, he is free to insist that its possession of this character is wholly constituted by facts (for example, neurophysiological or functional facts) which exclusively relate to its nature as a physical entity. In this way, the theorist could invoke metaphysical reductionism as the means of rendering his identity-claims intelligible.

Bearing in mind, then, that it has this double interest (both as an anti-dualist position in its own right and as a prop for the token-identity thesis), we must now explore the case of metaphysical reductionism in more detail. In doing so, it will be natural and convenient to focus on such reductionism in its standard, materialist form – a form which takes mental facts to be ultimately constituted by *physical* facts. The arguments I use, however, and the conclusions I draw from them, are intended to apply to metaphysical mental reductionism in general.

We must begin by trying to get clear about the notion of constitution which features in the reductionist's claim. So far, all I have said, by way of elucidating this, is that a fact F is wholly constituted by a fact or set of facts F' if and only if two conditions hold:

(1) F obtains in virtue of F'
(2) The obtaining of F is nothing over and above the obtaining of F'.[4]

But before we can hope to understand the nature of the reductionist's position, we need to spell out the content of these two conditions in more detail.

One thing which is implied by both conditions is that the obtaining of F' logically necessitates the obtaining of F. In other words, if F is the fact that p and F' is the fact that q (or the set of facts that q_1, that q_2, ...), each condition implies that it is logically necessary that if q (q_1, q_2, ...), then p. I am here using the term 'logical' (or 'logically') in a fairly broad sense, so that any necessity will count as logical if and only if it is stronger than mere *natural* (nomological) necessity. In other words, it is logically necessary that p if and only if there is no possible world, not even a world with different natural laws, in which it is not the case that p. The most important aspect of this is that, to qualify as logically necessary, a truth does not have to be establishable a priori. Thus, even though they can only be established by appeal to empirical evidence, both the identity of Hesperus (the Evening Star) with Phosphorus (the Morning Star) and the identity of water with H_2O qualify as logical necessities, since they are necessities of the relevantly strong kind.[5]

As I have said, both (1) and (2) separately imply that the obtaining of F' logically necessitates the obtaining of F. There are two reasons why such necessitation is not, on its own, sufficient for constitution, and it is these reasons which bring to light the further implications of, and consequential differences between, the two conditions.

In the first place, logical necessitation is not, as such, asymmetric. There are cases in which the obtaining of a fact (or set of facts) F_1 logically necessitates the obtaining of a fact (or set of facts) F_2, *and vice versa*. The obvious example is that in which the facts (sets of facts) are the same; for, trivially, the obtaining of any fact logically necessitates itself. Now we want the constitution-relation to be asymmetric, so that if F is constituted by F', then F' is not constituted by F. For we want constitution to be such that, where F is constituted by F', F *derives* its obtaining *from* (*owes* its obtaining *to*) the obtaining of F', in a way which precludes the same relationship holding in reverse. It is this element of asymmetric dependence which, in addition to mere logical necessitation, is expressed by saying (in condition (1)) that F obtains *in virtue of F'*.[6]

Secondly, there are cases where one fact is logically necessitated by some other fact or set of facts, but where its obtaining has, if I may put it thus, an ontological life of its own, separate from, and genuinely additional to, the obtaining of the fact or facts which necessitate it. For example, the fact that God (who is essentially omnipotent) decrees that there be light logically necessitates the fact that there is light; but there is still an obvious sense in which, simply because it concerns the nature of the physical world rather than the activities of God, the obtaining of this second fact, i.e. the existence of light, is something separate from, and genuinely additional to, the obtaining of the first. Or to take another, and in some ways analogous, example: the fact that the world is in a certain state S_1 at time t_1, together with the nomological facts recording the laws of nature, may logically necessitate the fact that the world is in a state S_2 at the later time t_2 (for it may be possible to deduce the t_2-state from the t_1-state together with the statements of law); but again, there is an obvious sense in which, simply because it concerns the state of the world at a later time, the obtaining of the second fact is separate from, and genuinely additional to, the obtaining of the first. Now we want the constitution-relation to exclude this kind of separateness, so that where F is constituted by F', the obtaining of F is wholly absorbed by, and included in, the obtaining of F'. It is this absorption, or inclusion, which is expressed by saying (in condition (2)) that the obtaining of F is *nothing over and above* the obtaining of F'.

Many instances of constitution are trivial and (except as clarificatory examples of how constitution works) devoid of philosophical interest. Such is the case by which I first illustrated the notion in my introductory discussion (1.2, p. 5) – the case in which we envisaged John's being heavier than Mary (F_3) as wholly constituted by the combination of John's weighing 14 stone (F_1) and Mary's weighing 10 stone (F_2). What makes this a trivial case is that it is part of our ordinary conception of facts of the F_3-type that they are constituted in this sort of way: it is part of our ordinary conception of a weight-relation that its holding between two objects is derivative from, and nothing over and above, the combination of their specific weights. This does not mean, of course, that we cannot know that John is heavier than Mary without knowing the details of how this fact is constituted; for we might not know the specific weights of the two individuals concerned. But it does mean that, in discovering that F_3 is constituted by F_1 and F_2, we do not learn anything new about the general nature or status of F_3, or of other facts of this kind. In contrast, the claim that mental facts are wholly constituted by physical facts is clearly far from trivial. For the recognition of this constitutional relationship is not something which forms part of our ordinary conception of mental facts; and, if we came to accept it, it would obviously make a profound difference to our philosophical understanding of their nature or status. It is this, of course, which gives the claim its reductive flavour. We only count a constitution-claim as reductive if there is a striking difference in perspective between viewing the relevant facts in their own terms and viewing them in the light of their envisaged constitution.[7]

As well as being trivial, the weight-example is also one in which the necessity-relationship involved in the constitution is a priori; that is, it is a conceptual, a priori establishable, necessary truth that if John weighs 14 stone and Mary weighs 10 stone, John is heavier than Mary. And, of course, the necessity will always be of this a priori kind in cases where the constitution is trivial – cases where our ordinary conception of the constituted facts involves a recognition of their being constituted in that sort of way. This point does not, however, hold in reverse. For it is easy enough to envisage cases in which the necessity would be a priori, but the constitution non-trivial. A good example arises in the context of analytical functionalism. The analytical functionalist claims that mental facts turn out, on conceptual analysis, to be functional facts. This is not, as such, a claim of constitution, since (given the requirement of asymmetric dependence) a fact can only be constituted by a fact or set of facts different from itself. But the functionalist is also likely to hold that, as functional facts, mental facts are ultimately constituted by physical facts.[8] Thus he is likely to think that a person's functional organization, and, at any time, his functional condition within the framework of this organization, are ultimately the product of, and nothing over and above, his physical makeup, the physical makeup of his actual and potential environments, and the basic physical laws of nature. Now such a constitution of mental facts by physical facts, if it obtained, would be highly non-trivial. But equally, it would allow the deduction of mental facts, psychologically specified, from the physical facts which constitute them. For it would be possible to deduce the relevant functional truths from the truths about physical conditions and physical laws; and it would then be possible to deduce the mental truths from these functional truths by invoking the functionalist analysis. So the result would be a form of non-trivial (philosophically significant) constitution in which the necessitation of the constituted facts by the constitutive facts – each instance of its being necessary that if physically p, then mentally q – was establishable a priori.

In this example, the constitution-claim is mediated by a step of analytical reduction. Thus it is claimed that mental facts are wholly constituted by physical facts because (i) mental facts turn out, on conceptual analysis, to be functional facts and (ii) functional facts are wholly constituted by physical facts. Because it involves this step of analytical reduction, the resulting position, though far from trivial, does not qualify as a form of *metaphysical* reductionism – at least, not of metaphysical reductionism about the *mind*. For although the metaphysical reductionist takes mental facts to be wholly constituted by physical facts, he also accepts that psychological statements are irreducibly mentalistic and that mental facts cannot be expressed in any but mentalistic terms; and while it is natural to represent this acceptance as a sort of concession (as the acknowledgement of a respect in which the dualist's conception of mentality is correct), it must still be viewed as an essential aspect of his position. The metaphysical reductionist's rejection of *analytical* functionalism does not, of course, exclude his being a functionalist in a broader sense. It is still open to him to insist that mental facts are directly constituted by functional facts, and that they are only constituted by physical facts via the functional facts which the latter sustain. The only requirement is that, whatever constitutional route he follows, he must not base it on a reductive analysis of psychological concepts.

Because he rejects analytical reductionism and takes mental facts to be, in their subject-matter, *sui generis*, the metaphysical reductionist is prevented from assigning an a priori status to the necessity-relationships involved in their constitution. It is not that the assignment of such a status is no longer a formally available option. But, without the backing of a reductive analysis, such an assignment would lack any rationale. For given the prima facie conceptual gulf between the mental and physical realms, the only chance of justifying the claim that mental truths are deducible from physical truths would be by showing that the distinctively mentalistic subject-matter of the former can be analysed away. This brings us to a crucial point. Given that he rejects analytical reductionism, and thereby removes the chance of any deductive route from the physical to the mental, on what basis can the metaphysical reductionist advance his constitutional claims? On the one hand, if he takes the metaphysically basic facts to be purely physical, but accepts that he cannot deduce any psychological conclusions from them, how can he avoid mental nihilism? On the other, if he acknowledges the reality of mental facts, but accepts that they are not deducible from any physical premises, how can he see them as physically constituted? These are not just rhetorical questions, designed to display the manifest incoherence of the reductionist's claims. But they do pose an obvious challenge to the reductionist to explain his position and show us how we can come to see things his way.

I think the reductionist does have a way of trying to meet this challenge. But to see how, we must begin by going back to the case of physical colour, by which we first illustrated the distinction between the analytical and metaphysical forms of reduction. The point of focusing on this case is that, though remote from the issues of the mind, it reveals an area in which the metaphysically reductionist approach is quite plausible.

As we saw, the philosophical problem in the area of physical colour arises from the tension between our common-sense beliefs and the findings of science. We ordinarily believe that physical objects (of certain types) are coloured, because that is how they visually appear to us. But science seems to show that this belief is wholly unwarranted. For it explains the colour-appearance of objects in terms of factors which do not ostensibly involve their possession of colour. Thus it explains their colour-appearance in terms of such things as the arrangement of their surface-atoms, the way this arrangement affects the reflection and absorption of light, the way in which photic input to the eye affects the human nervous system, and the effects of the relevant neural processes on human experience. All these factors can be understood and acknowledged without having to ascribe colour to the objects themselves. And if they fully account for colour-appearance, we seem to be left with no reason for supposing that the objects really have the colours which they appear to have, or indeed that they have any colours at all.

There are five ways in which, as philosophers, we could respond to this problem. First, in deference to our ordinary beliefs, we might simply reject the scientific 'findings' or claim that they have been misinterpreted. Secondly, in deference to science, we might conclude that our ordinary colour-beliefs are indeed unwarranted and should be abandoned. Thirdly, we might say that both science and our ordinary beliefs are correct, but that science reveals the real essence of physical colour, in the same way as it reveals the real essence of water and physical heat.[9] This would involve, for example, taking the greenness of grass to be a certain aspect of its microstructure – that aspect which, by its effects on the reflection and absorption of light, disposes grass to look the way it does when we view it in daylight. Fourthly, we might argue that both science and our ordinary beliefs are correct, not because physical colour can be identified with some scientifically specifiable property, but because our ordinary colour-ascriptions are to be analysed dispositionally – because, in saying that grass is green, we are only, on analysis, saying that it is disposed to look a certain way to the normal percipient who views it in standard conditions. Finally, we might claim that both science and our ordinary beliefs are correct, not because colour has a more fundamental scientific description, nor because it is to be construed as a dispositional property, but because the colour-facts and the scientific facts belong to different levels of reality. Thus we might say that physical colour is something *sui generis*, but that an object's possession of colour is derivative from, and nothing over and above, the more fundamental facts (about its microstructural properties and their effects on the human observer) which science reveals. It is this last response which is of particular interest in our present discussion. For, being the response of the metaphysical colour-reductionist, it offers an analogy with the metaphysical mental reductionism on which we are focusing. If we could discern a rationale for such reductionism in the case of colour, we might be better placed to find one in the case of the mind.

In taking physical colour to be *sui generis*, the metaphysical colour-reductionist is repudiating any reductive analysis of our ordinary colour-ascriptions and accepting that the relevant states of affairs cannot be described in any but colour-ascriptive terms. The question now is: given this conception of physical colour, how can he plausibly, or even coherently, represent physical-colour facts as wholly constituted by the non-colour facts (i.e. the non *physical*-colour facts) of his metaphysically fundamental reality? Thus suppose, for the sake of argument, we accept the proposed account of this reality. Suppose, that is, we accept that the underlying facts are as science describes them: facts about the microstructural properties of physical objects and the effects of these

145

properties on the transmission of light; facts about the physiology of the human nervous system and its responses to photic input; and facts about how certain kinds of states and processes in the human nervous system give rise to visual experiences. We have no difficulty in understanding how such facts would explain the facts of colour-appearance and thus explain why we come to hold the colour-beliefs that we do. Where there seems to be a problem is in understanding how such facts could make our colour-beliefs *true* – or at least, how they could do so granted (what the metaphysical colour-reductionist accepts) that colour-ascriptions cannot be analysed dispositionally and that colours cannot be identified with the microstructural properties on which the relevant dispositions are grounded. After all, it would be perfectly consistent with our acceptance of these facts to conclude (in line with the second of the five responses above) that the colour-appearances which they explain are illusory and that the colour-beliefs which the appearances induce in us are false. Indeed, when we consider the situation purely from the standpoint of the fundamental reality, this seems to be the only conclusion we could rationally adopt.

Now the reductionist's response, I think, will be to say that this is not the only viewpoint from which we can assess things. Thus he will argue that, although we cannot establish the truth of our ordinary colour-beliefs by appealing to the composition of the fundamental reality, we are still entitled to hold these beliefs on the basis of our ordinary sensory evidence (i.e. the basis of how things sensibly appear to us), and then – in the perspective of these beliefs – address ourselves to the question of how the relevant colour-facts (whose obtaining we are now taking for granted) are metaphysically related to the underlying facts which science reveals. His point would then be that, provided we acknowledge the *sui generis* status of physical colour (thus excluding any reductive analysis of colour-ascriptions or the identification of colours with scientifically specifiable properties), this way of considering the issue forces us to adopt the metaphysically reductionist account. After all, if physical colour is *sui generis*, the relevant colour-facts are not part of the scientifically revealed reality. But equally, we cannot suppose their obtaining to be genuinely additional to the scientifically revealed facts; for since the latter entirely account for the colour-appearance of physical objects, such a supposition would sever the perceptual link between physical colour and our visual experiences, and so would represent the colour-facts as ones to which we had no epistemic access. The only way of coherently combining our acceptance of the (*sui generis*) colour-facts on the basis of our visual evidence with the scientific account of the underlying reality is by assigning the colour-facts and the scientific facts to different metaphysical levels and concluding that the obtaining of the former is wholly derivative from, and nothing over and above, the obtaining of the latter. And this, of course, is just the position which the metaphysical colour-reductionist wants to defend.

In other words, to try to make sense of his theory, I think that the reductionist will take the constitution of colour-facts by scientific facts to be, from an epistemic standpoint, 'retro-spective'[10] – a constitution which we are only equipped to recognize if we have independent knowledge of the constituted facts. He will concede that a knowledge of the scientific facts would not, on its own, suffice to establish that physical objects have colours, and hence would not suffice to reveal that there are colour-facts which the scientific facts sustain. But he will insist that the colour-facts in question are ones of which we have prior knowledge, and that we can then invoke the scientific discoveries to establish that they are constituted in the envisaged way. In short, the reductionist will say that, to discern the relevant constitution, it is necessary to adopt the right epistemic perspective – not the perspective of someone who is focusing on the scientific facts from a purely abstract viewpoint and trying to work out what it is acceptable to say on their basis alone, but rather that of someone who is trying to gauge the philosophical significance of the scientific facts in the frame-work of the observational facts which he already knows.

This approach to the issue of physical colour strikes me as quite plausible, mainly because of the difficulties of finding an acceptable alternative. It would be hard to maintain that our ordinary ascriptions of colour to physical objects are simply erroneous – that grass cannot be correctly described as green, nor tomatoes correctly described as red. And it would be even harder, I think, to reject the scientific findings or deny that they fully account for the facts of colour-appearance. Again, it is not easy to accept a reductive analysis of colour-statements –

an analysis which construes our ordinary colour-ascriptions as merely purporting to say how physical objects are disposed to look. Nor, given our ordinary conception of it, is it easy to understand how an object's colour could be literally identical with some aspect of its microstructure.[11] But if all these alternatives are rejected, there is nothing left except the metaphysically reductionist account, which claims that physical-colour facts, while *sui generis*, are wholly constituted by facts of a quite different kind.

My purpose in discussing this account, however, is not to establish its correctness, but to shed light on the analogous form of reductionism in the case of the mind. We noted earlier that, because he rejects the analytical-reductive approach, the metaphysical reductionist will not be able to think of mental truths as deducible from physical truths. And this led us to wonder on what basis he could claim that mental facts are physically constituted. The answer should now be clear. The metaphysical reductionist in this area will represent his constitutional thesis as having a broadly similar rationale to the analogous thesis about physical colour. In effect, he will argue for his position by representing it as the only way of reconciling three claims which appear to be in conflict but which are all correct. The first is the claim that there are mental facts – a claim which he accepts on a common-sense basis, and which we have already fully vindicated.[12] The second is the claim that the metaphysically fundamental reality is purely physical – a claim which he accepts either on the basis of a scientifically motivated argument, or because he finds philosophical difficulties in any alternative, or both. The third is the claim that psychological facts and states of affairs are *sui generis* – that they cannot be re-expressed or re-described in non-psychological terms. He accepts this in deference to the philosophical objections to analytical reductionism and type-identity which we have already elaborated. The reductionist will insist that each of these claims is correct. And he will point out that, taken together, they oblige us to conclude that mental facts are wholly constituted by physical facts in the way he envisages.

As in the colour-case, all this crucially depends on looking at things in the right epistemic perspective. In rejecting any deductive route from physical to mental truths, the reductionist has to concede that a knowledge of the relevant physical facts would not suffice to reveal the mental facts which they sustain. But he insists that, through introspection and the common-sense criteria for third-person ascription, the mental facts are already revealed to us, and that we can then establish their physical constitution by invoking the appropriate scientific and philosophical arguments – arguments which establish the exclusively physical character of the fundamental reality and the *sui generis* status of mental facts and states of affairs. This approach only has a chance of success, of course, if, while representing them as *sui generis,* our prior knowledge of the mental facts does not involve a commitment to their being metaphysically basic, and so leaves room for the subsequent claim of constitution. But if we again focus on the analogy with physical colour, the claim that there is no such commitment does not seem too implausible. It seems reasonable to represent our common-sense colour-beliefs as neutral on the issue of metaphysical status; and it is at least not obvious that our ordinary mentalistic beliefs cannot be viewed in a similar way.

4 WHY THE REDUCTIONIST'S POSITION IS UNTENABLE

This way of defending metaphysical mental reductionism (MMR) is, as far as I can see, the only one available. And the suggested analogy with the case of physical colour may help to give it some initial plausibility. Even so, for reasons which I shall now explain, it seems to me that the defence fails and that the position itself is untenable. There are three points to be made here, of increasing importance.

The first, and most obvious, point is that, like all the other anti-dualist theories we have considered, MMR is counter-intuitive. For our ordinary intuition is that, despite its attachment to an embodied subject, and despite its intimate causal dependence on the relevant neural processes, mentality *cannot* be reduced to non-mental factors in the envisaged way – that facts about a subject's mental states and activities are *not* wholly constituted by facts about his physical condition and circumstances, or by any other set of non-mental facts which the theorist might cite. Predictably, this intuitive objection to the reductionist's position is especially clear-cut in the case of experiential mentality. Thus it just seems obvious that someone's being in pain, or someone's having a visual experience, involves something genuinely additional to all the non-mental factors to which the theorist might seek to reduce it.

This intuitive point puts pressure on the reductionist to justify his position. But it is not, on its own, decisive. After all, our initial intuitions on such matters are not infallible: further investigation might reveal them to be mistaken, and might also reveal the mechanism by which such a mistake was made. Moreover, in the present case, we can already discern a factor which might be misleading us. For we can see that even if the reductionist position were correct, the lack of a deductive route from the physical to the mental facts would be liable to make it *seem* that the former could obtain without the latter. And, of course, unless the mental facts are logically necessitated by the physical, they cannot be constituted by them in the relevant sense. For these reasons, then, I think we need to treat our initial intuitions on these matters with a certain caution – seeing them as posing a *challenge* to the reductionist position, rather than as a *refutation*.

A second objection which can be brought against MMR is that the metaphysical status it assigns to mental facts is at variance with their epistemological status. This is a much more complex point, and also more interesting. We must begin by taking note of a respect in which the cases of physical colour and the mind are crucially different.

Even if the reductionist's approach in the colour-case is a good one, the very considerations on which it is based reveal the possibility of coming to a different conclusion. For having established that the underlying facts are as science describes them, we at least have the option of rejecting our ordinary colour-beliefs and denying the existence of physical colour altogether. We have this option because the scientific account gives us a way of explaining away the sensory evidence on which these beliefs are founded – a way of fully accounting for the colour-appearance of things in terms which do not involve the ascription of colour to them. Thus, instead of retaining our common-sense beliefs and concluding that the facts which they record are wholly constituted by the underlying facts revealed by science, we could simply deny that physical objects ever have colour and interpret the experiences which make it seem as if they do as wholly illusory. Now, however unpalatable in the case of physical colour, this nihilist option is simply not available in the case of the mind. We cannot coherently suppose that there are no mental facts, since (for the reasons elaborated earlier[13]) no one can coherently deny the existence of his own mentality. Whatever conclusions we may reach about the content of the metaphysically fundamental reality, we could never interpret them as explaining *away* the evidence (if 'evidence' is the right term) on which our ascriptions of mentality to ourselves are founded, and thus as representing those ascriptions as unwarranted. In this respect, our ordinary acceptance of our own mentality is entrenched in our system of beliefs in a way that our acceptance of physical-colour facts, however natural, is not. And in fact this distinguishes the mental case not only from the case of physical colour, but from any other case in which an issue of metaphysical reduction arises.

Now, at first sight, it might seem that this epistemological entrenchment is to the reductionist's advantage. After all, nihilism is something he rejects. Indeed, his whole case is that we must start by taking mentality for granted, and then establish its derivative status by establishing its absence from the fundamental reality. Looked at in this light, what could suit him better than its turning out that nihilism is not an option? However, although, in combination, the existence of mentality and its exclusion from the fundamental reality would certainly entail the truth of the reductionist's position, the difficulty is in seeing how the impossibility of denying the first can be squared with the acceptance of the second. For if we can coherently suppose the fundamental reality to be wholly non-mental, how can there be an absolute obligation to recognize anything else? How can there be an absolute bar on our adopting an ontologically austere view, which refuses to acknowledge any facts apart from those which lie within that reality or are deducible from it? In short, does not the very absoluteness of our commitment to mentality oblige us to regard it as metaphysically basic?

Let me try to put the point more clearly. In any case where it is deployed, metaphysical reductionism exhibits a prima facie strangeness. Thus one is led to ask: given that the

151

relevant putative facts are neither part of nor deducible from the supposed fundamental reality, how can we preserve a commitment to the former without accepting some expansion of the latter? The reductionist's answer, as we have seen, is that we must approach the issue in the right epistemological perspective: we must start by taking the putative facts for granted, in accordance with our ordinary epistemic viewpoint, and then establish their derivative status by establishing the appropriate limits on the fundamental reality. But it seems that, in so far as this answer can be taken seriously, there is the implicit understanding (as it were a kind of metaphysical bargain) that, to compensate for their recognition as real, the reality-status of the facts is correspondingly diminished – a diminishing which precisely consists in the fact that it is a matter of theoretical and practical convenience, not of discovering how things really are, that one interprets the situation as a case of constitution rather than annihilation. In other words, once we have granted that the putative facts are not deducible from the metaphysically fundamental facts, it seems that the only way in which we can come to accept that they obtain at all (as derivative facts) is by building a sort of concession to (a compromise with) nihilism into the form of the acceptance – the concession that there would be no objective mistake in rejecting these supposed facts altogether and limiting our commitment to what we can establish on the basis of the fundamental reality alone. If this is right, then, paradoxically, the possibility of metaphysical reductionism in any area depends on the possibility of nihilism. And this would mean that the unavailability of the nihilist option in the case of the mind excludes the metaphysically reductionist option as well.

This objection to MMR seems to me well-founded, and, together with the intuitive point mentioned earlier, it may well be enough for my purposes. At the same time, I have to admit that the considerations on which it is based are not quite as clear-cut as I would like. If someone were to insist that the reductionist position does *not* require this concession to nihilism, I would be puzzled; but I am not sure how I could force him to see things my way. For this reason, I am going to rest my case against the reductionist primarily on a third point, to which I now turn, and which I believe to be decisive.

If a claim of constitution is to be taken seriously, there has to be some way of understanding how – by what logical or metaphysical mechanism, as it were – the supposed constitution works: we have to be able to discern some connection between the supposedly constitutive and constituted facts which we can see as effecting and accounting for the constitution. Often, the mechanism of constitution will be immediately apparent in our very conception of the facts in question; this will always be so, of course, in cases where the constitution is, in the sense explained earlier, trivial – for example, the case of a weight-relation between two objects being constituted by the combination of their specific weights. Where the mechanism of constitution is not immediately apparent in our initial conception of the relevant facts, the constitutionalist will usually try to defend his position by invoking some form of conceptual analysis – an analysis which converts our initial conception of the facts into one in which the constitutional mechanism is brought to the surface. A good example of this is the case of someone who, holding that mental facts are physically constituted, bases this position on a functionalist analysis of psychological concepts – an analysis which reveals how it is possible for mental facts to be constituted by physical facts with the appropriate functional significance. But, of course, neither of these possibilities is available in the case of metaphysical reductionism. The metaphysical reductionist recognizes a conceptual gulf between the supposedly constituted and constitutive facts – a gulf which precludes the possibility of deriving an understanding of how the constitution works merely from our ordinary understanding of the nature of the facts, or from what that understanding yields through conceptual analysis.

But if the metaphysical reductionist cannot make clear the mechanism of constitution merely by appealing to the content (explicit or implicit) of our ordinary conception of the relevant facts, how is he to proceed? Well, let us once again pursue the case of physical colour, where the reductionist's approach strikes us as reasonably plausible.

The fundamental reality which the metaphysical colour-reductionist postulates, though devoid of physical colour, does include, in a scientifically elaborated form, all the facts that concern physical-colour appearance – facts such as that objects with the appropriate microstructural properties reflect certain wavelengths of light, that light of certain wavelengths, entering the eye, has certain effects on the human nervous system, and that certain processes in the human nervous system give rise to certain kinds of colour-experience. From these facts, it is not possible to deduce that physical objects are coloured. But it is possible to deduce that they will appear coloured in certain ways to the human observer who views them in certain conditions – a deduction which, though not validating it, fully explains why our ordinary epistemic viewpoint on colour is as it is. We have already noted the role which this plays in the justification of the reductionist's position. Thus once we have endorsed the ordinary epistemic viewpoint – thereby acknowledging that physical colour exists and is visually accessible to us – and once we have accepted that physical colour is something *sui generis* (that it is not amenable to analytical reduction or scientific re-specification), it is precisely the fact that science fully accounts for the visual phenomena, without attributing colours to the objects themselves, which obliges us to accord colour-facts their derivative status. (The point is that, if the existence of physical colour is ultimately irrelevant to the explanation of the visual phenomena, colour-constitution is the only way of making sense of colour-accessibility.) But what now needs to be stressed is that, as well as contributing to the *justification* of the reductionist's position, this explanational link between the underlying facts and colour-appearance is crucial to its *explication*. For it is this link which provides the mechanism of constitution, this link which enables us to understand how, despite the conceptual gulf, it is possible for the constitutional relationship to hold. The point is that, even if we take colour itself to be something intrinsic and *sui generis*, we can still think of it as an essentially *observational* property, whose physical realization is relative to the viewpoint of human colour-experience – something for whose physical realization human colour-sensitivity provides, not just the evidence, but the ultimate criterion. And, in the context of the scientific findings, this allows us to think of such realization as derivative from the dispositions of objects to look coloured to the human observer, and hence as ultimately derivative from, and nothing over and above, the more fundamental physical and psychophysical factors (both categorical and nomological) by which these dispositions are logically sustained.

Now, while other forms of metaphysical reductionism may require different kinds of justification, it seems to me that any form, if it is to be comprehensible at all, will have to involve a mechanism of constitution of a broadly similar kind. Thus, given any specific reductionist position, the only way, as far as I can see, in which we could make sense of its constitutional claims would be if (i) the postulated fundamental reality, though not containing the supposedly constituted facts (or anything from which they could be deduced), afforded a complete explanation of our ordinary epistemic viewpoint on them – an explanation of why it ordinarily seems to us that such facts obtain – and (ii) this explanational link was built into the constitution itself, in such a way that the constitutive facts included (explicitly or implicitly) the relevant facts about, or about the influences on, human experience and/or cognition. How this works out in detail will vary from case to case. But the underlying idea is that, to understand how it is possible for the supposedly constituted facts *to be* constituted, we have to think of their obtaining as an obtaining *for us*, or *relative to our experiential/cognitive viewpoint*, thereby equipping ourselves to represent it as the product of, and nothing over and above, whatever it is that ultimately creates this viewpoint and invites us to acquire the relevant factual beliefs.

This brings us to the crunch. The above account of what is required if one is to make sense of the relevant constitutional claims allows for a wide range of comprehensible metaphysical-reductionist positions. Thus, in addition to metaphysical colour-reductionism, it allows one to make sense of such positions as: phenomenalistic idealism, which takes physical facts to be wholly constituted by facts about human sense-experience; metaphysical emotivism, which takes moral facts to be wholly constituted by facts about human feelings and attitudes; and various further forms of scientifically motivated reductionism, which work in much the same way as the metaphysically reductive account of colour. But, obviously, the one thing we cannot make sense of in this kind of way is metaphysical reductionism about the *mind*. For this way of making sense of a reductionist position is only available if there are the appropriate sorts of mental or mind-concerning fact among those which play the relevant constitutive role; and, in the case of mental reductionism, all such facts have to be constituted rather than constitutive. Thus while we can assign a derivative status to physical colour by taking it to be constituted by the powers of objects to look coloured to the human observer (and ultimately constituted by the physical and psychophysical factors which underlie these powers), and while we can assign a derivative status to the whole physical world by taking its existence to be constituted by the character of, and the law-like constraints on, human sense-experience, we obviously cannot assign a derivative status to mentality itself by taking it to be constituted by facts about, or about the influences on, the human mind. In short, the envisaged way of making sense of a metaphysically reductionist position does not apply to the case of *mental* reductionism, because it is expressly designed only to apply to cases in which the proposed reduction is wholly or partly in the direction of mentality itself.

The upshot of this is that the forms of constitution postulated by the mental reductionist are simply not comprehensible: given their *sui generis* character, we have no way of understanding how mental facts could be non-mentalistically constituted. It is not that the constitutional claims are semantically defective or involve some implicit contradiction. It is just that we can never achieve a perspective in which we can grasp how such constitutional relationships are possible – a perspective in which we can understand how such facts as Smith's being in pain and Mary's believing that dodos are extinct could be derived from facts of a non-mental kind. And, of course, we have to be able to achieve this perspective before we can take the reductionist's position seriously.

5 CONCLUSION

This rejection of metaphysical mental reductionism is of crucial importance in its own right: together with the rejection of analytical reductionism, it commits us to accepting the second claim of the dualist's thesis, that the mental realm is (conceptually and metaphysically) fundamental. But it also has an important bearing on the issue of token-identity. For it takes away the identity-theorist's last chance of escaping from the difficulties elaborated earlier. The refutations of analytical reductionism and type-identity had already forced the theorist to recognize the psychological character of a mental item as something *sui generis* – as something which cannot be specified or conceived in any but mentalistic terms. The refutation of metaphysical reductionism now forces him to concede that an item's possession of its psychological character is something metaphysically fundamental – something which is not constituted by facts of a different kind. The result is that the theorist is left with no resources for making sense of his postulated identities. Without a constitutional link between them, he cannot explain how it is possible for the same event to possess two such different natures. Nor, without such an explanation, can he show us how to avoid one or other of the two modal intuitions which, in combination, entail that mental and physical events are distinct.

In short, taken in the context of our previous findings, the rejection of metaphysical mental reductionism commits us to rejecting the token-identity thesis too. All that remains to be done, on this issue, is to expose the flaws in the arguments which defenders of the thesis have offered (or might offer) in its support. It is to this task that I turn next.

6

TOKEN-IDENTITY AND PSYCHOPHYSICAL CAUSATION

1 INTRODUCTION

The token-identity thesis claims that each mental item is identical with a neural item. The prima facie objection to this, as we have seen, is that we simply cannot understand how things of such seemingly different types can be identical – an objection which gets reinforced by Kripke's modal argument, to the effect that the psychological character of a mental item is essential to *it*, but *not* to its neural correlate. There are three ways in which the identity-theorist might try to answer this objection. First, he might adopt some form of analytical reductionism, claiming that the psychological concepts applicable to mental items are to be analysed in wholly non-mentalistic terms. The main option here would be that of analytical functionalism. Secondly, he might endorse the type-identity thesis, claiming that the psychological character of a mental item is to be empirically identified with some aspect of its physical character.[1] Thirdly, he might embrace the view of the metaphysical reductionist – conceding that the psychological character of a mental item cannot be specified in any but psychological terms, but insisting that the item's possession of this character is derivative from, and nothing over and above, certain non-mental facts about it. I have tried to show that none of these approaches is successful and that the objection to token-identity stands.

Even so, the identity-theorist can still offer arguments in support of his position, and although we have shown the position itself to be untenable, these arguments are ones which the dualist needs to rebut. Most of them are concerned,

158

in one way or another, with the topic of psychophysical causation – causation of the mental by the physical or of the physical by the mental – and it is on the issues in this area that I want to focus. The arguments divide into two groups: those which advance *a priori* objections to the dualistic form of psychophysical causation, and those which advance *empirical* objections. Over the next three sections, I shall confine my attention to arguments in the first group.

2 DUALISTIC CAUSATION: THE TRADITIONAL OBJECTION

Whether we are dualists or materialists – and the token-identity thesis qualifies as a (weak) form of materialism – we presumably have to accept the existence of psychophysical causation. We have to accept, for example, that when someone is stung by a wasp, he feels pain, and that this pain, whether it is physical or non-physical, is caused by some neural process which the sting induces. Likewise, barring epiphenomenalism, we have to accept that when someone takes a decision (e.g. to cross the road), the decision, whether it is physical or non-physical, will normally have a causal influence on his subsequent behaviour. The question we have to consider is whether the recognition of such psychophysical causation raises problems for the dualist – and in particular (at this stage of our discussion), whether it raises problems of an *a priori* kind. The general consensus is that it does, though opinions vary over the exact nature of the problem or problems involved. Curiously, many philosophers regard the problem as self-evident and not calling for further elucidation: they take it as just obvious that there is something deeply puzzling, perhaps even incoherent, in the notion of the non-physical mind coming into causal contact with the physical body. But if there is a genuine puzzle here, it is surely one which needs to be spelt out. Why should the fact that mind and body are so different in nature make it difficult to understand how there could be causal relations between them?

One reason why we may *think* that there is an a priori problem for the dualist is that our conception of the nature of causation tends to be strongly conditioned by the ways in which causality operates in the physical realm. Typically, when one physical event causes another, the two events are either spatially contiguous (or coincident) or are connected by a spatiotemporally continuous series of events through which the causal process passes. This feature of physical causation may make it seem that causation *has to* operate by means of spatial contact – that spatial contact is the *essential mechanism* for causal contact. And, of course, once this is accepted, causation between physical and non-physical events is automatically excluded, simply because the non-physical events have no spatial location.

If this is the supposed problem, then the dualist has a simple and effective answer. For even if physical causation typically, and perhaps always, operates through spatial contact, it is certainly conceivable, and unproblematically conceivable, that it should sometimes not. There is no conceptual difficulty in envisaging a case in which a physical event in one place causes a physical event a mile away, without there being any causal chain of events between them. Nor is there any difficulty in envisaging the sort of evidence which would persuade us that such cases occur – e.g. a constant correlation between the occurrence of the one type of event and the immediately subsequent occurrence of the other, an inability to detect any intervening mechanism, and an inability to provide a causal explanation of the second event in any other way. Indeed, it was once thought that gravitational causation operated over spatial distances in just this way, though I gather that this is not the view of *modern* physics. But if there is no conceptual difficulty in envisaging causation-at-a-distance in the physical realm, then dualistic causation should not be excluded, or regarded as conceptually problematic, purely on the grounds that there is no spatial contact between the non-physical mind and the body. And if there are other grounds for challenging the dualist's position a priori, these have still to be made clear.

Another way in which the problem is sometimes posed is by saying that, on the dualist view, we cannot understand *how* pyschophysical causation operates: we simply have to accept it as a brute fact, with no further explanation, that certain types of neural event directly cause certain types of mental event, and vice versa.[2] But again the point is not clear. For why should any explanation be demanded? Trivially, if the

causation is direct, there cannot be any question of an intervening mechanism. And presumably the notion of direct
causation is not as such problematic: indeed, whenever causation operates, there has to be *some* direct causation unless the
series of causally connected events is literally continuous (or
at least dense). Maybe the point is that we cannot understand
why the neural events have these mental effects or *why* the
mental events have these neural effects: the most we can hope
to do is bring the causal pairings under certain covering laws.
But I just cannot see why this why-question arises. In the
physical realm too our explanation of causation has to terminate
in the postulation of certain causal laws, without any further
explanation (other than in terms of divine volition) of why
these laws obtain. So why should the dualist be required to do
more? Why should he be called on to offer a deeper mode of
explanation than that which is available to physical science?

Admittedly, there are two factors which might make it *seem*
that we can sometimes supply a deeper explanation of causation
in the physical realm. The first factor, curiously, depends on a
certain respect in which we are necessarily ignorant of the real
nature of physical phenomena. Because we have no way of
discovering, beyond a specification of their geometrical properties, what physical objects are ultimately like in themselves
(what, as it were, they are like from a God's-eye view), we are
forced to identify their fundamental intrinsic properties by
the causal powers and sensitivities to which they contingently
give rise.[3] As a result, by employing predicates with the relevant
causal implications, our statements of physical causal law will
often have, or have to some extent, an *a priori* status. And this
can give the false impression that, abstracted from the perspective of their formulation, the laws themselves enjoy a
similar status and that the causal processes which they cover
are distinctively intelligible.

The second factor is that the very principle of individuation
for bodies (or at least what is commonly accepted as the
correct principle) can seem to have causal implications. This
principle, which states that, at any time, two portions of matter
are distinct if and only if the three-dimensional regions of
space they occupy are distinct, makes it logically impossible
for two bodies to occupy the same region simultaneously. This
seems to imply that when bodies come into spatial contact,

they are mutually obstructive; and the notion of obstructiveness seems to be a causal one. Thus it seems that, merely from the way bodies are individuated, we can deduce something about their causal powers and sensitivities in relation to one another. And this deduction would then provide a relevantly deep explanation of why these powers and sensitivities obtain.

All this again, however, is just an illusion. The principle of individuation certainly ensures that bodies are mutually impenetrable, since it does not allow us to describe anything as a case in which two bodies simultaneously occupy the same region. But it does not ensure that they are mutually obstructive in a *causal* sense. It would, for example, permit us to recognize a case in which everything was *as if* two moving bodies passed through each other: it is just that we would have to describe it as a case in which, over the period of the seeming spatial overlap, the total quantity of matter first diminished and then increased. It is only when we combine the spatial principle of individuation with the law of the conservation of matter that we can deduce that bodies are, in a causal sense, mutually obstructive. And the law of conservation is not itself knowable a priori.

Once we have seen through these illusions, it is clear that causation in the physical realm is not amenable to any distinctively deep explanation – that the only kind of explanation we can hope for in this area is to bring the various causal phenomena under covering laws. And, if this is so, then we have not yet identified anything about dualistic causation which renders it conceptually problematic, or makes it in any way different in general character from purely physical causation.

It is just at this point, however, that the materialist can launch a new attack. For while conceding that psychophysical causation does not require anything more than a nomological explanation, he might argue that it is precisely the business of subsuming such causation under covering laws which turns out to be problematic on the dualist view. In fact, there are two quite different lines of argument here. One line of argument, which arises from my own work on the topic of psychophysical causation,[4] tries to show that dualism does not allow for laws which cover the causal pairings of mental and physical events in a sufficiently determinate way. The other, which has been advanced by Donald Davidson, tries to show that dualism does not allow for covering laws at all. Let us look at these arguments in turn.

3 THE PROBLEM OF CAUSAL PAIRINGS

It is commonly assumed that where two events are causally related, their being so is wholly constituted by the way in which, via their non-causal properties and relations, they fall under some natural law or set of laws. Thus if, on a particular occasion, my heating of a lump of metal causes it to melt, it is assumed that what ultimately makes this true is that the metal is of a certain intrinsic type, that on the occasion in question it reaches a certain temperature, and that it is a law of nature (or the consequence of a law or set of laws) that whenever metal of that type reaches that temperature, it melts. And quite generally, it is assumed that whenever one event causes another, the obtaining of this causal relationship is derivative from, and nothing over and above, certain non-causal aspects of the situation and the obtaining of certain relevant covering laws. Let us refer to this as the 'nomological assumption'. The assumption, as I have said, is commonly made, and has gained a particularly strong hold among empiricist philosophers. It has its origins in Hume's first definition of cause (as 'an object precedent and contiguous to another, and where all the objects resembling the former are plac'd in like relations of precedency and contiguity to those objects, that resemble the latter'[5]), though some of the philosophers who have endorsed his general approach have taken the covering laws to involve genuine natural necessity, unlike the mere factual regularities of Hume's own theory.

Now when we try to apply the nomological assumption to the case of psychophysical causation, dualistically conceived, we encounter a problem. For where the mental or the physical event happens to have a simultaneous duplicate, it is not clear how the dualist can come up with laws that yield the appropriate determinacy of causal pairings. To take an example, suppose N is a neural event which occurs in Smith's brain at time t and which directly causes an experience E (say a pain) in Smith's mind a tenth of a second later. What psychophysical law can the dualist envisage which would account for this causal

163

episode? He might begin by envisaging a law of the following kind:

L1: It is a law that whenever an event of physical type Φ occurs in a brain of structural type Σ an experience of psychological type Ψ occurs a tenth of a second later

where it is understood that N is of type Φ, that Smith's brain is of structural type Σ at t, and that E is of psychological type Ψ. But, on the assumption that we have to be able to derive the causal relation between N and E from the nomological facts, together with the non-causal properties of the situation, a law of this kind could turn out to be inadequate. For suppose that the causal episode in Smith is simultaneously duplicated in another person Jones. Suppose, that is, that Jones's brain is also of structural type Σ at t, that an event N' of type Φ occurs in Jones's brain at t, and that N' directly causes, in Jones's mind a tenth of a second later, an experience E' of type Ψ. *Ex hypothesi*, N is the cause of E, and N' is the cause of E'. But these causal pairings would not be determined by the non-causal properties of the situation and the specified law. The only non-causal properties which are relevant to the law are: the Φ-ness of N and N'; the Ψ-ness of E and E'; the structural character of the two brains; and the fact that N and N' occur, simultaneously, a tenth of a second before E and E'. Clearly, these factors, together with the law, do not determine which neural event is paired with which experiential event. They are neutral between the correct claim, that E is the effect of N, and E' the effect of N', and the incorrect claim, that E is the effect of N', and E' the effect of N.

The inadequacy of L1 stems from the fact that it only links the specified physical type of event and the specified psychological type of event by means of a temporal relation. For, of course, this relation cannot help to settle the causal pairings of *simultaneous* events of either type. The natural remedy would be to supplement the temporal relation with some further relation, so that, in combination, the two relations would link the physical and psychophysical items in a sufficiently determinate way – a way which would leave at most only one psychological relatum for each physical event of the relevant type, and at most only one physical relatum for each psychological event of the relevant type. The question now becomes: what further relation is available to the dualist? Clearly the relation cannot be (as it is in the case of physical causation) spatial, since the dualist denies that mental events are genuinely located in space. Is there anything else?

The obvious candidate is the relation which holds between any mental event in some subject's mind and any physical event in the *same* subject's body – in other words, the relation signified by the expression 'x belongs to a subject in whose body y occurs'. Let us, for convenience, abbreviate this expression to 'x is subject-linked to y'. Then the dualist could suppose that, in the case of Smith and Jones, there is a covering law which nomologically links the relevant types of event both temporally and under this additional relation, i.e.

L2: It is a law that, for any Φ-event x in a brain of type Σ, there is a Ψ-experience y such that y is a tenth of a second later than x and y is subject-linked to x.

L2 yields unique causal pairings. Given any neural event of type Φ (in the relevant type of brain), the law tells us exactly where, in time and 'mental space', we will find its Ψ-effect, namely a tenth of a second later in the mind of that subject in whose body the neural event occurs. And, given any experience of type Ψ, the law tells us where, in time and physical space, we will find (if it has one) its Φ-cause, namely a tenth of a second earlier in the body of that subject in whose mind the experience occurs. So L2 tells us that N is the cause of E and that N' is the cause of E'. Moreover, it is surely very plausible to suppose that the psychophysical laws controlling the causation of mental events by physical events are of the L2-form, in which the relevant types of event are connected under the relation of being subject-linked.

However, the dualist cannot escape quite so easily. In envisaging psychophysical laws of the L2-form, he is taking for granted the notion of embodiment: he is assuming that we can speak, unproblematically, of a conscious subject's possession of a body, or of the union of a certain body and a certain mind in single person. The trouble is that, as the dualist conceives the relation between body and mind, the very notion of embodiment will turn out to be, in part, implicitly causal. An essential part of what makes it the case that a certain mind and a certain body belong to the same subject is that they are causally attached to each other in a special way – a way which equips the body to have direct causal interaction with this mind, and no other, and equips the mind to have direct causal interaction with this body, and no other. But how is this causal attachment to be nomologically construed? Obviously, the dualist cannot construe it in terms of laws, like L2, in which such attachment already implicitly features – that would be clearly circular. But if he falls back on laws like L1, in which the only psychophysical relation is temporal, then in certain circumstances the causal attachment would become indeterminate. Thus if the mental and neural biographies of two subjects coincided on every occasion, these weaker laws would not determine which body was attached to which mind. It may be objected that the possibility of such coincidence is too remote to be taken seriously. But it is not clear that it would be all that remote in the case of two monozygotic twins with very brief, e.g. entirely pre-natal, lives. And in any case, the mere fact that it is a *possibility* means that the dualist needs to be able to accommodate it.

Given these points, it might be argued that the only way of providing a satisfactory account of psychophysical causation would be by rejecting dualism in favour of token-identity. Certainly the identity-thesis would avoid the problem. For if mental events were physical, they would be located in physical space and hence stand in spatiotemporal relations to other physical events. And since such relations could be used to fix the exact spatiotemporal position of the effect relative to the cause, and vice versa, this would allow us to envisage laws which, by incorporating such relations, covered the causal pairings in the appropriate way. (Indeed, there would be a chance that we could settle here for purely physical laws.) The argument against the dualist would be that this is the *only* way of avoiding the problem – that unless we take mental events to be physical, and hence located in physical space, it is impossible to devise, in cases of simultaneous duplication, an adequate nomological account of the relevant causal pairings. If this is right, it turns out that the radical difference between mental and physical phenomena, dualistically conceived, does, after all, preclude a coherent account of the causal traffic between them – though for rather different, and more precisely statable, reasons than those ordinarily advanced.

In fact, however, I think that the dualist does have the resources to deal with the problem – and in two quite different ways. The argument against him rests on two premises. The first of these is the nomological assumption, that causal relationships between events are always constituted by certain non-causal properties of the situation, together with the relevant covering laws. The second is the claim that it is only by taking mental events to be physical that, in cases of duplication, we can envisage laws which cover the causal pairings in the way this assumption requires. Now it seems to me that the dualist is entitled to reject both these premises, the rejection of each constituting a separate solution to the problem. Thus, on the one hand, I think he can show that the nomological assumption is mistaken and that the demand for a nomological account of the pairings is therefore misconceived. On the other hand, I think he can show that, even in the framework of this assumption, an adequate account of the pairings can be found – that covering laws of the requisite sort are in fact available. It will be convenient to take the second of these points first.

As we have already noted, the failure of L1 to account for the causal pairings in the case of Smith and Jones stems from the fact that it only links the relevant types of event by means of a temporal relation. And, as we have also noted, the natural remedy would be to supplement this relation with some further one, so that the two relations together succeed in relating the neural and experiential items in a sufficiently determinate way. However, this is not the only remedy. Another way of ensuring that psychophysical laws yield unique causal pairings would be to restrict their scope to particular persons. Thus, for Smith and Jones, we could envisage the laws:

L(Smith): It is a law that whenever a Φ-event occurs in brain B^s at a time when B^s is of structural type Σ, a Ψ-experience occurs a tenth of a second later in mind M^s

L(Jones): It is a law that whenever a Φ-event occurs in brain B^j at a time when B^j is of structural type Σ, a Ψ-experience occurs a tenth of a second later in mind M^j

where B^s and M^s are respectively Smith's brain and mind, and B^j and M^j are respectively Jones's brain and mind. These laws would secure the right causal pairings. N and E would be causally linked under L(Smith), and N' and E' would be causally linked under L(Jones). The alternative pairings would not be sanctioned since they fall under neither law.

It might be thought a drawback of this solution that it postulates laws of this scope-restricted kind. We normally assume that laws are universal in scope, and that they can be formulated in purely general terms, without reference to any particular object. The suggestion that the identity of an object might turn out to be a nomologically relevant factor – a factor over and above the object's general properties – is, on the face of it, a rather strange one. Our expectation is that things are constrained to behave in the ways they do solely in virtue of the *kinds* of thing they are, and irrespective of *which particular* things they are. However, it seems to me that, in the present case, the restriction on the scope of the laws is unproblematic. For one thing, it is not as if it involves any element of nomological caprice. In postulating laws like L(Smith) and L(Jones) – and, of course, there would be an L(Brown), an L(Robinson), an L(Thatcher), and so on – we are not making the nomological constraints vary inexplicably from person to person. Quite the reverse. Where there is a law for one person, there are exactly similar laws for everyone else: the only thing which varies is the reference to the particular brain and particular mind in question. Moreover, even though the singular references cannot be eliminated in favour of some general relation, there is a sense in which all the restricted laws of the same type can be subsumed under one general and unrestricted law. Thus all the laws of the L(...)-type are, in a sense, specific instances of the general law:

L3: It is a law that there is some 1–1 correlation between human brains and human minds such that any Φ-event in a brain X of structural type Σ is a tenth of a second earlier than some Ψ-experience in that mind which is correlated with X.

It is not that the restricted laws can be *deduced* from L3; for L3 does not specify *how* the brains and minds are correlated. But L3 ensures that there is some correlation, and the restricted laws are what L3 yields for the correlation which actually obtains.

This, then, is the dualist's first possible solution, and, with one proviso, it seems to me entirely succesful. The proviso is that the dualist does not go on to account for the unity of the mind in terms (wholly or partly) of the causal relations of mental items to the same body or brain (what P. F. Strawson dubbed the 'no-ownership theory'[6]). The reason for this restriction is simply that, without it, the whole theory would become circular: the account of what constitutes a single mind would presuppose the availability of a prior account of psychophysical causation, while, by postulating laws with irreducible references to particular minds, the account of psychophysical causation would presuppose the availability of a prior account of what constitutes a single mind. As it turns out, the restriction will not prove troublesome, since (as we shall see) the dualist has better theories of the unity of the mind at his disposal.

The dualist's second solution is quite different, since it challenges the whole basis on which the problem was formulated. The problem only arises because of a certain assumption about the relationship between causation and natural law – the assumption that where two events are causally related, their standing in this relation is wholly constituted by the non-causal properties of the situation and the obtaining of certain covering laws. As I have said, this nomological assumption has been widely accepted by empiricist philosphers, following (more or less) the approach of David Hume. None the less, it can be shown to be mistaken. In fact, it can be faulted in two ways.

In the first place, the assumption does not do justice to the directionality of causation. And here the point is not just that, if it were correct, there would be no reason for excluding the possibility of backward causation, in which the effect precedes the cause. It is also, and more fundamentally, that the assumption is in conflict with our conception of causation as an inherently directional process – a process involving an asymmetrical dependence of one event (the effect) on another event (the cause). Thus suppose one billiard ball strikes another, causing it to move. Let us assume that the covering law is such that, in the cirumstances, the second type of event could not have occurred without the prior occurrence of the first, and the first could not have occurred without the subsequent occurrence of the second. The nomological relationship between the two types of events is then symmetric: the first is necessary and sufficient for the second, which is thereby sufficient and necessary for the first. Consequently, the nomological facts do not account for the directionality in the causal process: they do not explain the sense in which the first event is asymmetrically responsible for the second – the sense in which the second owes its occurrence to the first, but not vice versa. And this means that, contrary to the nomological assumption, their causal relationship transcends the obtaining of the relevant laws and the non-causal features of the situation.

Secondly, we can envisage cases in the physical realm in which the laws of nature do not account for the actual causal pairings. Thus (to use my favourite example[7]) suppose there is a certain kind K of metal, and it is a law of nature that when any spherical K-lump reaches a specified temperature, a flash occurs a tenth of a second later somewhere (unspecified) in the region of points which are no further from the centre of the sphere than twice its diameter. Suppose, further, that there is no stronger law to fix the location of the flash more precisely, and indeed that, at any moment when the critical temperature is reached, each position in the specified region has an equal chance of receiving it. Now we are surely entitled to construe the relationship between the occurrence of the critical temperature in a K-sphere and the subsequent occurrence of a flash in the specified region as a *causal* one: we are surely entitled to say that the temperature-event causes the flash-event. And normally, this interpretation creates no problems for the nomological assumption. But now imagine a case in which two K-spheres, which are sufficiently close together for their specified regions to overlap, reach the critical temperature simultaneously, and that, a tenth of a second later, two flashes occur within the region of overlap. It still seems right to suppose that each flash is the effect of just one of the temperature-events and that each temperature-event is the cause of just one of the flashes. But, because each flash falls within the specified region for each sphere, the causal pairings are not determined by the law and the non-causal conditions. So once again we have a situation in which the causal relationships transcend the factors which would wholly constitute them if the nomological assumption were true. Admittedly, the example is only fictitious; and for all I know, nothing like this occurs in the actual world. But its very conceivability is what matters in the present context. For unless the nomological assumption can be defended a priori, it cannot be invoked as part of an a priori objection to the dualist's position.

The dualist's second solution, then, is simply to reject the nomological assumption and so deny that the problem of pairings arises. Since the assumption is in fact mistaken, this solution too is entirely successful.

Given the success of this solution, it follows that the first is no longer needed: it is not necessary to postulate scope-restricted laws to bring psychophysical causation in line with the nomological assumption, since the assumption has been discredited. However, this does not mean that the first solution can now be forgotten. For its availability is likely to prove crucially important to the dualist's enterprise at another point, as I shall now explain.

In the case where a *K*-sphere reaches the critical temperature, it is entirely accidental at what point within the specified region the flash occurs. The flash is caused by the temperature-event, and it occurs at a particular point, but there is nothing in the prior conditions which forces it, or puts pressure on it, to occur at *this* point rather than at any of the others which lie within the relevant region. Now in the case where an event in someone's brain causes an event in his mind, or vice versa, the situation is quite different. Given the identity of the brain in which the neural cause (or effect) occurs, it is not merely accidental that its mental effect (cause) occurs in *that* mind rather than in another; and, given the identity of the mind in which the mental effect (or cause) occurs, it is not merely accidental that its neural cause (effect) occurs in *that* brain rather than in another. For the particular brain and the particular mind are linked by some special (and presumably relatively permanent) psychophysical arrangement, which ensures that *this* brain only directly interacts with *this* mind and that *this* mind only directly interacts with *this* brain. Indeed, such an arrangement, as we noted, is required for embodiment: it is, or is an essential part of, what makes it the case that the brain and the mind belong to the same person.

It is at this point that the first solution comes into its own. For while in theory there may be more than one form which this psychophysical arrangement could take, the obvious suggestion would be that it is secured by an appropriate system of scope-restricted laws – laws which, by their singular references to the relevant brain and mind, limit the fields of influence and sensitivity of each in the requisite way. Such a suggestion would not reinstate the nomological assumption. Nor would it even reinstate it for *psychophysical* causation. For the point of postulating the scope-restricted laws would not be to provide an account of how the relevant causal relations are constituted, but to explain why their occurrence is regular in a certain respect. Indeed, once we have recognized that causation is not reducible to law, it becomes quite plausible to suppose that the scope-restricted laws are themselves *explicitly causal* – that each one is to be explicitly formulated as a law about the causal traffic between a particular brain and a particualar mind.[8] In the case of the L(Smith) and L(Jones) laws, for example, this would mean putting the expression 'causally results' in place of the weaker 'occurs'.

I shall pick up the topic of embodiment again in Chapter 8. For the moment, we must return to the issue of psychophysical causation as such and consider one further line of argument by which materialists have tried to undermine the dualist's position.

4 DAVIDSON'S ARGUMENT

Donald Davidson has put forward an intriguing argument for token-identity.[9] He assumes both:

(1) There are causal relations between mental and physical events

and

(2) Singular causal relations fall under strict covering laws.

He further tries to establish:

(3) There are no strict psychophysical laws.

From these premises, he concludes that:

(4) Mental events are physical.

Set out in full, the reasoning here would run as follows (though Davidson himself does not set it out like this). (1), (2), and (3) jointly entail that causal relations between mental and physical events fall under strict, covering, non-psychophysical laws. So, in the case of any such relation, *either* both events are mental and the covering law is purely psychological *or* both events are physical and the covering law is purely physical. But, in asserting (1), the causal relations which we have in mind are (at least paradigmatically) relations between mental events and *non-mental* physical events.[10] So, in each case (at least each such paradigmatic case), both events are physical and the covering law is purely physical. But once we accept that those mental events which are causally related to physical events are physical, we cannot avoid concluding that all mental events (at least all within the human and animal domain) are physical. (This conclusion does not, of course, imply that such events are *purely* physical, in the sense that their intrinsic natures can be fully specified in physical terms.)

These steps of reasoning, from premises (1), (2), and (3) to conclusion (4), are basically sound, and I shall not query them in my present discussion. The only thing I might conceivably want to challenge is the assumption that the events which fill the overtly physical slot in psychophysical causation are (para-digmatically) non-mental. For this assumption ignores the mentalist possibility I mentioned at the end of Chapter 4. But, at worst, this complication would oblige Davidson to revise the formulation of the reasoning, not to abandon its substance.

Granted the validity of the reasoning, the assessment of the argument turns entirely on the status of the premises. It looks as if the main issue here will concern the status of premise (3) and the further argument by which Davidson tries to establish it. And certainly most of the discussions in the literature focus on this point. But let us start by taking a look at the other two premises, which might prove to be more straightforward.

Premise (1) asserts that there are causal relations between mental and physical events. This means, presumably, that there are cases in which either some mental event causes (or con-tributes to the causation of) a physical event or some physical event causes (or contributes to the causation of) a mental event. Thus construed, the premise seems uncontroversial. It is true that epiphenomenalists deny psychophysical causation in one direction, from the mental to the physical; this is an issue which I shall be examining in the next section. But surely there can be no denying that physical events sometimes have a causal influence on what takes place in the mind. For example, there is surely no denying that when someone is stung by a wasp, the stinging event brings about his subsequent pain, and that when someone is listening to the radio, the sounds emitted from the speakers bring about his auditory experiences. (In both these cases, of course, the relevant physical events do not cause the mental events *directly*, but only via some intervening causal process.) Davidson himself, it should be noted, accepts psychophysical causation in both directions, in line with common sense. Indeed, causation of the physical by the mental features prominently in his account of rationally motivated action. For he argues, with some plausibility, that when someone acts for a reason, his reason, consisting of some cluster of beliefs and desires, must be causally operative in the production of his behaviour.[11]

The meaning of premise (2) is not quite so clear. To begin with, there is the question of how we should interpret the notion of 'falling under a covering law'. If this is given a sufficiently strong sense, the premise as a whole could be taken as an endorsement of the nomological assumption discussed earlier – the assumption that any causal relationship between events is wholly constituted by certain non-causal properties of the situation and the obtaining of certain laws. And since we have already found fault with this reductive account of causation, we could simply reject Davidson's argument at this point. However, given what he says about causation in other places, I am fairly sure that Davidson does not intend the premise to be interpreted in this reductionist way.[12] Nor, indeed, is this interpretation required for the purposes of his argument. All he is claiming, I think, and all that his argument requires him to claim, is that, relative to some appropriate description of the events concerned and the circumstances of their occurrence, any singular causal relation can be represented as lawlike – as an instance of a purely general and law-ensured mode of causation. In other words, he is claiming that if an event x causes an event y, there is a covering law (or set of laws) which ensures that, in relevantly similar cirumstances, any event of the relevant x-type similarly causes, at a relevantly similar (space-time or mind-time) location in relation to it, an event of the relevant y-type. And such a claim does not imply that there is nothing more to the causal relationship than the obtaining of this law, together with those non-causal aspects of the situation by which the events fall under it. Indeed, it allows one to think of the covering laws as *explicitly causal*, in the sense explained earlier. And in fact this is how Davidson himself seems to envisage them in his most important article on this topic.[13]

There is one further aspect of premise (2) which needs to be clarified. Davidson is claiming that singular causal relations fall under *strict* covering laws – just as, in premise (3), he denies the existence of *strict* psychophysical laws. But what exactly is meant by 'strict'? I am not entirely sure. At one point, he formulates (2) as the claim that 'events related as cause and effect fall under strict deterministic laws',[14] and one might take 'deterministic' here as a gloss on 'strict'. But he also adds, in a footnote, that 'the stipulation that the laws be deterministic is stronger than required by the reasoning and will be relaxed'.[15] I think that, probably, 'strict law' just means 'genuine law', as opposed to a regularity which is purely or to some extent accidental, and this would allow statistical laws to qualify as strict in the relevant sense. Of course, counting statistical laws as strict would not commit one to regarding them as adequate for the purposes of covering causation: one could still insist that causal relations must fall under deterministic laws. But Davidson's comment in the footnote seems to imply that he *is* willing to allow for cases in which the covering laws are statistical. If so, then we need to modify slightly our earlier interpretation of premise (2). For the premise will no longer imply that whenever an event x causes an event y, there is a covering law which ensures that, in relevantly similar circumstances, events of the relevant x-type *always* cause events of the relevant y-type. However, since this whole issue is irrelevant to the core of Davidson's argument, it will simplify matters if we continue to think of the covering laws as deterministic, and simply bear in mind that there is room for manoeuvre on this point.

Granted that it does not imply the reduction of causation to law, premise (2) has some plausibility. Certainly we tend to work on the assumption that causation is nomologically uniform – that where certain factors are causally operative in one situation, natural law requires (or at least inclines) them to be operative in the same way in relevantly similar situations. Moreover, there seems to be some case for regarding this assumption as an a priori principle, governing our very concept of causation, rather than as something which rests on inductive evidence. For it is not clear that we can make sense of the supposition that one event happens *because* some other event happens, without also supposing that, relative to a description of the causally relevant factors, this instance of causation is lawlike. I confess I am not entirely sure about this: there are ways in which, as an a priori principle, premise (2) could be challenged. But since this would take us into a very different area of enquiry, and since my objections to Davidson do not depend on a rejection of this premise, I shall not pursue the issue any further here.

Premise (1) seems uncontroversial and premise (2) has some plausibility. But Davidson wants to combine (1) and (2) with a third, and seemingly more problematic, premise, which asserts that there are no strict (genuine) psychophysical laws. This further premise does not, of course, mean that there are no genuine *laws* covering the causal relations between mental and physical events – such an interpretation would be incompatible with premise (2). It means, rather, that the laws which cover psychophysical causal relations are to be formulated in purely physical, rather than psychophysical, terms – that they are laws which nomologically relate physical types with physical types. It is because of this that Davidson is able to reach his materialist conclusion. Mental events have to be identical with physical events, and thus have physical descriptions, in order for their causal relations with physical events to be covered by purely physical laws.

As I have indicated, Davidson has a separate argument to try to establish premise (3), and one which has attracted a great deal of attention. But before we look into this, there are two further ways in which the meaning of (3) needs to be clarified.

First, when Davidson denies the possibility of genuine psychophysical laws, I think he only intends this to apply to those types of mental phenomena, such as beliefs, desires, and decisions, which have propositional, or in some other way conceptual, content. It may well be that he thinks that all mental phenomena do have such content – in which case the denial of psychophysical laws will apply universally. But if there *are* wholly non-conceptual mental phenomena – and some philosophers would claim that there are such phenomena at the sensory level – he is not, as far as I can see, excluding the possibility of psychophysical laws concerning them. I am not sure that Davidson says this explicitly, but the point seems implicit in the way he tries to establish the premise.

Secondly, Davidson seems to equivocate between a stronger and a weaker thesis. The stronger thesis denies that there are genuine psychophysical laws of any form (though confined, as I have just indicated, to the relevant class of mental phenomena). The weaker thesis denies that psychological predicates are nomologically 'reducible' to physical predicates, i.e. denies that there are biconditional psychophysical laws of the form 'It is a law that, for any person P and any time t, P is in such and such a psychological state at t if and only if P is in such and such a physical state at t.'[16] There may be some real confusion in Davidson's thinking here. But, for the sake of our discussion, I shall assume that the stronger thesis is intended, since the weaker one would clearly not suffice for Davidson's overall argument. Someone who thinks that causal relations between mental and physical events are covered by psychophysical laws obviously does not need to postulate laws of this biconditional form.

Granted, then, that the area of interest is confined to mental phenomena of a propositional or at least a conceptual kind, and that the putative psychophysical laws are not restricted to any particular form, how does Davidson try to establish that no such laws exist? Well, the precise nature of the argument is somewhat elusive, but it seems to turn on what he sees as a radical contrast, or mismatch, between the epistemological methods of psychology and physical science. As he puts the point in 'Mental events':

> There are no strict psychophysical laws because of the disparate commitments of the mental and physical schemes. It is a feature of physical reality that physical change can be explained by laws that connect it with

other changes and conditions physically described. It is a feature of the mental that the attribution of mental phenomena must be responsible to the background of reasons, beliefs, and intentions of the individual. There cannot be tight connections between the realms if each is to retain allegiance to its proper source of evidence.[17]

And as he tries to explain it further in his subsequent essay 'Psychology as philosophy':

My general strategy for trying to show that there are no strict psychophysical laws depends, first, on emphasizing the holistic character of the cognitive field. Any effort at increasing the accuracy and power of a theory of behaviour forces us to bring more and more of the whole system of the agent's beliefs and motives directly into account. But in inferring this system from the evidence, we necessarily impose conditions of coherence, rationality, and consistency. These conditions have no echo in physical theory, which is why we can look for no more than rough correlations between psychological and physical phenomena.[18]

The questions now are: What exactly do these passages mean? And how does Davidson see them as constituting an argument for his third premise?

The situation is not at all clear. But looking closely at the passages, together with other things he says by way of elaboration, I am inclined to think that Davidson's intended argument can be set out, more fully and more explicitly, in the following steps:

(i) Our only evidence that another person P is in a certain mental state M is drawn from his behaviour and physical circumstances.

(ii) We cannot hope to obtain good evidence that P is in state M unless we also obtain good evidence about many other aspects of his psychological condition. This is because the behavioural evidence which we might take as directly bearing on the question of whether P is in state M can only be psychologically interpreted against the background of what we already know, or have good reason to believe, about his psychological condition. This in turn is because the sort of behaviour which we could reasonably expect to result from a person's being in a given mental state varies according to the other mental states with which it is conjoined.[19]

(iii) This means that any psychological interpretation of someone's behaviour on a particular occasion cannot be separated from our overall theory of his psychology, based on all that we know about his behaviour and physical circumstances, and perhaps all that we know about the behaviour and physical circumstances of other people. In constructing this theory, an essential guiding principle is that we should aim to maximize the degree to which we represent the subject as rational. This requires, in particular, attributing to him, as far as possible, propositional attitudes which form a coherent system, which harmonize with his sensory evidence, and to which his behaviour is rationally appropriate.

(iv) Such considerations of rationality do not constrain our theories about the physical world. Of course, *we* have to be rational in selecting these theories. But we do not have to attribute rationality to the physical conditions and processes in order to construct a rational theory about them.

(v) Because these considerations of rationality have, as Davidson puts it, 'no echo in physical theory', there can be no lawlike connections between the mental and the physical realms. Our theories of the mind impose order and system on mental phenomena and our theories of the physical world impose order and system on physical phenomena. But because the principles which determine what will count as relevantly orderly and systematic in the two cases are quite different, it is not possible for the two orders, or systems, to harmonize in a way which yields genuine psychophysical laws. In other words, because we are obliged to impose a rational order on the mental realm in order to be able to theorize about it at all, and because this order is quite different in kind from the nomological/mechanistic order we discover in the physical realm, there is no chance of the mental realm, qua mental, turning out to be nomologically orderly in relation to the physical.

I am inclined to think that this is the argument Davidson intends. The only trouble is that, when the reasoning is made explicit in this way, its faults become all too apparent. For it is shown up as a clear case of a *non sequitur*. Thus from the fact that the epistemological methods of common-sense psychology and physical science involve quite different principles, which impose quite different kinds of order on the phenomena with which they deal, it simply does not follow that there are no tight nomological connections between the two realms under their mental and physical descriptions. Consider, for instance, the case of the causal dependence of a person's beliefs on his neural condition. We can agree with Davidson that, to have grounds for ascribing a certain belief to someone, we need behavioural evidence which supports a more comprehensive psychological theory about him – a theory which represents that belief as an element of some larger system of propositional attitudes. And we can also agree that the behavioural evidence only supports this more comprehensive theory via considerations of rationality. But these points do not establish that there are no genuine psychophysical laws characterizing the causal dependence of beliefs on neural conditions. They do not preclude the existence of laws to the effect that, whenever a subject with a certain type of brain is in a certain neural state, he holds a certain type of belief.[20] Admittedly, given that an individual belief can only exist as part of a larger system of beliefs (for the holism of the mental is not just epistemological), such laws are bound to be highly complex on their physical side, and indeed to be consequences of laws which are highly complex on both sides. For it would ultimately be a matter of certain kinds of very complex neural structure (or perhaps structure plus pattern of occurrent events) being nomologically sufficient for certain kinds of very complex cognitive system – or at least, of their being sufficient given the presence of a suitably embodied mental subject. But while this complexity would distinguish such laws from those which are operative in the purely physical realm, as well as, presumably, making them harder to discover, it is not a reason for denying their existence.

Nor does the envisaged argument fare any better in the case of psychophysical laws running in the other direction, i.e. from the mental to the physical. It may well be that we can only legitimately ascribe a certain intention to someone within the framework of some more comprehensive psychological theory, and that the confirmation of this theory depends on considerations of rationality. But again there is nothing here which precludes the existence of the relevant kinds of psycho-physical law – laws to the effect that certain kinds of intention, occurring in certain larger mental contexts, and belonging to subjects with certain kinds of brains in certain kinds of neural condition, give rise to certain kinds of motor-neural effect. Indeed, in both cases, the fact that the rationality-conditions which constrain our ascriptions of mentality have 'no echo in physical theory' seems to have no bearing at all on the isssue of whether, independently of our theorizing, mental phen-omena, qua mental, and physical phenomena, qua physical, are nomologically linked.

Now it may be that I have simply misrepresented Davidson's reasoning here. Certainly, there is much more to be said on this issue: in particular, I think more needs to be said about Davidson's conception of natural law, and about the relevance, if any, of his acceptance of Quine's thesis of the indeterminacy of translation.[21] Fortunately, however, we can avoid any further entanglement in this difficult area. For we can demonstrate the failure of Davidson's *overall* argument (from (1), (2), and (3) to (4)), without having to decide at exactly what point the error occurs. More precisely, we can show that, whatever its status, Davidson cannot consistently combine an acceptance of (3) with an acceptance of the other two premises. Let me explain.

When one event causes another, there are certain properties of the first which are distinctively relevant to its role as cause: properties which are, as we may put it, *causally operative.* Likewise, there are certain properties of the second event which are distinctively relevant to its role as effect: properties which are, as we may say, *causally responsive* or *sensitive* to the operative properties of the first. Thus suppose I strike a match, causing it to ignite. It is a causally operative property of the striking-event that it involves friction between phosphorus and a rough surface, but not that it takes place in the vicinity of (say) my gas-fire. Likewise, it is a causally responsive property of the ignition-event that it involves the combining of the phosphorus with oxygen, but not that it occurs at the same time as (say) Tottenham score their first goal. None of this, of course, is to deny that the causal relation holds between events as such. Nor is it to imply that the events have to be designated under their causally relevant descriptions in order for a statement recording their causal relationship to be true.

Now we have said that premise (1) seems uncontroversial; and, as we noted, Davidson himself accepts psychophysical causation in both directions. But it is surely also undeniable that, prior to the acceptance of the token-identity thesis, whatever grounds we have for believing that mental and physical events are causally related are grounds for believing in the causal relevance of their respective mental and physical properties. Thus any grounds we have (independently of the identity-thesis) for believing that (say) electrical events in the optic nerves are causally involved in the production of visual experiences are surely also grounds for believing that the physical character of the electrical events causally affects the psychological character of the experiences (the physical properties of the one being causally operative and the psychological properties of the other being causally responsive). Likewise, any grounds we have (independently of the identity-thesis) for believing that a person's decisions are causally involved in the production of his behaviour are surely also grounds for believing that the psychological character of the decisions causally affects the physical character of the behaviour (the psychological properties of the one being causally operative and the physical properties of the other being causally responsive). In both cases, of course, the crucial point, in the present context, concerns the causal status of the relevant *psychological* properties. Thus what needs to be stressed is that, unless we have already established that mental events are physical, we do not have any grounds for believing that mental events have physical causes or physical effects except by having grounds for believing that their psychological properties are responsive or operative in the appropriate ways. And the reason for this is simply that, so long as we are only thinking of the mental events as mental, there is no way in which their causal relations could become apparent to us except in terms which concern their character *as* mental events. (In all this, of course, I am taking it for granted that we have already rejected analytical functionalism and any other form of mental reductionism.)

It follows from this that Davidson cannot employ (1) as a premise in his argument unless he accepts the causal relevance of psychological properties – accepts that such properties are causally operative in causation from mind to body and causally responsive in causation from body to mind. But this raises a problem. For if he accepts the causal relevance of psychological properties, it is difficult to see how he can also accept, in combination, premises (2) and (3). The point is simply this. Whatever reason Davidson has for accepting that singular causal relations always fall under covering laws, it seems that it must also be a reason for thinking that each such relation falls under a covering law, or set of laws, *relative to a description of the causally relevant factors*. In particular, it seems that it must be a reason for thinking that, if x causes y, and P is a property of x which is operative in x's causing of y, and Q is a property of y which is causally responsive to P in y's causation by x, then there is some law, or set of laws, which not only nomologically links x-type and y-type events (thus covering the causal relationship in a minimal sense), but does so in a way which, by according an appropriate nomological relevance to P and Q, makes clear their respective operative and responsive roles. But then how can Davidson apply this model to the case of psychophysical causation if he both accepts the causal relevance of psychological properties and denies the existence of psychophysical laws? For if the covering laws are purely physical, it will only be the physical properties of mental events which they represent as causally relevant. In short, it seems that, whatever case can be made out for each premise on its own, Davidson cannot be in a position to accept all three together. His acceptance of (1) commits him to recognizing the causal relevance of psychological properties. This, together with his acceptance of (2), seems to commit him to recognizing the nomological relevance of psychological properties. And the nomological relevance of psychological properties, in the area of psychophysical causation, is just what gets excluded by (3).

I think Davidson's only possible reply to this would be to say that the operativeness and responsiveness of psychological properties in the context of psychophysical causation are ultimately constituted by causal facts which obtain at the *physical* level. When one billiard ball displaces another, we can describe the causal process in 'common-sense' terms, picking out such causally relevant factors as the shape, size, and weights of the balls, and their speeds and directions at the moment of impact. But there is also a description of the causal process in scientifically fundamental terms (in terms of such factors as the motion of the elementary particles, the influence of electromagnetic forces, and the presence of gravitational fields), and the causal relationships which obtain at the common-sense level are presumably derivative from, and wholly constituted by, these more fundamental causal facts. Analogously, then, Davidson might say that, while psychological properties are to be assigned a causal relevance at the level of common-sense (the level at which we ordinarily think about psychophysical causation), these common-sense causal facts are derivative from, and wholly constituted by, causal facts of a purely physical kind – facts which are at present largely unknown, but which may one day be brought to light by neurophysiology. The point of this reply is that it allows Davidson to accept both the causal relevance of psychological properties and the lawlike character of psychophysical causation, without having to accept that such causation is lawlike under its psychophysical specification. For if the psychophysical causal facts are wholly constituted by physical causal facts, it will not be surprising if the only genuinely nomological uniformities in psychophysical causation have to be specified in purely physical terms. In other words, Davidson's acceptance of premise (2) does not, after all, commit him to accepting the nomological relevance of *all* causally operative and responsive factors, but only to accepting the nomological relevance of all such factors which emerge at the fundamental level of description – all factors which are, as causal factors, metaphysically basic.

This distinction between basic and derivative causal facts is a good one, and well-illustrated, in the physical realm, by the relationship between causality at the level of common sense and that at the level of particle physics. Moreover, if Davidson could exploit it in the way envisaged, it would solve his problem. But the point which now needs to be stressed is that the envisaged solution is already ruled out by our earlier results. For Davidson would only be able to represent the facts of psychophysical causation as ultimately constituted by the facts of purely physical causation if he could also take psychological facts as such to be wholly constituted by physical facts. And we have already shown that no such reductive account of mentality is tenable. Whether Davidson wants to offer such an account I am not sure. His official position is merely that psychological properties 'supervene on' physical properties, by which he means that it is logically impossible for two situations to differ in their psychological features without some difference in their physical features.[22] And this does not formally entail that psychological facts are constituted by physical facts, since it does not entail that the physical features of a situation logically necessitate its psychological features. At the same time, it is difficult to see why Davidson should want to make the supervenience claim unless he accepts (and accepts as something logically necessary) the constitutionalist position as well.[23]

At all events, whether or not it is something which Davidson himself endorses, the envisaged solution is not now available. Nor, as far as I can see, is any other: there is simply no way in which, within the framework of our findings, we could avoid a commitment to psychophysical laws, while accepting both that all singular causal relationships are covered by laws and that psychological properties are operative and responsive in psychophysical causation.

If this is right, then we are in a position to reject Davidson's argument without having to identify the exact point where it has gone wrong. For we can see that whatever case he may be able to construct for each of the premises individually, he is not entitled to assert their conjunction. Since premise (3) has the least prima facie plausibility, and since Davidson's attempt to establish it seems wholly ineffective, we may suspect that the fault lies here. But, in rejecting Davidson's argument, this is not a point which we need to press.

5 THE SCIENCE-EFFICACY ARGUMENT

We have considered three ways in which, in the area of psychophysical causation, dualism has been attacked on a priori grounds. Thus we began by considering the traditional objection to dualistic psychophysical causation, that there is something deeply puzzling about the notion of the non-physical mind making causal contact with the body. We then examined a rather more technical objection, which concerned the issue of psychophysical causal pairings and involved the endorsement of a nomologically reductionist account of causation. Lastly, we looked at Davidson's objection, that the dualist cannot, in the way he needs, bring psychophysical causation under covering laws. In each case, we found the points brought against the dualist to be misconceived.

I want now, and finally, to turn to a quite different kind of argument against dualism. This new argument is still very much concerned with the topic of psychophysical causation; and it is still directed towards establishing token-identity. But what makes it quite different in character is that it appeals to the findings of empirical science and so does not have a purely a priori foundation. I shall refer to it as the 'science-efficacy argument'.[24]

The argument runs as follows:

1 On the basis of physical science, we should accept:

   (a) To the extent that they can be causally explained at all, the physical conditions obtaining at any time can, from a God's-eye view, be fully causally explained purely in terms of the preceding physical conditions and the framework of physical laws.

The point of the qualifying-clause 'To the extent ... at all' is to leave room for the possibility that the physical system is not fully deterministic. And the point of the qualifying-phrase 'from a God's-eye view' is to indicate that, given the limitations on our knowledge of the physical conditions and laws, the causal explanation may be one which we are not in a position to specify. Strictly speaking, there should also be a third qualification. It is possible, and perhaps even plausible to suppose, that the physical universe had a beginning, so that there is an earliest time when physical conditions obtain. This means that (a) should really be formulated so as only to apply to physical conditions *other than such initial conditions* (if there are any). It will be convenient, however, to leave (a) in its present form and just bear in mind the need for this modification.

2 From (a), we can legitimately conclude:

   (b) The physical world is a 'closed system', in the sense that the only causal influences on what occurs within it (at least at any time later than its initial time, if it has one) are themselves physical.

(b), of course, leaves room for the possibility that there is an external non-physical agency which is responsible for the physical laws. And, even ignoring the point about the initial conditions, I imagine we can also interpret it in a way which leaves room for the possibility of an external agency which is responsible for the system as a whole.

3 But irrespective of physical science, it is clear that:

(c) Mental events often have a causal influence on the subsequent course of the physical world.

For example, if I decide to cross the road, the decision can be expected to bring about a certain behavioural response, namely that of my crossing the road. Or again, if I hear the telephone ring, my auditory experience, together with my beliefs and desires, will normally lead me to answer it.

4 The only way of reconciling (c) with (b) – the only way of reconciling the causal efficacy of the mental with the fact that the physical world is a closed system – is by concluding:

(d) Mental events are themselves physical.

In other words, given that the only causal influences on what occurs in the physical world are themselves physical, we are forced to say that the causal influence of the *mental* on the physical is just a special case of the causal influence of the *physical* on the physical – a special case of the causal influence of earlier physical conditions on later physical conditions in accordance with physical laws. And this, in turn, forces us to say that the mental events which exert this causal influence are physical events. Of course, from the proposition that all such *causally influential* mental events are physical, it does not strictly follow that *all* mental events are physical. But presumably no one would want to dispute the stronger conclusion once he had accepted the weaker. Or at least, no one would want to dispute it with respect to the domain of human and animal mentality which here concerns us.

With this slight and unimportant qualification over the strength of the conclusion, it is clear, I think, that the move from (b) and (c) to (d) is logically valid. And this means that, if we are to resist the argument, we must either dispute premise (a), or dispute the move from (a) to (b), or dispute premise (c). I shall look at each of these options in turn, starting with the last.

Premise (c), which asserts the causal efficacy of the mental, or, more precisely, the causal influence of the mental on the physical, is intuitively plausible, and indeed is endorsed by dualism itself in its traditional form. Admittedly, in the case of those traditional dualists who are also traditional libertarians (i.e. libertarians who believe in a contra-deterministic freedom), it might be better to speak of the 'causal or *quasi-causal*' influence of the mental on the physical. For the libertarian will insist that the route from mentality to behaviour is often mediated by the exercise of free choice – choice which, while genuinely responsive to, and so in some sense influenced by, the mentality in question, is not (mechanistically) caused by it. But, for the purposes of the present discussion, I shall simply allow the notion of the causal influence of the mental on the physical to be sufficiently broad to cover this sort of case.[25]

Traditional dualism, then, in line with common sense, accepts the causal influence of mental events on the physical world. But of course there is a version of dualism which does not – a version known as *epiphenomenalism*.[26] Thus while traditional dualists hold that the mind and the body causally *interact*, with each exerting a causal influence on the other, epiphenomenalists claim that the lines of psychophysical causation run in only one direction, from the body to the mind. Thus, when someone is stung by a wasp, epiphenomenalists accept that the subsequent pain is caused by the sting; but they deny that this pain has any causal bearing on the subject's oral complaint, or that his decision to apply vinegar to the affected region helps to bring about the subsequent movements of his body. And, quite generally, they accept that processes in the body causally affect the mind in all the ways we ordinarily believe, but deny that events in the mind ever causally affect the body or anything else in the physical world. Most epiphenomenalists, as well as denying that the mind has any causal influence on the physical world, also deny that it has a causal influence on anything at all. In particular, they deny that mental events cause, or contribute to the causation of, the occurrence of other mental events. But this is not an essential element of the position I am here using the term 'epiphenomenalism' to signify – though it may be that my usage is non-standard.

Like the token-identity theorists in the science-efficacy argument, epiphenomenalists tend to base their position on the assumption that physical science shows the physical world to be a closed system. But they see this as having a quite different implication. Thus whereas the identity-theorist argues:

> *The physical world is a closed system.*
> *Mental items causally affect the physical world.*
> *Therefore, mental items are physical.*

The epiphenomenalist argues conversely:

> *The physical world is a closed system.*
> *Mental items are non-physical.*
> *Therefore, mental items do not causally affect the physical world.*

So if the identity-theorist is to invoke the science-efficacy argument, his first task must be to show that epiphenomenalism is untenable.

It would be tempting to reject epiphenomenalism simply on the grounds that it is in radical conflict with our ordinary conception of ourselves as agents. If mental states have no causal influence on behaviour, then behaviour cannot be thought of as intentional in any decent sense, even if the subject happens to have certain intentions which it fulfils. And if behaviour is not intentional, it does not qualify as action in any sense which would distinguish it from mere bodily movement. It is true that, even in the epiphenomenalist's system, the general conformity of our behaviour to our intentions is presumably not purely accidental: it is presumably ensured by the very structure of our brains and their muscular extensions in the framwork of physical and psychophysical laws. In other words, the epiphenomenalist will presumably take us to be so constructed that the neural states which cause intentions are made to play a functional role appropriate to what they cause. But even so, the behaviour which results is not intentional in the requisite sense, since the intentions and the psychophysical laws are irrelevant to its production: given the antecedent physical conditions and physical laws, the same behaviour would have occurred even if (with a change in psychophysical law) the appropriate intention had been absent; and conversely, even with the presence of the intention, this behaviour would not have occurred in the absence of either the physical conditions or the physical laws.

Another factor which might be thought to count against epiphenomenalism is that the supposition of efficacy plays a causal role in the explanation of human behaviour. Such behaviour exhibits certain complex regularities which call for explanation and which, at present, we explain (at least partly) in psychological terms. These psychological explanations, though typically of a rational rather than a mechanistic kind, attribute a causal efficacy to the mental: they represent the subject's behaviour as falling under the control of his beliefs and desires, or under the control of his decisions and intentions, which are responsive to his beliefs and desires. The claim might then be that such explanations gain credibility from the fact that, as well as being in their own terms successful, they cannot at present be replaced by non-psychological explanations which cover the same ground.

These common-sense points against the epiphenomenalist are not, to my mind, decisive. There is no denying the conflict between epiphenomenalism and our ordinary conception of ourselves as agents. But the fact that this is our *ordinary* view of the situaton does not mean that it is correct. Just what grounds do we have for supposing that human behaviour *is* intentional, and *does* qualify as action, in the relevant sense? Again, there is no denying that, for ordinary purposes, we need to make use of psychological explanations. But it could still be claimed that the *ultimately* correct explanations (maybe only discernible from a God's-eye view) are purely physical. And indeed this is something which the defender of the science-efficacy argument himself accepts. The most that follows from these lines of reasoning is that the onus is on the epiphenomenalist to try to justify his unusual position. But presumably he is happy to take on this challenge. For he can say that what supplies the justification is the scientific evidence in favour of the view that the physical world is a closed system, together with the already established case against token-identity.

However, it seems to me that epiphenomenalism is open to a much more powerful objection than either of these. For I cannot see how, if epiphenomenalism were true, the mind could form a topic for overt discussion. Certainly, if mental items have no causal access to our speech centres, the notion of an introspective report collapses: even if the subject retains an introspective knowledge of his mental states, his utterances do not count as *expressing* that knowledge if it contributes nothing to their production.[27] But I cannot even see how, on the epiphenomenalistic view, our language, as a medium for our utterances, makes semantic contact with the mind at all. In what sense, for example, could the word 'pain', as overtly used, be said to signify a certain type of sensation, if neither the occurrence of the sensations nor our introspective conception of their type affects its overt use? Quite generally, it seems to me that if the mental contributes nothing to the way in which the linguistic practices involving 'psychological' terms are developed and sustained in the speech-community, and in no other way affects the production of utterances employing these terms, then, in respect of their overt use, the terms should be analysed in a purely behaviourist or functionalist fashion – which would deprive the epiphenomenalist of the linguistic resources to enunciate his thesis. It is true, of course, that each language-user may *mentally* interpret each term as signifying a certain kind of (dualistically conceived) mental item. But I cannot see how such private interpretations could have any bearing on the objective meaning of the terms, as employed in speech and writing, if, with respect to this employment, they are causally idle. (This is not, of course, to endorse Wittgenstein's private language argument. The sort of private interpretations which Wittgenstein was trying to exclude would not, on my interactionist-dualist view, be causally idle.[28])

It does not follow from this that the state of affairs which epiphenomenalism postulates is one which could not obtain – that there could not be a world in which the mental had no causal influence on the physical. Nor does it even follow that we can know *a priori* that the actual world is not of this kind. For it cannot be established a priori that the mental actually is a topic for overt discussion. None the less, if the point is correct, there is a sense in which, as overtly expressed, epiphenomenalism becomes self-refuting. For if it is only possible to provide a publicly audible or visible formulation of the thesis if the mental is causally efficacious, then any attempt to provide such a formulation can only succeed if the thesis is false. In effect, then, we either have to accept that the thesis is false, or abandon the attempt to make its truth or falsity an issue for public debate, or even for private but vocal soliloquy. If this does not quite refute epiphenomenalism, it at least renders it the sort of position which cannot be seriously entertained – the sort of position whose falsity (to echo Hume on the existence of body[29]) we are forced to take for granted in all our reasonings, even of a philosophical kind.

Having pressed this objection against epiphenomenalism, I must now add a qualification. In claiming that if epiphenomenalism were true, the mind could not form a topic for overt discussion, I have been assuming that if mental events have no causal influence on the physical world, then their occurrence will be, in every way, irrelevant to any explanation of physical phenomena. This assumption is a very natural one – and something which orthodox epiphenomenalists are unlikely to dispute. However, so long as we grant the coherence of theism, I think we can envisage two situations in which the assumption would be false.

The first situation is that in which, while mental items have no *causal* influence on physical phenomena, they serve as 'occasions' for God to bring about certain physical events. For example, it might be that whenever a human subject decides to act in a certain way, God, taking note of the decision, causes the subject's motor-neurons to fire in the appropriate way. The decision itself does not cause the neuronal event; it does not even *indirectly* cause it, by causally influencing God's decision, since God is here thought of as entirely active and free, and hence as not subject to any kind of external pressure. It is just that God chooses to control the physical on-goings in such a way as to match the subject's state of mind.

The second situation is one in which, instead of controlling the physical on-goings in a piecemeal fashion, God deliberately arranges things, in advance and globally, so that the biological creatures which evolve are constituted in a way which secures a match between the functional roles of their neural states and the psychological character of the mental items which these states causally generate. Everything which occurs in the physical world has an efficient cause in the preceding physical conditions, and the mental items caused by neural states and events are themselves causally idle. But since God has selected the physical and psychophysical laws and the initial physical conditions of the universe with a view to ensuring that the mental and the physical realms harmonize in the appropriate way, there is still a sense in which the fact that neural states and events have certain psychological effects features in the ultimate explanation of the physical phenomena. Thus when a subject makes a decision and his muscles contract appropriately, we can say that, although it does not contribute anything causally to the muscular movement, this decision does have an ultimate explanatory bearing on the movement; for it is only because the preceding central-neural event is empowered to produce that sort of decision that it is also empowered, by the structure of the organism and the physical laws, to produce that kind of physical effect.[30]

Now of these two situations, it is only the second which has any real relevance to the issue which concerns us. For the first, in which God takes human mental items as occasions for causing physical events, is not really an epiphenomenalist situation in the intended sense. It does not deny the causal efficacy of the mental *in deference to the claims of physical science*, and, if anything, it looks more like an occasionalistic version of interactionism than a form of epiphenomenalism. In any case, it would be hard to find any rationale for it except as part of a quite general occasionalist theory, such as that of Malebranche, which denies the causal efficacy of mental and physical events alike. The second situation, however, in which the physical world is a closed system and God is the transcendent architect of the psychophysical harmony, does yield a form of epiphenomenalism in the intended sense. And it might be that, if such a situation obtained, the explanatory link between mentality and behaviour would be enough to render the mind a topic for overt discussion – and, indeed, enough to allow us to retain some conception of ourselves as agents. I shall return, briefly, to this point presently. But, for the time being, let us continue with the assumption that epiphenomenalism represents the mind, not merely as having no causal influence on physical events, but as having no explanatory role either.

On this assumption, as we have seen, epiphenomenalism is a position which, even if logically coherent, cannot be seriously entertained. And here the crucial point is not that it conflicts with common sense (i.e. in respect of our conception of ourselves as agents and our employment of psychophysical explanations), but that the supposition of its truth would oblige us to suppose that the mind was not a topic for overt discussion. In this respect, then, things are looking good for the identity-theorist. All he needs to do, it seems, is to vindicate premise (a) of the science-efficacy argument, and then validate the move from (a) to (b), and the identity of mental with physical events will automatically follow.

However, while it is certainly true that claim (b), together with the falsity of epiphenomenalism, would be enough to establish the token-identity thesis, it would be wrong to conclude that our argument against epiphenomenalism has made the prospects for this thesis any better. Quite the reverse. For a little reflection shows that the argument in question should be taken as an argument against the acceptance of claim (b) rather than as a step in the direction of token-identity. Let me explain.

Claim (b) asserts that the physical world is a closed system. Taken in the context of premise (a), from which it is inferred, this implies not just that the only events which cause (or contribute to the causation of) physical events are physical, but also that the only qualitative factors which are ultimately (i.e. metaphysically-fundamentally) operative in the causation of physical events are physical. But, thus interpreted, it is easy to show that, combined with what we have already established, claim (b) itself generates a sort of epiphenomenalism. For although it leaves room for the causal efficacy of mental items, it does not leave room for the causal efficacy of their psychological properties. Thus it allows us to say that a person's decision to cross the road caused the subsequent firing of his motor-neurons; but it does not allow us to say that its being a decision, or its being a decision of that specific psychological type, played any causal role in bringing about this effect. In short, it obliges us to conclude that, with respect to the causation of the physical by the mental, psychological properties are causally idle. Now I am not suggesting that this conclusion immediately follows from claim (b) *taken on its own*. After all, someone might accept that it is only physical factors which are causally operative, but secure the causal efficacy of psychological properties by identifying them with physical properties. Or again, he might accept that it is only physical factors which are ultimately operative, but, by pressing some form of metaphysical reduction of mental facts to physical facts, allow psychological properties to enjoy a derivative efficacy. Or yet again, he might accept that it is only physical factors which are ultimately operative, but provide a *sort* of causal role for psychological properties by construing them in a functionalist way, so that such properties are partly defined as causal powers of mental items to affect behaviour.[31] But all these positions are ones which we have already shown to be untenable. For we have already established that psychological properties are *sui generis* and metaphysically fundamental. It is against the background of these already established results that an acceptance of claim (b) would force us to say that psychological properties are causally idle.

Now, of course, the claim that psychological properties are causally idle is not the full-blooded 'ontological' epi-phenomenalism which we characterized earlier: it does not imply that mental items (mental events) have no causal influence on the physical world. It is merely what we might call 'property-epiphenomenalism'. But the crucial point is that the considerations which seem to count against the ontological (or event-) version of epiphenomenalism count equally against the property-version. Thus the claim that psychological properties have no causal influence on behaviour conflicts with common sense (in respect of both our conception of ourselves as agents and our employment of psychological explanations) in the same way as the full epiphenomenalist claim. And, more importantly, short of invoking the divine harmony hypothesis, it still leaves no way in which the mental, qua mental, could be a topic for overt discussion. In short, all the factors which would persuade us that the mind has a causal efficacy and that full epiphenomenalism is false would also persuade us that the mind has a causal efficacy *qua mind* and that mental events exert a causal influence on the physical world *by means of their psychological features*.

We can see now why the argument against epi-phenomenalism has not improved the prospects for the token-identity thesis. We are working on the assumption that the identity-theorist is trying to establish his position by invoking the science-efficacy argument, as we have set it out. It had initially seemed that the argument against epiphenomenalism would help him in this enterprise by establishing premise (c). But the trouble is that, if it succeeds in establishing this premise, it thereby serves to refute claim (b). For any case which it provides in favour of the causal efficacy of mental events is an equally strong case in favour of the causal efficacy of psychological properties; and the closed-system view does not allow for the efficacy of psychological properties unless it is combined with one of the positions (the type-identity thesis or some kind of mental reductionism) which we have already refuted. So, instead of improving his prospects, the argument against epiphenomenalism, if successful, would actually prevent the identity-theorist from establishing his position in the envisaged way.

This, on its own, is enough to discredit the science-efficacy argument, and in a sense we could afford to leave matters there. However, there are still two further aspects of the argument which it is worth discussing. These aspects respectively concern the move from premise (a) to claim (b) and the status of premise (a) itself. I shall look at these issues in turn.

Premise (a) states that, to the extent that they can be causally explained at all, the physical conditions obtaining at any time can, from a God's-eye view, be fully causally explained in terms of the preceding physical conditions and the framework of physical laws. And, from this premise, it is inferred that (claim (b)) the physical world is a closed system, so that the only factors which causally influence what occurs within it are themselves physical. Now the first thing which needs to be stressed about this inference is that, whatever its plausibility, it is not deductively valid: there is no logical contradiction in asserting the premise but denying the conclusion. The reason for this is that we cannot exclude a priori the possibility of 'causal overdetermination' – the possibility of a single event having two causes which operate separately, rather than in combination, to produce it.[32] Thus the fact (if it is a fact) that each physical event can be fully causally explained in terms of the preceding physical conditions in the framework of the relevant physical laws does not as such rule out the possibility that some physical events (for example, certain events in the brain) can also be causally explained, quite separately, in terms of certain not-wholly-physical preceding conditions in the framework of certain not-purely-physical laws. And if this possibility obtained, then the physical world would not be a closed system in the relevant sense: it would not be something whose events and conditions were subject exclusively to the influence of physical factors. In particular, of course, the possibility of overdetermination allows someone to combine an acceptance of premise (a) with the acceptance of the causal efficacy of psychological properties, conceived as fundamental and *sui generis*. Thus in the case where a person's decision to cross the road (event D at time t_1) is followed by a certain firing of his motor-neurons (event F at time t_2), someone could hold *both* that F is causally determined by the neural conditions obtaining at t_1 in accordance with the ordinary laws of physics and chemistry *and* that F is separately causally determined by the psychological character of D, in the context of certain other psychological and/or physical conditions, in accordance with some irreducible psychophysical law. And, quite generally, he could hold that psychological properties (as fundamental and *sui generis*) are causally efficacious in the way we ordinarily believe, but that, in each case where they are causally operative on the physical world, there is an additional and purely physical process of causation which has exactly the same effect.

Admittedly, such a view, considered on its own, does not strike us as very plausible. It seems rather peculiar if things are so organized that psychological factors have a causal influence on the physical world, but one which, given the prior physical conditions and physical laws, is wholly redundant. And here the main point is not that a causal influence which can only duplicate the independent influence of the physical factors may seem only notionally different from epiphenomenalism, but that the systematic way in which the envisaged overdetermination would operate surely cries out for explanation. In reply, it might be hypothesized that the system is divinely ordained for our benefit: the purpose of granting a causal efficacy to psychological properties would be to ensure our capacity for intentional action and meaningful utterance; the purpose of maximizing the reign of physical law would be to make the physical world as orderly, and hence as predictable, as possible. Even so, one cannot help thinking that God could have made a better job of things by allowing the psychological factors to express themselves through action and utterance in a more distinctive way. A measure of neural unpredictability at the physical level seems a small epistemological price to pay for a psychological efficacy which can make a real difference to what takes place in the physical world. Admittedly, our preference for a form of efficacy which is not constrained by overdetermination is closely bound up with our desire to possess some genuine and efficacious freedom of choice with respect to the actions we perform; and if, as some philosophers hold, the very notion of a genuinely free choice is incoherent, it might then be suggested that overdetermination is the best that God can achieve. Since I reject such an attack on the notion of free choice, this suggestion is not one which I need to take up.[33] But, in any case, I am inclined to think that, without the accompaniment of volitional freedom, efficacy would be of no value and God would have no reason to prefer overdetermination to the nomologically simpler system postulated by the epiphenomenalist.

To the extent that we find the overdetermination hypothesis implausible, we shall be prepared to accept the inference from (a) to (b), despite its lack of deductive validity. And if we do accept this inference, the issue over the status of premise (a) becomes of paramount importance. This importance, of course, does not relate to the evaluation of the science-efficacy argument, since we have already seen that this argument fails: there is no way of defending premise (c) which does not undermine claim (b). What makes it crucial to examine the status of (a) is that, if we exclude overdetermination, the acceptance of (a) would force us to deny the efficacy of psychological properties – which would be, to put it mildly, an embarrassing consequence.

Premise (a) is supposed to be based on the findings of physical science. It is physical science which, allegedly, reveals, or makes it rational to believe, that, to the extent that they are causally explicable at all, the physical conditions obtaining at any time are causally explicable in purely physical terms. But exactly how is science supposed to reveal this? Suppose we concede that, in general, physical events have a purely physical explanation, but insist that, in the case of the human brain (and perhaps the brains of animals too), things are different. Suppose we insist that, in the case of the human brain, the non-physical mind exerts a direct causal influence on what goes on, and that because this influence is not (as on the overdetermination view) merely a redundant duplicate of the influence exerted by the physical conditions, no adequate explanation of the workings of the brain can be given without reference to it. How are the findings of science supposed to discredit this traditional interactionist position?

We ought to begin by distinguishing two ways in which science might provide grounds, or what are taken to be grounds, for believing that the workings of the human brain are explicable in purely physical terms. The first way would be by direct research on the brain itself. Thus by monitoring neural activity and chemical states in its various parts (perhaps by some yet-to-be-discovered method which does not disrupt normal functioning), neuro-scientists might be able to establish a strong inductive case for the conclusion that everything which takes place in the brain can be causally explained in terms of preceding physical conditions and ordinary physical laws. The second way would be by investigating physical phenomena *in general*, without any specific reference to the brain. Thus it might be discovered that, in so far as it has been investigated, the physical world seems to be governed by laws of a sort which, assuming they hold universally, guarantee that the workings of *any* physical system are explicable in purely physical terms. Now I take it that the supposed case for thinking that the workings of the brain are physically explicable rests predominantly on scientific evidence of the second kind. For while there has been considerable research on the brain, it could hardly be thought sufficiently extensive and revealing to provide, on its own, a strong case against the interactionist position envisaged above. I assume that the basic case against such interactionism is that the investigations of physics and chemistry into the general nature of physical phenomena yield findings that are in line with premise (a), and that, in default of any evidence to the contrary, it is a reasonable presumption that the brain will not constitute an exception. In short, the argument is not that we have much in the way of direct evidence that what takes place in the brain can be adequately explained in purely physical terms, but that we have a great deal of direct evidence for a certain general view of the world, and that this general view implies the adequacy of physical explanation for the functioning of any physical system – the brain included.

But if this is the nature of the scientific case for supposing that the workings of the brain can be causally explained in purely physical terms, then it is a conspicuously weak one. For since the crucial evidence is of this indirect kind – evidence drawn, not from brain research, but from the more basic investigations of physics and chemistry into the nature and behaviour of things in general – it has to be evaluated in the light of whatever else we independently know, or have reason to believe, about the special relationship between the human body and the human mind, and about the role which the brain plays in this relationship. Of course, if all we knew about the brain was that it was a physical object of a certain physical type, it would be reasonable, prior to direct investigation, to suppose that its functioning would turn out to be explicable in terms of the same laws of physics and chemistry as other physical things – that anything distinctive in its internal behaviour would be attributable to its distinctive physical properties rather than to some distinctive set of causal principles or to some *sui generis* source of causal influence. But, in fact, we already know that the brain is the seat of the mind; and all that we pre-scientifically know about ourselves suggests that the mind, qua mind, has a causal influence on behaviour. When the scientific evidence is evaluated in the light of this information, and when we also take account of our refutation of the type-identity thesis and the various forms of mental reductionism, the rational conclusion to draw is that the brain is subject to certain non-physical influences which do not affect the other physical systems which science investigates; and, in default of any special reason for postulating overdetermination, this in turn would make it rational to believe that the workings of the brain are not fully explicable in purely physical terms. The point is not that the scientific evidence gets *overruled* by other considerations (though such an overruling would be legitimate if the contrary considerations were sufficiently powerful). It is rather that the significance of the evidence can only be properly assessed in a wider context, and that, in this context, it simply does not support the conclusion that the brain functions in a way which could be wholly accounted for (even from a God's-eye view) on the basis of its physical character and physical laws.

All this, of course, is relative to our present state of scientific knowledge. It is *conceivable* that future research on the brain will provide strong evidence in favour of the view that its workings are fully explicable in terms of the ordinary laws of physics and chemistry. And if such evidence were sufficiently strong, it would become rational to accept the conclusion to which it points – leaving us with an embarrassing choice between, on the one hand, accepting the overdetermination account and, on the other, denying the causal efficacy of psychological properties altogether. In such circumstances, I think I should probably opt for the second alternative and invoke the divine-harmony hypothesis, discussed earlier, to salvage some kind of explanatory role for psychological properties – a role which might be sufficient both to preserve the possibility of intentional action and meaningful utterance and to allow the mental, qua mental, to be a topic for overt discussion. Neither option, of course, would further the purposes of the science-efficacy argument: the overdetermination account would leave us free to assign the operative psychological properties to events which were non-physical; and denying the causal efficacy of psychological properties would be compatible with full-blooded (ontological) epiphenomenalism. The science-efficacy argument can only succeed if there is some way of establishing the causal role of mental events within the framework of the closed-system view. And, for reasons which we have already elaborated, this cannot be done.

In any case, whatever embarrassment we *would* feel if we had to choose between overdetermination and property-epiphenomenalism, the point to be stressed is that our present evidence does not give us good reason to expect that we shall have to face this choice. The rational position to accept, in our present state of knowledge, is that premise (a) is false and that any adequate causal explanation of the functioning of the brain would have to take account of the influence of psychological factors.

7

THE MENTAL SUBJECT

1 THE ISSUES

The dualist takes the mental and the physical realms to be ontologically separate (claim [5], or [5a], of the dualist doctrine, as formulated in Chapter 1). This separation has two aspects. One we have already covered. It is simply that the dualist gives a radically non-physicalistic account of what exists or occurs within the mind: he takes sensations, thought-episodes, decisions, instances of belief, and so on, to be wholly non-physical – to be devoid of any intrinsic physical attributes or location in physical space. In this respect at least (though with one qualification which I shall deal with presently), we have shown the dualist's position to be correct. The other aspect we have not yet covered. It concerns the dualist view of the *mental subject* – of the sort of thing which has sensations, engages in thought, takes decisions, and so on. Admittedly, it is a little misleading to speak of *the* dualist view here. For on this issue, as we shall see, there are two rival and radically different dualistic theories. But it is still possible to identify a common thesis which these rival theories share and which, in conjunction with the non-physicalistic account of the ingredients of the mind, captures the sense in which the dualist takes the mental and physical realms to be ontologically separate. So I shall start by trying to formulate this common thesis.

We might begin by noting that, while we can straightforwardly represent the dualist as claiming that the ingredients of the mind are wholly non-physical, we cannot, in the same way, straightforwardly represent him as claiming that mental subjects are wholly non-physical – that they too have neither intrinsic physical attributes nor location in physical space. The reason is simple. Something will qualify as a mental subject if and only if it has mental states or engages in mental activities. If we take the dualist to be claiming that *all* mental subjects are wholly non-physical, then we commit him to saying that we cannot, in any sense, correctly ascribe mental states or activities to animals. And worse, we commit him to saying that we cannot correctly ascribe them to human beings, construed as members of an animal species. But, as well as being at variance with our ordinary view, these are not conclusions which most dualists would be prepared to accept. Nearly all dualists would acknowledge that, construed as members of the species *homo sapiens*, human beings still qualify as mental subjects – that we can correctly speak of them as perceiving, thinking, feeling, deciding, and so on. And most (though, notoriously, not Descartes) would be prepared to ascribe some modest degree of mentality to the higher non-human animals too. Clearly, then, we want to formulate the dualist's thesis in a way which, while effecting the relevant ontological separation of the mental and physical realms, gives him the appropriate latitude in these respects – a way which enables him to accommodate these aspects of our ordinary ascriptive practice.

How, then, should we formulate it? Well, the first and most crucial step is to draw a distinction between the general concept of a mental subject and the more specific concept of what I shall call a *basic* mental subject. An entity qualifies as a mental subject if and only if it is something which has mental states or engages in mental activities. It qualifies as a *basic* mental subject if and only if it is a mental subject and is represented as such in the *philosophically fundamental account*. That is, it qualifies as a basic (mental) subject if and only if it is represented as a mental subject in the *conceptually funda-mental account* (i.e. in terms not amenable to further conceptual analysis) of the *metaphysically fundamental reality* (i.e. the reality of metaphysically basic facts). There are two ways in which a mental subject may fail to qualify as a basic subject in this sense. In the first place, it may be something which does not even feature as an entity in the philosophically fundamental account – something whose very existence is analysed away or taken to be constituted by facts about other things. In such a case, we may say that the entity fails to qualify as a *basic entity*.

Secondly, it may be something which, though a mental subject and a basic entity, does not retain its status as a mental subject in the fundamental account. That is, it may be an entity whose existence is fundamental, but whose role as a subject is conceptually or metaphysically reducible to something else. One way, of course, in which the second type of situation could arise would be by our acceptance of a reductive account of mentality itself. But since we have already rejected all forms of mental reductionism, this possibility will have no interest for us in the present context.

Given this notion of a basic subject, we can now formulate the relevant dualist claim as:

All basic subjects are wholly non-physical.

Combined with the non-physicalistic account of the ingredients of the mind, this separates the mental and physical realms in the requisite way: thus, in line with the requirements initially specified (1.2, pp. 8–9), it ensures that, apart from time-entities (moments and periods), the mental and physical ontologies do not overlap at the level of the philosophically fundamental account. At the same time, the claim permits the dualist to ascribe mental states and activities to human and non-human animals, whose natures are wholly or partly cor-poreal. The dualist is able to make such ascriptions, compatibly with his position, by construing such corporeal mental subjects as non-basic. For example, assuming that he counts human beings (construed as members of an animal species) as mental subjects, he might say that each such subject derives its subject-status from the fact that it in some way embodies a purely non-physical subject to which its mentality primarily belongs.

I have formulated the relevant dualist claim as '*all* basic subjects ...'. I intend this to be interpreted in a way which does not imply that there *are* any basic subjects. Indeed, I intend it to be interpreted in such a way that the non-existence of basic subjects would guarantee its truth. In other words, we are to take the claim as equivalent to:

For anything *x*, if *x* is a basic subject, then *x* is wholly non-physical

where the 'if ... then' functions in exactly the same way as the material-implication operator of propositional logic. Or made even more explicit, we are to take it as equivalent to:

For anything x, either x is not a basic subject or x is wholly non-physical.

This point is important. As I mentioned at the beginning, there are two radically different dualist theories of the mental subject. But these theories differ precisely on the question of whether or not we should recognize an ontology of basic subjects. So it is crucial that we formulate the relevant claim (which is intended to be what both theories endorse) in a way that leaves this issue open. These rival theories originate from Descartes and Hume, and it is now time to explain the difference between them.

The issue on which the Cartesian and Humean forms of dualism differ concerns the ontological structure of the mind, as represented in the philosophically fundamental account. The Cartesian dualist claims that, in providing such an account, we must represent each item of mentality as an element in the biography of a mental subject. Thus if P is a pain-sensation occurring at a certain time t, he claims that we should ultimately represent the occurrence of P as the event of a certain subject's being in pain at t. And if D is a decision occurring at t, he claims that we should ultimately represent the occurrence of D as the event of a certain subject's taking a decision at t. Quite generally, he claims that, for the purposes of the philosophically fundamental account, we must represent each episode of mentality as the event of a subject's being in a certain mental state at a certain time, or performing a certain mental act at a certain time, or engaging in a certain mental activity over a certain period of time. Since something qualifies as a basic subject if and only if it is represented as a mental subject in the fundamental account, it follows that the Cartesian is accepting an ontology of basic subjects and claiming that mental events are always and necessarily events concerning the mentality of these subjects. In effect, basic subjects become the primary ingredient of the Cartesian's mental ontology, on which everything else that exists or occurs in the mental realm is ontologically dependent.

The ontological outlook of the Humean dualist is quite different. He claims that, for the purposes of the philo-

sophically fundamental account, we must represent the ingredients of the mind, not as the token-states (state-realizations)
and activities of subjects, but as things with an independent
and self-contained existence. Thus when someone is in pain
or takes a decision, the Humean will say that, to represent
things in their conceptually and metaphysically fundamental
perspective, we are to record the occurrence of the mental
item without assigning it to a subject: we are to speak of the
occurrence of the pain-event or the decision-event without
recognizing anything as the entity which suffers the pain or
takes the decision. And quite generally, he will say that, in the
fundamental account, the notion of a mental subject drops
away and each mental item is represented as something ontologically autonomous rather than as an element in the mental
biography of some other kind of thing. In short, while a
Cartesian accepts an ontology of basic subjects and construes
the ingredients of the mind as their token-states and activities,
the Humean rejects this ontology altogether and sees mentality
as fundamentally subjectless.

There are two issues, then, which we need to discuss with
respect to the mental subject. First, there is the issue over the
dualist claim itself – the claim that basic mental subjects, if
there are any, are wholly non-physical. Second, there is the
issue which divides the Cartesian from the Humean – over
whether an ontology of basic subjects should be recognized at
all. Let us consider these issues in turn.

2 CAN CORPOREAL OBJECTS BE BASIC SUBJECTS?

So far, the aspects of dualism which I have been trying to
defend have all been, more or less, in accord with 'common
sense'. Before we are exposed to the arguments of the reductionists and materialists, we have, I think, a natural inclination
to think of mentality as something both fundamental and non-
physical – an inclination which would lead us to reject any
conceptual analysis of mental statements in non-mentalistic
terms or any metaphysical reduction of mental facts to non-
mental facts or any identification of mental events with
physical events. In contrast, the dualist's thesis about the
subject – the claim that basic subjects (if there are any) are

wholly non-physical – does not initially strike us as very plausible. Thus suppose Jones (an ordinary human person) is in pain. Our natural inclination is to accept the following three propositions. First, the pain belongs to a basic subject; in other words, whatever the possibilities for conceptual and metaphysical reduction, there being something which is *in* pain is an irreducible feature of the situation and requires recognition in the philosophically fundamental account. Second, the basic subject who suffers the pain is Jones himself; that is, the fundamental psychological description of the situation is simply that Jones is in pain at the relevant time. Third, as a *human* individual, Jones has a corporeal nature: he is not a purely spiritual entity, like an angel or a disembodied soul; he is, whatever else, a member of an animal species (*homo sapiens*), with shape, size, and material composition; a solid occupant of physical space; something to which physical as well as psychological attributes can be ascribed. But the claim that all basic subjects are wholly non-physical would not allow us to construe the situation in this way. Thus if we accepted the claim, we should have to reject at least one of the propositions which we are initially inclined to accept: we should have to conclude *either* that the pain does not belong to a basic subject at all *or* that it belongs to a basic subject distinct from Jones (e.g. a non-physical self or soul which in some sense 'inhabits' Jones's body) *or* that Jones, while the basic subject, does not possess a corporeal nature. So if we try to defend this aspect of the dualist's position, we shall be defending something which runs counter to the common-sense view – counter to our ordinary modes of thought. This is not to deny that there are some things which a great many people believe which seem to support the dualist claim. For example, many people in our own culture believe that human individuals continue to exist in a purely spiritual form after their biological death, and many in other cultures believe in reincarnation. These beliefs are hard to make intelligible without the assumption that the human individual himself is a purely spiritual entity, which is capable of existing apart from a body and capable of migrating from one body to another. However, it still seems correct to say that, whatever other views we may (and perhaps inconsistently) combine with it, the central core of our common-sense outlook construes the living human individual as something which (to echo the language of Chalcedon[1]) hypostatically unites two natures, being both a biological organism in physical space and the basic subject of mental states and activities.

The crucial question is whether we can really make sense of this common-sense position, given our radically dualist construal of the mental phenomena themselves. The basic problem is the same as the one we encountered in the case of the token-identity thesis: the problem of understanding how it is possible for the same thing to possess two such different natures; how it is possible for something both to be a physical object and to have, in a way which is not amenable to conceptual or metaphysical reduction, additional intrinsic attributes which are extraneous to its physical character. If pain is a wholly non-physical state, how can we think of it as genuinely and irreducibly characterizing the very thing which is extended and material?

It might be suggested that we can understand how a corporeal object can be the basic subject of non-physical mental states by appealing to the intimate causal relationship between the occurrence of these states and the object's physical condition. Thus when Jones is in pain, the pain itself is non-physical; but it is presumably causally generated by some state or process in Jones's brain; and it is also, presumably, likely to have certain neural effects which could make a difference to Jones's behaviour. So, if we take Jones to be a member of an animal species, and thus the possessor of a corporeal nature, perhaps we can construe his ownership of the pain in causal terms: perhaps we can say that his being in pain consists in the fact that a pain-sensation is causally related to his physical system in a certain way.[2] There are a number of different specific proposals which we could adopt here. Thus we might say that what makes the sensation Jones's is that it is directly caused by some physical state or process in his body. Alternatively, we might say that what makes the sensation Jones's is that it exerts, or has the potential to exert, a direct causal influence on his body. Again, we might say that Jones's ownership of the sensation depends on *both* these factors – that the links of causal dependence and (potential) causal influence *combine* to make Jones the subject. Or again, we might say that what makes Jones the subject is that, as well as having this two-way causal attachment to his body, the sensation is thereby equipped to play a functional role (in relation to this body's sensory input and behavioural output) appropriate to its psychological character. And there are further (and still more complicated) options which I shall not attempt to formulate. The question we have to consider, then, is whether, by adopting one of these proposals, and generalizing it to cover similar cases, we could come to understand how a corporeal object can qualify as a basic mental subject.

But if this is the question, then the answer is obvious. It may be that, by construing its possession of mental states in causal terms, we can understand how a corporeal object can qualify as a mental *subject*; but we certainly cannot, in this sort of way, gain any understanding of the object's supposed status as a *basic* subject. For, in order for something to qualify as a basic subject, it has to feature as a subject in the philosophically fundamental account; and, *ex hypothesi*, it will not feature as a subject in this account if the fundamental way of describing its possession of mental states is in terms of the causal relations between its physical states and certain mental items. So whether or not we should accept a causal account of what it is for a corporeal object to be a mental subject – of what its possession of mental states, or its engaging in mental activities, ultimately amounts to – such an account will not help to make sense of the claim that such an object is a *basic* subject.

The problem for this claim, as I have said, is the difficulty of seeing how two such different natures could be co-instantiated – how something could both be a physical object and have, irreducibly, intrinsic properties extraneous to its physical nature. Now so far, we have only focused on the *obvious* aspect of this problem – that aspect which is *manifest* in the contrasting character of the natures in question. But the problem has a further aspect, which is less obvious but just as crucial. This further aspect turns on the fact that, even if we could gain some rudimentary conception of what it would be for a corporeal object to qualify as a basic subject, there seems to be nothing in the ultimate facts which could objectively determine how that conception applied. For, given any mental item, there seems to be nothing which could make it objectively true that it was to be ultimately represented as the token-state or activity of one particular corporeal object rather than of some other. Let me explain.

Someone treads on Jones's foot – and, for the sake of the example, let us continue to think of Jones as a member of an animal species, with a corporeal nature. As a result of the stimulus, a neural event occurs in Jones's brain which directly causes a sensation of pain, and this sensation in turn (though only via some intervening neural process) causes, or in some way prompts, a certain vocal response. Our normal practice is to ascribe the pain-state to Jones himself, the corporeal being whose foot receives the pain-inducing stimulus and whose mouth emits the vocal response. But why not ascribe it instead to some corporeal part of Jones, e.g. to his brain, or to that part of his brain in which the relevant neural event occurs? Or alternatively, why not ascribe it to some larger corporeal object of which Jones is a part, e.g. to Jones together with the room in which he is currently located, or even to the whole physical world? No doubt there are reasons why, for ordinary purposes, we find it more convenient to select the human being as the subject rather than one of these smaller or larger alternatives. But it is very hard to see what, in the ultimate situation, could make this selection objectively right and the others objectively wrong. Since the pain-state itself is non-physical, and thus not an aspect of the physical nature of the corporeal object to which we assign it, our conception of it does not force us to assign it to one kind of corporeal object rather than another. If we say that what is ultimately in pain is Jones's brain, or that it is the whole physical world, we do not seem to be making an objective mistake, except in so far as there may be a general objective mistake in treating any corporeal object as a basic subject. But, presumably, if it were legitimate to treat corporeal objects as basic subjects, then the question of *which* objects qualified for this role would have an objective answer. For we can hardly suppose that corporeal subjects feature in the philosophically fundamental account (in the conceptually fundamental description of the metaphysically fundamental reality), while conceding that it is ultimately indeterminate, or a matter for stipulation, as to what things they are. The nature of the fundamental reality, as fundamentally described, must surely be fully objective and determinate.

In fact, the problem here is even worse than I have

indicated. In focusing on the question of what we could select as the basic corporeal subject of Jones's pain, I have so far confined my attention to candidates which contain the neural structures in which the immediate cause of the pain-event is located. But this restriction would only have a rationale if we wanted to keep open the possibility of token-identity. Once we have accepted, as we have, that, not only the pain-*state*, but also the concrete pain-*event* (the event of the pain-state's being realized in Jones's mind at the relevant time) is non-physical, and hence is not identifiable with any neural event, the range of candidates will include *all* material objects which exist at the relevant time. Thus if we are free to assign the pain-state to Jones's brain or to the whole physical world, then we are equally free to assign it to the moon or to Mount Everest or to the dome of St Paul's. And quite generally, we are free to select any material object which exists at every time at which Jones exists and re-assign the mental states and activities in Jones's supposed mental biography to this object. The problem is not so much that we would not know how to discredit these bizarre selections, as that there seems to be no sense in which we could think of any selection as objectively correct or mistaken. Whatever object we choose to regard as the basic subject makes no difference to the account we give of the psychophysical causal process in which the mental events feature: thus if we take the moon to be what is ultimately in pain, we are still allowing that the pain is generated by neural events in Jones's brain, and that it exerts its causal influence on the physical world exclusively via Jones's body. The title 'basic subject' seems here to be a purely honorary one, which we may find it more natural to bestow on the object, or one of the objects, with which the pain is functionally linked, but which does not itself imply the performance of any objective function.

These difficulties with the acceptance of an ontology of basic corporeal subjects seem to me insuperable. I cannot see how anyone advocating such an ontology could secure the requisite objectivity and determinacy in its composition; nor can I see how he could even do this with the help of the token-identity thesis – though, by restricting the range of subject-candidates to those which contain the relevant neural structures, this thesis would at least have the effect of reducing the area of indeterminacy. All this, of course, just serves to bring out, in a more specific and sharply-focused form, the general difficulty in understanding how, at the fundamental level, the corporeal and psychological natures could be co-instantiated – how a corporeal object could be the irreducible possessor of intrinsic psychological attributes which lie outside its physical nature.

From now on, then, I shall assume that the corporealist position has been refuted and that the dualist claim is correct: I shall assume that anything which qualifies as a basic mental subject is wholly non-physical. Despite its conflict with the 'common-sense' view, this conclusion is hardly surprising given the dualist account of mentality which precedes it and on which it rests. And, of course, as we have stressed, it does not prevent the dualist from recognizing human and non-human animals as mental subjects in a weaker sense.

3 DESCARTES VERSUS HUME

Having established the truth of the subject-claim which all dualists endorse, we must now turn to the issue over the Cartesian and Humean alternatives. Should we, following Descartes, recognize an ontology of basic subjects and represent mental items as elements in their biographies? Or should we rather, following Hume, reject this ontology and think of mental items as ontologically autonomous?

Our initial intuitions are unequivocally on the side of the Cartesian. We may feel some initial reluctance to think of the basic subjects in the sphere of human and animal mentality as wholly non-physical. But that mental items can only occur as the token-states or activities of subjects, and that this ontological dependence on subjects forms part of our fundamental understanding of their nature – these are things which initially strike us as self-evident. Thus just as it seems intuitively absurd to suppose that there could be an instance of shape without there being something which possesses that shape, or an event of motion without there being something which moves, so, in the same way, it seems intuitively absurd to suppose that there could be an instance of belief without there being something which holds that belief, or an episode of thought without there being something which thinks. And likewise, it seems intuitively absurd to suppose that there could be some more profound understanding of the nature of belief and thought in which their assignment to subjects drops away. I shall refer to these intuitions, and others of the same kind (covering other types of mental states and activities), as our *intuitions about ownership*.

In his famous discussion of personal identity, Hume tried to discredit these intuitions and to establish, in their place, a quite different conception of the ontological structure of the mind.[3] Like Descartes, he assumed that basic subjects, if they existed, would have to be wholly non-physical. He further supposed, as a consequence of his empiricist outlook, that if we were to have any genuine idea (or as we might say, any coherent notion) of such a subject, it would have to be derived from an introspective impression: we would have to be able to give empirical content to the idea by appealing to some impression of the self and, as it were, saying: 'That's me, and a basic mental subject is a thing of that sort.' But, insisted Hume, there is no such impression, and hence no such idea:

> For my part, when I enter most intimately into what I call *myself*, I always stumble on some particular perception or other, of heat or cold, light or shade, love or hatred, pain or pleasure. I never can catch *myself* at any time without a perception, and never can observe anything but the perception.[4]

His conclusion was that the mind is 'nothing but a bundle or collection of different perceptions, which succeed each other with an inconceivable rapidity, and are in perpetual flux and movement',[5] and that it is only because of the unifying relations in which these perceptions stand to one another (relations of contiguity, resemblance, and causation) that we come to suppose that there is some persisting thing (a substantival self) in which they all inhere. Hume, of course, was using the term 'perception' in a fairly broad sense, to cover any kind of conscious experience.

One weakness in this argument is that the radically empiricist view on which it relies is open to question. The underlying assumption is that any genuine idea (coherent concept) must draw its whole content, either directly or by analysis, from the data of sensory and introspective experience. And it is far from clear why this principle should be accepted. Hume employs the principle in several other areas – most notably in the area of causation, in an attempt to undermine the notion of an objective necessary connection between cause and effect.[6] And, in each case, it is open to the defender of the notion which Hume regards as spurious to reply that Hume is begging the question – that he is just assuming, without argument, that the empiricist principle discredits the notion, when one might equally say that the respectability of the notion discredits the principle. Moreover, there are areas in which the principle seems clearly untenable. For example, it is surely beyond dispute that we possess a genuine concept of logical entailment. But it is very hard to see how we could represent this concept as drawing its whole content from the data of experience. And this, of course, is just one of a whole range of cases of a similar kind, in which the abstract nature of the relevant concept seems to preclude the provision of an empiricist account.

A further weakness in the argument is that, even if the empiricist principle is accepted, it is not clear why we need to have an *impression* of the self in order for our concept to pass the empiricist test. After all, Hume does not insist that *every* idea should be ostensively definable – should be, as he put it, a copy of an impression. Rather, his principle allows for cases in which an idea earns its empiricist credentials by being *analysable into* ideas which are ostensively definable. So even by Hume's own standards, the lack of an impression of the self would not be decisive. We might still be able to achieve an empirically respectable conception of the self in some more complex way – presumably in terms of its role as a basic subject with respect to the introspectible items of mentality.

However, even if we reject his empiricist principle or conclude that it is not effectively employed in this particular case, it could still be claimed that Hume's introspective argument poses a threat to the Cartesian position. For on what basis could we postulate a non-physical substantival self if no such entity is revealed by introspection? It might be replied that the basis is provided by our intuitions about ownership, together with the points we have already established. In other words: we introspectively detect some mental item, such as a pain or a thought; we reason that such an item can only exist as the token-state or activity of a basic subject; and we appeal to the established fact that all basic subjects are wholly non-physical. But while all this is very plausible, there will at least be some suspicion that our intuitions about ownership are erroneous if introspection fails to confirm them. Maybe we are just so accustomed to thinking of the mind in terms of a subject with mental states that, without some deep reflection, we fail to appreciate the possibility of a different ontological framework.

Clearly, the status of our ordinary intuitions is something which we must examine more closely. And we must begin by looking at the introspective argument itself. Is Hume right in claiming that the self is not introspectively revealed?

A natural response to Hume would be to say that, even if we cannot detect ourselves *apart from* our perceptions (our conscious experiences), we can at least detect ourselves *in* them – that when I introspectively detect an experience, what is revealed is the complex of myself-experiencing-something or myself-experiencing-in-a-certain-manner. Indeed, it is not clear in what sense an experience *could be* introspectively detected without the detection of its subject. Hume seems to be supposing that introspection works like sense-perception: a mental item is presented as the object of introspective awareness in the same way as a colour-pattern is presented as the object of visual awareness. On this presentational model, it is hardly surprising that he finds no room for self-awareness. But it seems to be the model itself which is at fault. Thus suppose I am looking at something. My visual awareness, divorced from interpretation, is of some spatial array of colours – an array which the naive realist takes to be a portion of my physical environment and which the sense-datum theorist takes to be a purely internal object, logically inseparable from the awareness. As well as having this visual awareness, I am also, let us assume, introspectively aware of it. But I am surely not aware of it as a kind of phenomenal object – as something detached from, but presented to, me. Surely I am aware of it, so to speak, *from the inside* – not as something presented, but as something which *I have* or as the experiential state which *I am in*. In short, it seems that I introspectively detect my visual awareness by being aware of *being visually aware*; and this is equivalent to saying that I detect it by being aware of *myself* being visually aware. On this view, then, even if Hume was right to insist that he could not catch himself without a perception, he should also have acknowledged that he could not catch a perception without himself.

As far as I can see, the only way in which Hume could try to avoid this objection would be by denying the traditional conception of sense-experience as involving a sensory act (or state) of awareness and a phenomenal object, and claiming that the phenomenal object is the only item involved. This is the line taken, for example, by A. J. Ayer, when he comes to the defence of Hume in *Language, Truth and Logic*:

> We must make it clear that we do not accept the realist analysis of our sensations in terms of subject, act, and object. For neither the existence of the substance which is supposed to perform the so-called act of sensing nor the existence of the act itself, as an entity distinct from the sense-contents on which it is supposed to be directed, is in the least capable of being verified.[7]

Thus, in the visual example just considered, Ayer would deny that there was any genuine self-awareness by denying that there was any visual awareness distinct from the visual colour-array. All that I can introspect, he would insist, and all that my visual experience involves, is the occurrence of a visual sense-content. I do not detect *myself* in the experience, because I only detect the experience as a phenomenal object, not as an experiential act or state. Applied to sense-experience in general, Ayer would see this account not only as discrediting all claims to self-awareness, but as undermining our a priori intuitions about ownership: if there are no acts of sensing, then there is no need to postulate subjects to perform them, and so the sense-contents can stand on their own as things which are ontologically autonomous.[8]

For various reasons, I find this approach unsatisfactory. One difficulty with it is that it seems to be very limited in its application. For even if we can eliminate any irreducible mental act in the case of sense-experience, it is hard to see how this could be done for mental items in general. To begin with, it is hard to see how thoughts, judgments, and decisions, and other conscious items with a propositional or conceptual content, could be represented as quasi-phenomenal objects, analogous to visual colour-patterns and phenomenal sounds. How could Ayer avoid thinking of these items as ultimately acts or activities of a subject? And how could he avoid conceding that our introspective awareness of them is an awareness of doing something – of thinking, judging, deciding, and so on? Moreover, it is even harder to see how Ayer could apply his analysis to introspective awareness itself. Granted that we are often directly conscious of our own mentality, or at least of certain aspects of it, how is this consciousness to be represented without the acknowledgment of a basic subject to possess it? I suppose Ayer might reply that the only irreducibly mental ingredients of such things as thoughts, judgments, and decisions are mental images of the ordinary sensory type, and that everything else is the product of the functional system in which these images are located.[9] And he might then insist that even the supposed acts of introspection are merely mind-monitoring judgments, to be construed in a similarly imagist and functionalist way. In both cases, his point would be that, since these items have no irreducibly mental ingredients other than sensory images, and since sensory images can be handled in the same way as the phenomenal objects of ordinary sensory experience, there is no need to postulate any irreducible mental acts or any basic subjects to perform them. But such an austere account of human psychology would surely be desperately implausible. Indeed, since the only irreducibly mental entities which it recognizes are sense-impressions and sensory images, and since the only psychological roles it assigns to these entities are ones which, being purely mechanistic, could be equally played by non-mental entities (e.g. by neural items), it is scarcely any improvement on the forms of total mental reductionism which we have already rejected. How, for example, if we accepted such an account, could we avoid (absurdly) ascribing an intellectual life to a man-made machine which replicated the functional organization of a human being and which was furnished with the appropriate physical analogues of human sense-impressions and images?[10]

However, even if we ignore the other areas of the mind and focus exclusively on the case of sense-experience, I think that Ayer's account is still vulnerable to two decisive objections. In the first place, there are some types of sensory experience for which, in so far as it is appropriate to deny the traditional act-object analysis, this denial would take the form of absorbing the putative sensory object into the sensory act rather than vice versa. A clear example is that of sensory pain. The experience in this case is not to be ultimately represented as the presentation of a pain-quale, analogous to the visual presentation of a colour-array or the auditory presentation of a sound. The subject is aware of the pain, but he is aware of it as an episode of sensing or feeling, not as a quality-item presented. And although the pain has a qualitative content, and one which is introspectively manifest, this content characterizes the sensing adverbially, as the qualitative mode of the sensory act or state, rather than as its object. This is why we feel no temptation to ascribe pain-qualia to the external objects which cause our pain-experiences, in the way that we ordinarily ascribe colour and sound qualia to the objects which cause (i.e. have a certain crucial role in causing) our visual and auditory experiences. But once it is agreed that pain is to be ultimately represented as a form of sensing, there seems to be no way of denying its ultimate attachment to a sensing subject; nor does there seem to be any reason to deny that, in being introspectively aware of the sensing, the subject is introspectively aware of himself *as* subject.

Secondly, even if we confine our attention to those sorts of sense-experience which seem most amenable to Ayer's analysis, I still cannot see how a commitment to basic subjects can be avoided. Take again the case of my visual experience. Ayer wants to say that, at the purely sensory level, my experience ultimately consists in the occurrence of a certain phenomenal object, or sense-content, namely a visual colour-array. But if this array qualifies as a phenomenal object, as something visually presented, then surely there must be something *to which* it is visually presented. And if there is something to which it is presented, then we are back with the conscious subject, along with his acts or states of consciousness, which Ayer was trying to eliminate. Ayer's only possible reply to this would be to insist that the colour-array is not as such (i.e. in its essential nature) phenomenal, and that it only qualifies as something visually presented in so far as it gets monitored by other items, whose only irreducibly mental ingredients are images. But unless it is essentially phenomenal, the colour-array will simply not qualify as something mental at all (as something occurring in the mind), and hence will not qualify as that in whose occurrence my sensory experience consists.

(It is difficult, indeed, to see what, in this sub-phenomenal form, we could take it to be, except perhaps the physical pattern of colours on my retina.) Moreover, assuming that Ayer wants to extend the same account to all sense-contents and sensory images, the consequence would be the total elimination of all irreducible mentality; and this would be in conflict with the dualist position which we are now taking as established.

It seems to me, then, that neither Hume's introspective argument nor Ayer's account of sense-experience do anything to undermine our intuitions about ownership. Nor can I think of any other way in which these intuitions can be effectively challenged. In short, it seems to me that there is no escaping from what initially strikes us as self-evident, that mental items can only occur as the token-states and activities of subjects, and that this ontological dependence on subjects forms part of our fundamental understanding of their nature.

4 FILLING IN A GAP

Let us take it as established, then, that mental items are attached to basic subjects, in the sense defined, and that basic subjects are wholly non-physical. The main question now concerns the nature of these subjects: granted that they are non-physical, what kinds of thing are they? But before we progress to this crucial issue, I want to use our latest results to fill in a small gap in our previous discussion. The reason for this gap is that there is still one aspect of the dualist thesis, in its full-blooded form, that I have not succeeded in establishing.

In our earlier discussion (3.5, pp. 80–2), we saw how analytical functionalism could be either *fully comprehensive*, where the functionalist analysis applies to *all* psychological concepts, or *scope-restricted*, where it applies to only *some*. We also saw how the scope-restricted positions, in turn, divide into two kinds: those that are *fully reductive*, in the sense that they provide wholly non-mentalistic analyses of the psychological concepts which they cover, and those that are *less-than-fully reductive*, in that, as well as recognizing certain psychological concepts as primitive, they actually employ these concepts in their analyses. Now our earlier arguments refuted analytical functionalism in its fully comprehensive form; and they also ruled out all scope-restricted positions of the first (fully reductive) type. But they explicitly left room for certain kinds of scope-restricted position of the second (less-than-fully reductive) type. In particular, they left room for positions which take the psychological character of a propositional attitude to be definable in terms of the attitude's functional role in relation to (conscious) propositional acts. (For example, such a position might take *being an instance of the belief that p* to be definable as (something like) *being an instance of a state which disposes the subject, whenever he consciously addresses himself to the relevant question, to perform the conscious act of judging that p.*)

Now these less-than-fully-reductive forms of functionalism, which our previous arguments do not exclude, are not as such in conflict with full-blooded dualism. After all, the second claim in the dualist thesis, that the mental realm is (conceptually and metaphysically) fundamental, was explicitly interpreted (1.2, p. 8; 3.5, pp. 81–2) as allowing for the possibilities of conceptual analysis and metaphysical stratification *within the mental realm*: it was only *wholly non-mentalistic* reductions which were excluded. None the less, a functionalism of this sort could be used against the dualist in another way. For, as we saw (5.2, p. 137), it could be invoked as part of the rationale for a scope-restricted form of token-identity. The point is that, if the psychological character of a mental item consists in its functional character (i.e. the functional role characteristic of things of its intrinsic type), then, irrespective of whether the latter can be specified without the use of mentalistic concepts, the former sets no restrictions on the item's intrinsic character, and so there is no difficulty in understanding how the item could turn out to be intrinsically physical. And this means that a less-than-fully-reductive form of functionalism could be used to facilitate the acceptance of token-identity in the case of those types of mental item to which the functionalist analysis is applied. In this respect, then, our arguments leave open the possibility of a position which is incompatible with dualism in its most full-blooded and comprehensive form.

However, now that we have established the non-physical character of the basic subject, we can reject even this limited form of token-identity. The point is simply that a *physical* mental item cannot be the token-state or activity of a *non-physical* mental subject. It may be that propositional attitudes are, at all points, causally sustained by neurophysiological states; but given that these states are wholly extraneous to the entity (the non-physical basic subject) to which the attitudes primarily belong, we cannot identify instances of the former with instances of the latter.

Conceivably, the identity-theorist might reply that beliefs and desires are not really states of this non-physical subject, but of something wholly or partly corporeal. But given that we are obliged to assign conscious judgments and conscious wishes to the non-physical subject, such a position would be manifestly absurd. Clearly, the propositional acts and the propositional attitudes have to be assigned to the same thing.

5 THE NATURE OF THE SELF

But to what sort of thing? What is the essential nature of a basic mental subject? Or more specifically, what is the essential nature of this subject in our own (the human) case?

The question, of course, is one about *real* rather than *nominal* essence. We already know what conditions something has to satisfy to qualify as a basic subject: to qualify as a mental subject, it has to be something to which mental states or activities can be truly ascribed; and to qualify as a basic mental subject it has to be something which features as a mental subject in the philosophically fundamental account – something which is both ontologically basic and whose role as a subject of mental states and activities is not reducible to factors of a different kind. The question we are posing, then, is: What is the essential nature of those things which (or which in the human sphere) qualify as basic subjects in this sense? What are such things like, and essentially like, in themselves?

So far the only thing we have established which directly bears on this question is purely negative: whatever their nature, basic subjects are wholly non-physical. We have arrived at this conclusion because we cannot make sense of the suggestion that something could both be a physical object and have, irreducibly, additional intrinsic properties (i.e. psychological ones) which are extraneous to its physical nature. But this, of course, does not tell us what, positively, basic subjects

221

are like. Nor, obviously, would it be enough to add that basic subjects are both simple (not divisible into parts) and continuants (things which persist through time). These further claims seem relatively uncontroversial, and I shall take them for granted in the context of the present discussion. But we are still left wanting to know what sort of a thing it is whose indivisibility and persistence are being asserted. The Cartesian position is commonly thought to be especially vulnerable at this point.[11]

Since basic subjects are wholly non-physical, and since they are, whatever else, the things to which mental states and activities are to be ultimately ascribed, it would be natural to begin by trying to characterize their essential nature in psychological terms. But how exactly are we to proceed? Three points are clear. First, and trivially, given any basic subject, any psychological attribute which we take to be part of its *essential* nature will have to be something which it possesses, and necessarily possesses, at every moment of its history. For this reason, we cannot take the essential nature to include any relatively *specific* form of mental state or activity, like sensing or judging or deciding, since, in each such case, it is possible for the subject to exist at a time when the relevant state or activity is absent. Secondly, given any basic subject, any psychological attribute which we take to be part of its essential *nature* will have to be intrinsic and categorical. It will have to be something which pertains to what the subject is like in itself, rather than something which concerns the subject's psychological relations to other things or its psychological capacities and dispositions. Thirdly, whatever psychological attribute, or complex of attributes, we take as forming the subject's essential nature, it must enable us to understand how it is possible for the subject to possess, or engage in, all the more specific mental states and activities which occur on particular occasions. Thus even though such things as sensing, judging, and deciding are not parts of the essential nature, the account we give of this nature must explain how it is possible for them to feature in the subject's psychological repertoire: it must reveal the subject as the sort of thing which we can intelligibly suppose to have sense-experiences, to make judgments, to take decisions, and so on. In the light of these three considerations, it seems that what we are looking for, to constitute the subject's essential nature, is some psychological attribute which is not only intrinsic, but highly generic – sufficiently generic both to form a necessarily constant feature throughout the subject's varying mental condition and to be that of which the subject's more specific and contingent mental states and activities can be seen as the various modes or specific forms.

But is there a psychological attribute which will meet these requirements? Descartes thought that there was. He claimed that all the specific mental states and activities – sensing, judging, deciding, doubting, and so on – were modes of a single attribute, *cogitatio*, and that, in the human realm at least, *cogitatio* constituted the whole essence of each basic mental subject. As he put it in *Meditation* VI: 'I ... conclude that my essence consists solely in the fact that I am a thinking thing [*res cogitans*].'[12] He also thought that the various specific modes of *cogitatio* could be subsumed under the two general modes of *perception* (or understanding) and *volition* (or willing):

> All the modes of thinking that we observed in ourselves may be related to two general modes, the one of which consists in perception, or in the operation of the understanding, and the other in volition, or the operation of the will. Thus sense-perception, imagining, and conceiving things that are purely intelligible, are just different methods of perceiving; but desiring, holding in aversion, affirming, denying, doubting, all these are the different modes of willing.[13]

In the same way, of course, these specific modes of perceiving and willing would themselves be generic with respect to their determinates. Thus imagining the Eiffel Tower would be a specific mode of imagination, and disliking the taste of garlic would be a specific mode of aversion.

One could quibble over the details of these classifications: for example, it is not clear in what sense doubting is a mode of willing; nor clear that affirming and denying, as mental acts, are modes of willing in the same sense as desire and aversion. But these issues are not relevant to our present concern. What matters is the claim that the whole essence of the mental subject is *cogitatio* and that all the various more specific mental states and activities are (in whatever hierarchical structure) modes of this essence. And it is here that the crucial problem arises. For what interpretation can we assign to Descartes's notion of *cogitatio* which will allow it to play this role? The natural translation of the Latin word, taken out of its Cartesian context, would be 'thought' or 'thinking', as signifying a certain kind of intellectual activity; and this indeed was how it was rendered in the translations of the passages I cited. But obviously, in this sense, *cogitatio* would not be a sufficiently generic attribute for Descartes's purposes. Descartes wants to classify all the specific mental states and activities as modes of *cogitatio*; and thinking, in its ordinary sense, is just one member of this diverse group rather than its common factor. Some commentators have offered the translation 'consciousness'.[14] But even this does not seem to be sufficiently generic. For surely I can be said to have propositional attitudes, such as beliefs and desires, at times when I am not consciously rehearsing them, and even at times, such as during sleep, when I am not conscious at all. It seems that if *cogitatio* is to cover *all* mental states and activities, we must translate it simply as 'mentality'. But the problem now is that while, trivially, mentality is sufficiently generic to cover all the relevant states and activities, it is hard to see how to construe it as a *unitary* intrinsic attribute rather than as merely the disjunction of the things it covers. And unless it can be construed as a *unitary* intrinsic attribute – as the genuine common factor uniting the various types of specific states and activities which are allegedly its modes – it has no chance of forming the mental essence for which Descartes was looking. If we define *cogitatio* merely as the disjunction of sensing, judging, deciding, desiring, and so on (or even as the disjunction of Cartesian perceiving and willing, if these turn out to be sufficiently generic), then in characterizing himself as a *res cogitans*, Descartes has not yet identified his essential nature as a thing: he has not specified what he, who undergoes or engages in these various types of *cogitatio* is like in himself – what he is like qua *res*.

It might be objected that there is bound to be something which is common to the various types of mental state and activity – something in virtue of which they all qualify as mental. And surely it will then be this common factor, whatever it is, which forms the unitary attribute of which these states and activities are the modes, and which constitutes the essential nature of the subject in which they occur. But the difficulty is in finding a common factor which can be seen as an *intrinsic attribute* of the subject. On the face of it, all that the various mental states and activities have in common, apart from being non-physical and attached to a non-physical subject, is that they are all accessible to introspective awareness at times when their subject is conscious. This indeed seems to be what Descartes himself sees as the common factor, in virtue of which they all qualify as forms of *cogitatio*. For, under the heading 'What thought [cogitatio] is', he writes: 'By the word thought I understand all that of which we are conscious as operating in us. And that is why not only understanding, willing, imagining, but also feeling are here the same thing as thought.'[15] But in defining thought as covering all that is accessible to introspective awareness, Descartes has not revealed the specific forms of thought as modes of some common intrinsic attribute. He has not specified any intrinsic respect in which all mental states and activities resemble one another, but only specified the common way in which the subject can be directly conscious of their presence when they occur in him.

I said that the objection to translating 'cogitatio' as 'consciousness' was that the latter does not seem to be sufficiently generic for Descartes's purposes. The point I was making was that Descartes wanted *cogitatio* to cover *all* mental states and activities, and that the propositional attitudes cannot be classified as modes of consciousness, since they can be present at times when the subject is not consciously rehearsing them, and even at times when he is not conscious at all. Now, against this, it might be suggested that propositional attitudes should not be construed as genuine mental states, but as mere dispositions (i.e. propensities) to perform the corresponding sorts of propositional act – so that the belief that p gets equated with the disposition (propensity), in appropriate circumstances, to judge that p, and the desire that p gets equated with the disposition, in appropriate circumstances, consciously to wish that p. This would mean that Descartes no longer had to think of such attitudes as modes of *cogitatio*, and so the equation of *cogitatio* with consciousness would still be available. And thus interpreted, *cogitatio* would have a prima facie claim to qualify as a unitary intrinsic attribute.

However, even if, by thus narrowing the range of things that have to be covered, it were possible to classify all mental states and activities as modes of consciousness, it is not clear how this would improve Descartes's overall position. For what Descartes needs is not just a unitary intrinsic attribute under which all the different forms of mental state and activity can be subsumed, but one which he can take to constitute the subject's essential nature. And there is no getting away from the fact that, however we construe propositional attitudes, there seem to be occasions, such as those of dreamless sleep and general anaesthesia, when subjects exist without being conscious. If Descartes insists that his essence is *cogitatio* and if he equates *cogitatio* with consciousness, then he faces an embarrassing choice between two unappealing alternatives. He either has to say that, during these periods of supposed unconsciousness, there really is a continuous stream of consciousness, of which he has no memory and gives no physical manifestation. Or he has to say that such periods are interruptions in his existence, so that he ceases to exist when he falls asleep and comes back into existence when his consciousness returns. In this respect, excluding the propositional attitudes (along with any other mental states of a not essentially-conscious kind) from the scope of *cogitatio* seems positively disadvantageous from Descartes's point of view. For, unless he is willing to embrace one of these implausible alternatives, he needs *cogitatio*, as the subject's essence, to be something which continues to characterize the subject during these periods of unconsciousness.

This said, it is still not clear that according *cogitatio* the broadest scope would eliminate the problem entirely. For, leaving aside the question of whether, thus construed, *cogitatio* would be a unitary attribute, it could still be thought that the subject is capable of existing at times when he has no psychological attributes at all. For example, it might be thought that, in the case of human beings, the basic subject (the non-physical soul or self) comes into existence at a time (e.g. biological conception) which precedes the onset of its mental life. Certainly, I find this view quite plausible, though, in the nature of things, it would be difficult to prove. But even its conceivability would be awkward for Descartes, since he wants the identity of his essence with *cogitatio* to be something he can establish *a priori*.

However this further issue is to be resolved, the main difficulty with Descartes's approach remains. If we construe *cogitatio* very broadly, so as to cover all states and activities which we ordinarily classify as mental (including, in particular, the propositional attitudes), it is hard to see it as a *unitary intrinsic* attribute, of which the specific states and types of activity are different modes or forms. For there does not seem to be any genuine common factor which unites all the different cases, and renders each a form of mentality, other than the fact that each is non-physical, has a non-physical subject, and is (when the subject is conscious) accessible to introspective awareness. On the other hand, if we construe *cogitatio*, more narrowly, as consciousness (and perhaps, along with this, construe propositional attitudes dispositionally), it is hard to see how it can be an *essential* attribute of the subject. For, on the face of it, there are times (e.g. the cases of sleep and anaesthesia) when subjects exist without being conscious. In the light of these problems, there seems to be a strong case for abandoning Descartes's approach altogether. And since we were allowing ourselves the freedom to construe *cogitatio* in whatever way would best suit its role as the subject's mental essence, the abandonment of this approach would, in effect, be the abandonment of any attempt to equate the essential nature of a subject with some psychological attribute. Let us then consider what other approaches are available.

We are taking it as established that basic subjects are wholly non-physical – that they have no intrinsic physical attributes nor location in physical space. So, *a fortiori*, we are barred from taking the essential nature of a subject to be something physical. If we also give up the attempt to equate the essential nature of a subject with something psychological, then it seems we are left with only two possibilities. On the one hand, we might say that basic subjects do not have essential natures at all: each subject is just a pure particular, which has no qualitative essence, but in which, at certain times or over certain periods, various psychological attributes contingently inhere. On the other hand, we might say that basic subjects do have essential natures, but ones which, being neither physical nor psychological, lie beyond the scope of our knowledge and conception: each subject has a qualitative essence, which it necessarily possesses throughout the period of its existence, but one which, being neither revealed introspectively (as something psychological) nor revealed through sense-perception (as something physical), is from our standpoint a know-not-what. I shall call these two positions respectively, the 'no-nature' theory and the 'noumenal' theory.

The no-nature theory is a restricted version – a version applied to the mental realm – of that more general theory, apparently endorsed by Locke, that, underlying every qualitatively replete object, there is an in-itself-featureless substratum, which is capable of existing without qualities, but in which, contingently, certain qualities inhere.[16] In so far as we can be certain of anything in metaphysics, we can surely be certain that this theory, both in its general form and in its mind-specific version, is mistaken. It is surely self-evident that there cannot be anything which is in-itself-featureless – which could continue to exist as a thing even if all its intrinsic properties (other than that of being a thing) were removed. This is not to imply that concrete objects (whether in the mental realm or in the physical realm) are just collections of particularized qualities, without anything which ultimately instantiates them. We do not, for example, have to think of a table as a series of momentary tables, each of which is just a spatial arrangement of such qualities as shape, size, colour, and hardness. We can still think of it as a substantial thing, which is characterized by its qualities and which persists through time. It is just that we cannot think of the table, or something else which lies within it, as having an existence and identity independent of the qualities which make it the sort of thing it is. We cannot coherently suppose that the ultimate instantiator of the tabular qualities is something which is not essentially a thing of a tabular sort or any qualitative sort at all. And, in the same way, we cannot coherently suppose that the ultimate instantiators of psychological attributes, i.e. basic subjects, are things which have no qualitative essence even of a non-psychological kind.

What then of the noumenal theory, which accepts that subjects have essential natures, but ones which, being neither physical nor psychological, lie beyond the scope of our knowledge and conception? This too might seem, at first sight, unappealing. For if we cannot frame any positive conception of what the Cartesian self is or might be like, how can we intelligibly suppose that such a thing exists? A similar challenge is often directed against the orthodox theist, who both claims to believe in God and, when asked to clarify the content of this belief, pleads that God is incomprehensible.

However, we must be careful not to exaggerate the difficulties for the noumenal theory here. As I stressed at the beginning, the question which concerns us, and to which the noumenal theory itself is a response, is one about *real* rather than about *nominal* essence. We already know what we mean by the term 'basic subject': we know what conditions have to be satisfied for something to qualify for this description. So the admission that we cannot form any positive conception of the essential nature of a basic subject does not show that we cannot understand – and understand fully and perfectly – what is meant by saying that such subjects exist. Nor, of course, could it be said that, while this existential claim is comprehensible, the noumenal theory deprives us of any grounds for believing it true. For the argument to establish that mental items are the token-states and activities of basic subjects is still available, and it is quite unclear why the cogency of this argument should be in any way affected by the admission that the natures of the subjects lie beyond the scope of our knowledge and conception. In any case, it seems we encounter a similar situation of inscrutability in the case of the physical realm. For, granted the truth of the structuralist thesis, we cannot discover anything about the intrinsic nature of physical space, beyond its geometrical structure, nor anything about the intrinsic nature of the fundamental occupants of space, beyond their shape and size. Nor, designed as it is to suit the needs of empirical theorizing, does our system of physical concepts even equip us to speculate on what these natures might be. In these respects, the noumenal theory is keeping what we would normally regard as good company.[17]

However, even if there is no general principle against postulating inscrutable natures, there is, I think, a real problem with this in the case of the basic subject. The problem is that if we take the essential nature of the subject to be something non-psychological – something whose constitutive attributes are quite different from the psychological attributes revealed by introspection – then it is no longer clear how such an entity could qualify as a basic mental subject: it is no longer clear how it could be something of which, at the fundamental level, mental items are the token-states and activities. For let us remind ourselves of the reason why we rejected the 'common-sense' view that certain types of corporeal object (e.g. human beings as members of an animal species) qualify as basic subjects. Our objection to this view was that there was no way of understanding how a corporeal object could have, irreducibly, additional intrinsic properties which were extraneous to its physical nature – an objection which, in its sharpest form, became the point that there would be nothing to determine *which* corporeal objects possessed these additional properties. But it seems that, whatever the difficulties in understanding how a corporeal object could have the status of a basic subject, there would be analogous difficulties in assigning this status to *any* sort of object unless the psychological attributes we wish to ascribe to it can be thought of as, in some way, modes or aspects of its essential nature. And if this is so, then the noumenal theory becomes as problematic as the common-sense view, simply because it takes the essential natures of basic subjects to be non-psychological. It is true, of course, that the theory also takes the natures of these subjects to be non-physical, and, in this respect, their natures resemble the psychological attributes we ascribe to them. But this negative resemblance is not enough for our purposes. To make sense of such ascriptions, we have to suppose that there is some positive respect in which their natures equip them to serve as basic subjects. And if we assign these natures to the noumenal rather than to the psychological realm, we seem precisely to deny that such a respect obtains.

To this objection, the noumenal theorist might reply that we can understand how subjects with underlying inscrutable natures can possess psychological attributes in the same way as we understand how physical objects with underlying inscrutable natures possess sensible qualities. In the latter case, it is a matter of something with an underlying insensible nature having sensible qualities relative to the viewpoint of human sense-perception. In the former case, it would be a matter of something with an underlying non-psychological nature having psychological attributes relative to the viewpoint of introspection. However, a little reflection reveals that, for two reasons, this analogy cannot be pressed. In the first place, the sense in which physical objects are endowed with sensible qualities relative to the viewpoint of sense-perception is merely that, given their underlying properties and our physiological make-up, such objects are empowered to appear to us in certain ways (to produce certain kinds of sense-experience in us) when we observe them in certain conditions. This means that, whether we think of the relevant reduction as analytical or as metaphysical, the attribution of sensible qualities to physical objects is not an element in the philosophically funda-mental account. But since his position is being offered as a version of Cartesian dualism, thus presupposing the funda-mental status of mentality and its subject, the noumenal theorist cannot afford to endorse an account of psychological attributes of this reductive sort. Secondly, if applied quite generally, this 'secondary-quality' construal of psychological attributes is clearly incoherent, simply because introspective appearance is itself a psychological phenomenon. Thus even if we were to take the occurrence of something like pain or anger to be just a matter of how things introspectively seem, or are liable to seem, to the subject, there would still be the question of the introspective experiences themselves. And, plainly, it would generate an infinite regress if *their* occurrence was construed in a similar way.

We seem, then, to be in something of a dilemma. Our earlier arguments apparently established that mental items are attached to basic subjects and that basic subjects are wholly non-physical. But we seem unable to find any coherent account of what sort (or sorts) of thing such subjects might be. If we suppose that they have a qualitative essence of a non-psychological kind, it seems that we can no longer make sense of their role as basic subjects: it seems that we are in no better position to understand how *they* could be the irreducible possessors of pschological attributes than to understand how such attributes could irreducibly characterize physical objects. On the other hand, if we suppose that their essential natures are purely psychological, we ought to be able to identify the psychological attribute, or complex of attributes, involved. And here, as we saw, there seems to be no suitable candidate: if we take the mental essence to be consciousness, we get something which, on the face of it, fails to cover all periods of the subject's existence; while if we try to find something more generic than consciousness (for example, something which would be exemplified both by episodes of consciousness and by propositional attitudes), there seems to be nothing available of a suitably unitary kind.

Can we find a way out of this dilemma? I think that we can. But to see how, we must start by correcting two misconceptions which have affected our approach so far. These two misconceptions are closely related, though one has been mainly operative in our discussion of Descartes's account and the other mainly operative in our assessment of the noumenal theory. I shall begin with the latter.

I have said that the objection to the noumenal theory is that it does not allow us to think of the entities which possess the inscrutable essential natures as equipped to serve as basic mental subjects. And this objection, I think, is right. But, in elaborating it, I have given the impression that the reason why we cannot think of these entities as thus equipped is that we cannot think of their essential natures as ones of which the various types of mental state and activity constitute modes, or specific forms. And this, I think, while on the right lines, is not exactly right. For while it is right to insist that the essential nature of a basic subject must belong to the psychological realm and must be introspectibly discernible to fit the needs of the subject's psychological repertoire, we are not entitled to assume that the only kind of nature which could meet these conditions is one which stands as mental genus to the various species of mental states and activities which the repertoire contains – one which plays the role of *cogitatio* in the way that Descartes conceived it. So the real objection to the noumenal theory does not rest on the narrow point, that the specific types of mental state and activity could not be modes of an essential nature which was non-psychological (for this point is not as such decisive), but rather on the broader point, that if an essential nature is not introspectible, and not even such that we could form an introspective conception of it, then it is not the right sort of nature to equip the entity which has it to be the irreducible subject of states and activities whose own essential natures can only be introspectively grasped. In other words, what is wrong with the noumenal theory is that, by putting the essential nature of a basic subject beyond the reach of introspective knowledge and conception, it does not allow this nature to harmonize with the subject's psychological attributes in the requisite way.

Now for the second misconception. In discussing Descartes's view that the essential nature of the self is *cogitatio*, I have probably given the impression that our only reason for rejecting this view is that there is no way of construing *cogitatio* which will allow it to meet, in combination, two conditions: first, that it be a unitary intrinsic attribute of which the more specific mental states and activities are modes; and second, that it be something which is genuinely essential to the subject – something which necessarily characterizes him at every moment of his existence. However, it seems that even if these conditions could be met, Descartes's view would not be acceptable. For let us suppose, for the sake of argument, that we have found a construal of *cogitatio* which meets them. If you like, let us pretend that we can take consciousness to be something which both covers all the specific mental states and activities and is necessarily present at each moment of the subject's existence. Even so, we would surely feel that this is not enough to specify the subject's whole essential nature. We would surely feel that there is some more fundamental qualitative element which constitutes the subject's 'substantial' character as a continuant thing – something more basic about how the thing which is conscious, or which 'cogitates' in whatever sense, is *as a thing*. The difficulty with taking *cogitatio* to be the whole essence (assuming we can find a suitable way of construing it) is that such a view does not, in the end, seem to provide a *real thing*, or *substance*, to be the subject of the *cogitatio* or of its specific modes, and, in this way, fails to do justice to our intuitions about ownership.

Putting these two points together, the way forward – or at least the way we must *try* to move forward – becomes clear. In order to escape from the dilemma, we need to identify the essential nature of a basic subject with some attribute which, on the one hand, belongs to the psychological realm – an attribute of which we can form an introspective conception and which we can see to equip the entity it essentially chararac- terizes to serve as a basic mental subject – but which, on the other, is not a psychological attribute in the ordinary sense –

233

not even a very generic psychological attribute like Descartes's *cogitatio* – but rather something which constitutes the subject's character as a substantial thing. In other words, we need to find an attribute which is accessible to introspection and which characterizes the subject qua *mental* subject, but which, by embodying the character of his thinghood, characterizes him in abstraction from the mental life which it equips him to have.

Is there such an attribute? It seems to me that there is. Thus it seems to me that when I focus on myself introspectively, I am not only aware of being in a certain mental condition; I am also aware, with the same kind of immediacy, of being a certain sort of thing – a sort which characterizes me independently of my mental condition. And it further seems to me that what I thus know, in knowing introspectively that I am of this sort, reveals to me, quite clearly, how it is that I am equipped to be a basic mental subject – to be an irreducible possessor of mental states and performer of mental acts. Moreover, I can only assume that the same kind of introspective knowledge is available to any other adult human being of normal intellectual capacities – though no doubt my prior commitment to the Cartesian position (which I take as already established) helps me to recognize this self-kowledge for what it is. My contention then is that this introspectively revealed sortal attribute constitutes my essential nature and that of all other basic human subjects.

It will now be asked: 'Well, what *is* this nature, this sortal attribute? Let's have it specified!' But such a demand is misconceived. Of course, I can give it a verbal label: for instance, I could call it 'subjectness' or 'selfhood'. But unless they are interpreted 'ostensively', by reference to what is revealed by introspective awareness, such labels will not convey anything over and above the nominal essence of the term 'basic subject'. In this respect, however, there is no difference between this attribute, which constitutes the subject's essential nature, and the specific psychological attributes of his conscious mental life. It is for this reason that there is no way of conveying the psychological character of visual experience to someone who is congenitally blind or the psychological character of auditory experience to someone who is congenitally deaf. Both the essential nature of the subject and the character of his conscious states can only be grasped introspectively – by, in the one case, knowing from the inside what it is like to be a subject, and, in the other, knowing from the inside what it is like to be in a certain mental condition. This does not mean that basic subjects and their conscious mental lives are not *objective* – that they do not exist from a God's-eye view. It only means that there is no more to be said about their natures from a God's-eye view than is accessible to introspection.

Admittedly, the feeling that there must be more to be said from a God's-eye view dies hard. The reason is that, even when we have acknowledged that basic subjects are wholly non-physical, we still tend to approach the issue of their essential natures in the shadow of the physical paradigm. We can only investigate physical objects as external observers, relying on the data of sense-perception and the methods of empirical science; and, in so far as it is framed in physical terms, any conception we can form of their natures is tied to this externalist perspective. Because the physical realm has such a dominant role in our conceptual scheme, we become conditioned to treating physical objects as the model for *all* concrete objects, and so come to suppose that an objective conception of the nature of a basic subject must have a similarly externalist form. Thus we come to suppose that, to characterize such subjects as they are in themselves, we have to be able to stand back from them and specify how they would appear to an ideal observer who could veridically perceive their spiritual substance, or how they would be characterized by some fully developed spiritual science. It is this, indeed, which, taken to its extreme, sometimes seduces us into picturing the Cartesian soul as a parcel of ghostly, but spatially voluminous, stuff – a fuzzy-edged portion of some form of etherial protoplasm, which is lodged within the person's body, though without making obstructive contact. Such pictures strike the reflective philosopher as absurd – and rightly so. But even philosophers often fail to diagnose the deeper error which underlies the absurdity. They fail to see that it is not merely the quasi-physicalistic picture which is misconceived, but the very quest for some characterization of the soul from an external viewpoint. Indeed, the philosophical presumption that, to achieve an objective conception of our natures and our mentality, we have to find some way of focusing on ourselves from the outside, without the supposed distortions of introspective (subjective) appearance, is, I think, more than anything else, what gives materialism its spurious philosophical appeal.

The irony is that, if we grant the truth of the structuralist thesis, then, even in the physical realm, the externalist approach does not deliver (all) the goods. And here the point is not just that observation and science do not reveal the fundamental intrinsic content of physical objects. It is also that externalist concepts do not even supply the resources to speculate on what this content might be. Indeed, the only way of bringing the content within the scope of our conception would be by construing it mentalistically, thus enabling us to characterize it by means of concepts drawn from introspection.[18] Whether this provides a reason for accepting a mentalistic account is another matter, and one which it would be inappropriate to pursue in the present context. My own approach, as it happens, is to use the structuralist thesis as a stage in an argument against physical realism, rather than as a reason for accepting such realism in a mentalistic form.[19]

6 NON-HUMAN ANIMALS

It is hardly surprising that, in developing my Cartesian account of the mind, I have concentrated on the case of human beings. And this will continue to be the focus of my attention. But I want to round off the present discussion with three brief comments on the case of non-human animals. The brevity of these comments is not an indication that I regard the issues as unimportant.

1. I take it as now established that *all* mental items are attached to basic subjects and that *all* basic subjects are wholly non-physical. So if non-human animals have minds (or at least if certain species of non-human animals have minds), there must be non-physical basic subjects appropriately attached to their bodies – just as there are non-physical basic subjects attached to ours.

2. If non-human animals do have minds, the non-physical basic subjects attached to their bodies must be of the same general kind as those attached to ours. In particular, whatever their own introspective and intellectual capacities, their na-

tures, like ours, must be ones which are only transparently conceivable in introspective terms. It does not follow, of course, that human and animal subjects are of *exactly* the same kind (*exactly* the same essential nature). It may well be that they are different, and that the points of difference help to explain the differences in their psychological capacities. It is also possible that, within the domain of non-human animals, there are different kinds of subject attached to the members of different species.

3. I am not entirely sure that non-human animals *do* have minds. Like everyone else, of course, I take their mentality for granted in the ordinary course of life: when my cat purrs, I suppose it to be *happy*; when it stalks a bird, I assume it to be *watching* its quarry and pursuing it with a *purpose*. But from a philosophical standpoint, I find the situation less clear. This is not because there would be any difficulty in accommodating animal mentality within my Cartesian system. It is simply that, in the case of animals, the traditional problem of 'other minds' is especially acute. This is partly because, with the conspicuous differences between their behavioural practices and ours, there is less prospect of our being able to justify the ascription of mental states to animals by means of an 'argument from analogy'. And it is also because, to the extent that animal behaviour is, in mind-relevant respects, less sophisticated than ours, there is a greater likelihood of its being wholly explicable in physical terms. The fact that animals do not have language, or any other behavioural facility suggestive of a similar level of intellectual power, is obviously the most crucial factor here.

8

PERSONAL IDENTITY, EMBODIMENT, AND FREEDOM

1 PERSONS IN THE ORDINARY SENSE

Granted that mental items are attached to basic subjects and that basic subjects are wholly non-physical, how should we construe persons in the ordinary sense – the human mental subjects to which we ascribe mental states and activities in the ordinary course of life? Thus when I say 'Jones is in pain', to what kind of entity does the name 'Jones' refer? To what sort of thing am I ascribing the pain? On the face of it, there are just two possibilities. One would be to say that persons in the ordinary sense *are* basic subjects: Jones and the non-physical subject to which the pain is attributed in the philosophically fundamental account are one and the same. We may call this the 'simple' view. The other possibility would be to say that persons have two natures: Jones has both a non-physical nature, which equips him to be the subject of mental states and activities, and a corporeal nature, as something with shape, size, material composition, and location in physical space. We may call this the 'complex' view. It is important that we interpret the complex view in the right way. The view should not be represented as claiming that persons are meriologically complex entities, each of which contains, as parts, a non-physical basic subject and a purely corporeal object (a body or biological organism) to which this subject is in some way attached; for such a claim would not allow us to ascribe psychological attributes or corporeal attributes to the person as a whole. Rather, the view should be represented as claiming that each person is a unitary entity whose existence is wholly constituted by the existence of a non-physical basic subject,

238

the existence of a purely corporeal object, and the attachment-relationship between them, and that this unitary entity takes on the twin natures of the entities which feature in its constitution.

It is not easy to decide between these rival views. On the one hand, it is part of our ordinary, 'common-sense' outlook that persons are basic subjects: in ascribing pain to Jones, we ordinarily take ourselves to be ascribing it to the entity to which it fundamentally belongs. And this aspect of our ordinary way of thinking could be plausibly represented as implicit in our very concept of a person. On the other hand, it is also part of the 'common-sense' outlook that human persons have corporeal properties. For we would ordinarily say that Jones, the person, is a human being, and that human beings are, whatever else, members of a certain animal species. And this aspect too of our ordinary way of thinking could be plausibly represented as implicit in our very concept of a person – at least as we employ it in the human realm. (Both these aspects, of course, were noted in the earlier discussion in 7.2.) Perhaps we should conclude, then, that, from the standpoint of our Cartesian philosophy, our ordinary concept of a person is incoherent, and that, prior to some revision of its content, neither of the rival views can be adopted. Perhaps we should say that our ordinary concept represents a person as something which *both* qualifies as a basic mental subject *and* possesses a corporeal nature, and that we have to eliminate one or other of these components before we can give an account of persons in Cartesian terms. The issue would then be: Which of the possible revisions would best suit our theoretical purposes? Which of the rival views would yield a revised concept with the highest theoretical rationale? But again, I cannot see this issue as having any clear-cut answer. One might take the concept which fits the simple view to be superior, since it preserves the perspective of the philosophically fundamental account. On the other hand, one might regard the concept which fits the complex view as better, since it reflects (by as it were ontologically institutionalizing) the peculiar intimacy and theoretical importance of the relationship between a basic subject and the organism to which it is attached. All things considered, I am inclined to think that there is no genuine issue here at all. We can adopt whichever concept of a person we like; or, perhaps better still, simply speak of 'persons$_1$', when we mean the non-physical basic subjects, and of 'persons$_2$', when we mean the dual-nature entities created by the special attachment of these subjects to bodies. What remains an important issue, of course, is the nature of this special attachment: what is it about the relationship between a basic subject (or person$_1$) and a certain body which makes it appropriate to speak of the body as *his* and makes it possible to recognize a futher mental subject (a person$_2$) ontologically constituted by, and reflecting, that relationship? For the time being, however, I shall put this question on one side.[1]

2 PERSONAL IDENTITY

If the question of how we should construe persons in the ordinary sense were merely a question of choosing between the simple and the complex views, as we have defined them, it would not, then, as far as I can see, be a genuine philosophical issue: we could make out a reasonable case for either view; or, if we liked, we could have it both ways, by introducing two distinct concepts of a person in the way just envisaged. However, the question of what we should take persons to be has another aspect – an aspect which we are simply ignoring if we regard these two views as the only options. This further aspect is concerned with the topics of personal identity and the unity of the mind. I think the best way of introducing it is to consider the account of persons and their identity offered by John Locke.[2]

Like Descartes before him, Locke accepted that mental items are always the token-states or activities of basic subjects – subjects that he referred to as 'thinking substances'. He also took these thinking substances to be continuants, i.e to be things which persist (preserve their identity) through time; and, despite a certain degree of agnosticism on the issue, he was inclined to the view that they were non-physical. In this Cartesian framework, he addressed himself to the question of whether persons could be identified with thinking substances, and returned a negative answer. But his reason for giving such an answer was not that he thought that persons have corporeal natures and that thinking substances (probably) do not; indeed, his willingness to envisage cases in which persons are transferred from one body to another, together with his acceptance of the Christian doctrine of the Day of Judgment, could be taken to show that he thought of them as wholly non-physical. His reason for refusing to equate persons with the thinking substances to which their mentality primarily belongs was that he took personal identity through time to be logically independent of substance-identity. Thus he thought that it was logically possible for the same thinking substance to coincide, at different times, with different persons, and likewise possible for the same person to coincide, at different times, with different thinking substances. The reason why he thought that substance-identity and personal identity could diverge in this way was that he thought that two momentary substance-stages qualified as stages of the same person if and only if they shared the same consciousness; and he took this sharing of the same consciousness (this 'co-consciousness' as we may call it) to be a purely psychological relation, which is capable of holding between stages of different substances and of failing to hold between stages of the same substance. In effect, then, while following Descartes in his acceptance of an ontology of basic subjects, he anticipated Hume in his account of personal identity. For he held that the grouping of mental items into a single personal biography was effected by the unifying psychological relations between them (or between the substance-stages to which they belonged) rather than by their co-attachment to the same basic subject (the same persisting thinking substance).

Now, at first sight, it might seem that such a position would be just perverse. Once we have accepted an ontology of non-physical basic subjects, there may be some question as to whether we can equate them with persons in the ordinary sense; for we may wonder whether we can properly regard persons as wholly non-physical. But if we are happy to think of persons as non-physical, and hence to approach the question of their identity through time from a purely psychological standpoint, why should we feel any temptation to drive a wedge between the person and the basic subject? Surely the only natural thing to say, in this framework, is that persons are basic subjects and that it is their attachment to the same basic subject which assigns mental items to the same personal biography. Any other view would seem to be a gratuitous complication.

However, the issue is not quite so simple. One of the factors which complicates matters is that, granted their non-physical character, there seems to be no way of telling, in general, when basic subjects are the same and when they are different. And, in consequence, we can entertain hypotheses which represent the distribution of subjects over bodies and mental items as systematically at variance with what, employing our ordinary criteria, we would normally take to be the distribution of persons. For example, we might suppose that basic subjects, though genuine continuants, are literally ephemeral (each subject persisting for only a day), and that what we ordinarily take to be the mental biography of a single person (because it exhibits a certain psychological unity and is causally attached to a single persisting organism) is really the biography of a series of basic subjects, each of which, when it comes into existence, takes on the psychological characteristics of the subject which it replaces. Or, at the other extreme, we might suppose that there is really only one basic subject – a kind of 'world soul' – which is causally attached in the same way to every human organism, and that what we take to be the mental biographies of different persons (because they are psychologically separate and attached to different organisms) are really the separate biographies of this single thing. But when we focus on such hypotheses, we can begin to see a rationale for refusing to equate personal identity with basic-subject identity. In the first place, because they postulate such a *systematic* divergence between the distribution of basic subjects and the commonly accepted distribution of persons, we find it plausible to think of these hypotheses not as challenging the correctness of our ordinary criteria, but as merely envisaging a certain, and prima facie surprising, way in which, from a God's-eye view, persons might turn out to be ultimately constituted. Thus focusing on the situation postulated by the first hypothesis, we find it plausible to interpret this, not as one in which there are many more persons than we normally suppose, but as one in which the history of a single person incorporates a multiplicity of basic subjects. Likewise, focusing on the situation postulated by the second hypothesis, we find it plausible to interpret this, not as one in which there are considerably fewer persons than we normally suppose, but as one in which a multiplicity of persons inhere in a single basic subject. Moreover, since we cannot look at things from a God's-eye view, it seems that we have no way of telling whether these hypotheses are true or false. And this would mean that if we were to equate persons with basic subjects, we would be forced to acknowledge that almost all questions of personal identity and difference were wholly undecidable. But, as well as being unpalatable, such a conclusion could be thought to show that the concept of a person which is relevant to our theoretical and practical concerns must be of some other kind – a kind which allows the decidability of its application by reference to the evidence available to us. And presumably this relevant concept would be the one whose application is governed by our ordinary criteria.

It seems, then, that a case can be made out for distinguishing persons and basic subjects, and for developing an account of personal identity which allows mental items belonging to different subjects to be 'co-personal' and mental items belonging to different persons to be 'consubjective'. It would not follow from this that the correct account was that provided by Locke. And indeed Locke's account is vulnerable to a number of familiar objections.[3] As I have said, Locke held that two substance-stages qualify as stages in the history of the same person if and only if they are co-conscious. And he went on to construe co-consciousness in terms of memory, so that a later stage S_2 counts as co-conscious with an earlier stage S_1 if and only if S_2 has the capacity to recall, as its own, some of S_1's experiences. This is clearly defective in at least three ways. In the first place, on the assumption that co-personality is transitive,[4] it generates a contradiction in cases, like that of Reid's gallant officer, where S_3 can recall the experiences of S_2, and S_2 can recall the experiences of S_1, but S_3 cannot recall the experiences of S_1.[5] Secondly, it is clearly wrong to insist that a person cannot suffer total amnesia with respect to some phase in his past history. And thirdly, unless we build a requirement of personal identity into our concept of memory – which would make the Lockean account circular – it is at least conceivable that a person should remember, as if they were his own, the experiences of someone else (think here of a case in which memory-traces are transplanted from one brain to another). The first of these defects could be corrected by replacing the memory-relation by its 'ancestral', so that two substance-stages qualify as co-conscious if they are connected by a series (not necessarily in temporal order) of substance-stages whose successive members are directly linked by memory.[6] And this proposal would also do something to mitigate the problem of amnesia. But it is still surely conceivable that a person's earliest experiences – e.g. pain during the process of birth – are ones which he is never subsequently able to recall. And the problem of paramnesia – the remembering of someone else's experiences – would not be affected at all.

The fact that Locke's account is defective does not mean that the general strategy it exemplifies is misconceived. It does not mean that it is wrong to look for an analysis of co-personality in terms of the relations in which mental items, or the substance-stages to which they belong, stand to one another, rather than in terms of the persistence of the same basic subject. And indeed Locke's main point, that the preservation of the same person is really the preservation of the same consciousness has a certain plausibility, even if his construal of what this involves is mistaken. What we must now consider, then, is whether the general strategy can be implemented in some more effective way.

There is one general point which needs to be stressed in advance. Assuming that our actual concept of a person has some rationale, we can expect any account of what constitutes the identity of a person *through* time (of what renders mental items at different times co-personal) to have some natural affinity with, and to be something we can represent as a natural development of, our account of what constitutes the identity of a person *at a* time (of what renders simultaneous mental items co-personal). Thus if we decide that what makes simultaneous items co-personal is their standing to one another in a certain psychological relation, then it would be very strange if we went on to claim that what makes non-simultaneous items co-personal is a relation of a wholly different kind, such as the fact that the items are causally dependent on the same body or nervous system. Likewise, if we decide that what makes simultaneous items co-personal is that they causally depend on the same body, it would be very strange if we went on to claim that what makes non-simultaneous items co-personal is their standing to one another in some psychological relation, like that of memory. The point is that, if we were to adopt quite different, and, as it were, ideologically contrasting, criteria of co-personality in respect of simultaneous and non-simultaneous mental items, then the two species of co-personality would not have sufficient in common to warrant their subsumption under a single generic concept. There would be simply no point in having a concept of co-personality of that internally disjointed kind.

Now I think that Locke was trying to provide a unitary account of co-personality when he took personal identity through time to consist in some kind of identity of consciousness. Locke took it for granted that what makes simultaneous experiences co-personal is that they are united by a single consciousness. And he then saw memory as a way in which a person's consciousness at one time can reach back and encompass experiences which occurred at an earlier time, so that the earlier and later experiences are also united by a single consciousness. Of course, the way in which my present consciousness encompasses my present experiences is not the same as the way in which, by memory, it may encompass my past experiences. My present experiences, including my present memory-experiences, are literally elements of my present consciousness, whereas my past experiences are, at best, merely objects of my present consciousness – items of which I am currently recollectively aware. And I think it was in failing to give due weight to this difference that Locke's account went astray. None the less, it is not difficult to see why Locke saw memory as playing the role he accorded it. For, from the phenomenological standpoint of the recollecting subject, it does seem as if the experiences he recalls are being re-lived in the context of his present consciousness and as if he is as directly aware of them as he is of the experiences which are objectively current.

Let us then see if we can improve on Locke's account while preserving its basic insights. For the time being, I shall continue with the assumption from which Locke himself began, and which I think is substantially correct, that simultaneous experiences qualify as co-personal if and only if they are components of a single complex experience – elements of a single episode of consciousness and accessible to the same introspective awareness. Let us speak of experiences which are rendered co-personal in this way as 'strictly co-conscious'. Our next task must be to see whether we can find some relation, other than memory, which can hold between experiences at different times and which has the right sort of affinity with strict co-consciousness to allow us to count the experiences thus related as co-personal too. I shall argue that we can find such a relation by looking more closely at the connection between experience and time.[7]

The first point to be stressed – and I think it originates from William James[8] – is that a single sensory awareness can take in a temporal spread of phenomena. Thus suppose I see a bird fly past my window. The movement of the bird-shaped patch is surely as much a visual datum – part of the sensory content of my visual experience – as its colour and shape. Or again, suppose I hear a tune. The duration and succession of notes is surely as much an auditory datum – part of the sensory content of my auditory experience – as their pitch and loudness. It might be objected that what seems like the direct awareness of a temporal pattern is really the recollection of a mental succession – for example, that if I seem to see the movement of the bird, this is only because at each time when I see its current position, I remember what positions I successively saw it occupy over the preceding period. But this objection fails. There is a clear phenomenological difference between the kinds of experience I have when, on the one hand, I witness the movement of a bird through the series of points from P_1 to P_2, and when, on the other, seeing it at P_2, I remember that, some twelve hours earlier, I successively saw it occupy the successive points in the same series. This phenomenological difference cannot be eliminated or diminished merely by reducing the time-interval from twelve hours to twelve minutes or to one minute or even to a fraction of a second. Of course, it is diminished, though not eliminated, if we suppose the remembering to be accompanied by an image of the previous movement – an image whose content includes a temporal succession of bird-patch positions. But such a supposition would defeat the point of the objection. For if motion can be visually imaged, then it can also be visually sensed. And if motion *can* be sensed, it would be sheer perversity to deny that it *is* sensed on those occasions, like seeing the bird in flight, when it seems to be.

In any case, the reasons for accepting that sensory awareness can take in a temporal spread of phenomena are not
merely phenomenological. For, at least in the case of the
auditory realm, we cannot even conceive of there being an
experience whose content lacks a temporal element. Thus just
as it is inconceivable that there should be an experience of
colour which was not the experience of a colour-pervaded
region, so, equally, it is inconceivable that there should be an
experience of sound which was not the experience of a sound-
filled period.[9] Phenomenal time is the essential medium for
the sensory presentation (sensory realization) of sound-qualia,
as phenomenal space is the essential medium for the sensory
presentation (sensory realization) of colour-qualia. A mere
pitch-loudness, abstracted from a time-field, cannot form a
complete auditory datum, just as a mere colour, abstracted
from a space-field, cannot form a complete visual datum.[10] I
am not sure whether phenomenal time is, in the same way, an
essential ingredient of the other (non-auditory) sense-realms.
But if it is essential to the auditory realm, it is at least available
to the other realms. And, granted its availability, we have no
reason to doubt its presence in these realms, given the phenomenological evidence in its favour.

Now I am not suggesting that whenever we watch some
moving object or listen to some sequence of sounds, the entire
sequence of events, however long, is taken in by a single act of
awareness. Clearly this is not so. Rather, my claim is that, as we
watch or listen, there is a sequence of complex experiences,
each of which presents some temporal pattern of phenomena
– this pattern corresponding to, and representing, some (perhaps relatively small) portion of the entire sequence of observed
external events. Nor am I suggesting that the portions of the
sequence which are successively observed are entirely discrete.
For, clearly, if our observation is uninterrupted, the successively
observed portions will largely overlap, and this will generate a
matching overlap in the successively presented patterns. A
typical, if slightly oversimplified, example would be this. I
listen to someone playing the scale of C major, with, let us
suppose, no pauses between the successive notes. I undergo a
series of total auditory experiences, the first presenting the
pattern *2 units of silence before 1 unit of C*, the second the pattern
1 unit of silence before 1 unit of C before 1 unit of D, the third the

pattern *1 unit of C before 1 unit of D before 1 unit of E*, the fourth the pattern *1 unit of D before 1 unit of E before 1 unit of F*, and so on. As we run through the series of patterns, we see that some last portion of each is always the same as some first portion of its successor; and each of these overlaps indicates a corresponding overlap between two successively heard portions of the physical sound-sequence. When I speak here of a 'total' auditory experience, I mean one which is not part of a larger auditory experience. A total *auditory* experience need not, of course, be a total experience *simpliciter* (one which is not a part of *any* larger experience), though, for convenience of exposition, I shall assume that what feature in my example *are* total experiences in this stronger sense.

I warned that the example would be oversimplified. What makes it so is that it is unrealistic to suppose that the succession of experiences will exactly keep pace with the succession of notes in this way. Thus, preceding what I have labelled as my first total experience, there will be a sequence of experiences taking in only fragments of the 1-unit C-period (e.g. there will be an experience of 2.5 units of silence before 0.5 units of C). And, in a similar way, between what I have listed as my first and second total experiences, there will be a sequence of experiences taking in only fragments of the 1-unit D-period. Indeed, it may be that the whole series of experiences is literally continuous (or at least dense) and that the qualitative change in their phenomenal time-patterns is likewise continuous (or dense). But I think it will be best, initially, to focus on the oversimplified example, in which the essentials of the situation can be more clearly seen.

It is to the overlap of the successively presented temporal patterns that I want us to pay particular attention. On the face of it, this overlap is rather puzzling. For it seems to imply that, while each total pattern is heard only once, its parts are heard more than once. Indeed, it seems to imply that the smaller the qualitative part, the more times it is heard. For example, consider the qualitative item *1 unit of C*. This item features, in different positions in the time-field, in each of the patterns presented by the first three total experiences. So it seems that I have to hear this C-period three times – on these successive occasions. But, of course, this is just not the case. When I listen to the scale, I hear each note, or note-period, only once.

At least, this is how it seems.

The conclusion we should draw from this, I think, is not that the example has been wrongly specified, nor that our impression of the number of times that each note-period is presented is mistaken, but that where the successive patterns overlap, the experiences which present them overlap in a corresponding way. Thus let us call the first three total experiences E_1, E_2, and E_3, and let us call the three patterns they respectively present P_1 (*2 units of silence before 1 unit of C*), P_2 (*1 unit of silence before 1 unit of C before 1 unit of D*), and P_3 (*1 unit of C before 1 unit of D before 1 unit of E*). Then we should say: that E_1 and E_2 contain, as a common component, an experience of that smaller pattern (*1 unit of silence before 1 unit of C*) which is the common component of P_1 and P_2; that E_2 and E_3 contain, as a common component, an experience of that smaller pattern (*1 unit of C before 1 unit of D*) which is the common component of P_2 and P_3; and that all three total experiences contain, as a common component, an experience of that sound-period (*1 unit of C*) which is the common component of P_1, P_2, and P_3. By construing the situation in this way, we allow the smaller patterns and sound-periods to feature in the total patterns presented by different total experiences, but we avoid having to say that they are presented more than once: there is only one hearing of *1 unit of silence before 1 unit of C*, though it is a component of two total hearings; there is only one hearing of *1 unit of C*, though it is a component of three total hearings. This means, of course, that we have to take each experience to extend over a period of real time in a way which exactly matches the phenomenal period it presents. And it means that the sense in which E_1 precedes E_2, and E_2 precedes E_3, is not that E_1, E_2, and E_3 occur at successive real moments, but that they occupy successive, but largely overlapping, real periods.

By allowing total experiences to be extended in real time, we are allowing the relation of strict co-consciousness (the relation which holds between experiences which are parts of a single experience) to relate experiences which occur at different times. Thus E_1 will contain three successive and non-overlapping experiences – a presentation of *1 unit of silence* followed by another presentation of *1 unit of silence* followed by a presentation of *1 unit of C* – and these successive experiences, being parts of E_1, will qualify as strictly co-conscious. Moreover, by allowing successive total experiences to overlap, i.e. to contain a common component, we allow for cases in which two experiences which are not themselves strictly co-conscious are connected by a series of links of strict co-consciousness. Thus since E_1 overlaps with E_2 and E_2 overlaps with E_3, there is such a series connecting the earliest component of E_1 with latest component of E_3. And, of course, this series of links will continue through the whole sequence of auditory experiences which our example envisages. Where two experiences are either strictly co-conscious or connected by a series of links of strict co-consciousness, let us speak of them as 'serially co-conscious'. Serial co-consciousness is then the ancestral of the relation of strict co-consciousness.

Now we were looking for a relation which can hold between experiences at different times and which has the right sort of affinity with the co-personality sustained by strict co-consciousness to allow us to count the experiences thus related as co-personal too. Serial co-consciousness seems to be just what we want. It has a clear affinity with strict co-consciousness; and, on the natural assumption that co-personality is an equivalence-relation – reflexive, symmetric, and transitive – it is easy to prove that, since strictly co-conscious experiences are co-personal, serially co-conscious experiences are co-personal as well. The point is simply that its transitivity will ensure that co-personality is preserved through the series of links of strict co-consciousness by which serially co-conscious experiences are connected.

Can we then simply define co-personality as serial co-consciousness? The answer is no. Serial co-consciousness allows us to account for the co-personality of experiences which belong to an uninterrupted stream of experience, like the stream of auditory experience in our example, and like the longer and richer streams of experience which characteristically span our continuous periods of consciousness from waking in the morning to falling asleep at night. But these streams of experience are separated by periods of unconsciousness – periods which the relation of serial co-consciousness cannot bridge. Unless we are willing to draw the implausible conclusion that a new person comes into existence each morning (assuming a nocturnal period of dreamless sleep), we need some further relation to explain how these separated streams can belong to the same personal biography. Presumably this new relation too will have to have some natural affinity with serial co-consciousness and thereby with strict co-consciousness.

I think that the new relation which meets these requirements is what we might call *potential* serial co-consciousness. In the sense in which I am here using the term, a *stream* of experience can be defined as any temporal sequence of successively overlapping total experiences; and a *total* stream will then be any stream which is not a portion of a larger stream. Given two total streams *A* and *B*, where *A* is earlier than *B*, and where there is a temporal interval between them, let us say that *A* and *B* are *directly joinable* if and only if there is something which ensures (whether logically or nomologically) that, with *B* held constant, a hypothetical continuation of *A* to the time when (or just after) *B* begins would join up with *B*; and let us say that two total streams are *indirectly joinable* if and only if they are connected by a series of total streams whose successive members are directly joinable. We can then say that two experiences are *potentially serially co-conscious* (or, for short, *potentially co-conscious*) if and only if the total streams in which they occur are either directly or indirectly joinable. Strictly speaking, and for reasons which will emerge in due course, the definition of direct joinability will need to be a little more complicated if this relation is to play the role marked out for it. But it would only confuse things if we took account of the complication at this stage.[11]

The connection between potential (serial) co-consciousness, thus defined, and co-personality can be illustrated by the following example. Last night, before falling asleep, I had a series of auditory experiences, which were mainly caused by the drone of the washing-up machine downstairs. This series formed the last portion of yesterday's total stream (call this *A*). About seven hours later, after a period of dreamless sleep, I had a further series of auditory experiences caused by my radio alarm-clock. This series formed the first portion of today's total stream (call this *B*). Now, in the actual world, *A* and *B*, while belonging to the same personal biography, were separated by a period of unconsciousness. But imagine a hypothetical world which includes *B*, and which is the same as

251

the actual world up to the end of *A*, but in which *A* continues to the time when (or just after) *B* begins – this continuation being composed, let us suppose, of various other auditory experiences, such as the roar of cars on the eastern bypass or the sounds of the all-night party next door. Then this continuation would join up with *B* to make *A*, *B*, and the continuation itself portions of a single stream. So, in the actual world, *A* and *B* qualify as directly joinable, and their constituent experiences qualify as potentially co-conscious. In contrast, if *A'* is my wife's total stream yesterday, terminating in a similar series of auditory experiences, then *A'* and *B* are not directly joinable. For even if *A'* had continued to the time when *B* began, it would not have joined up with *B* – though it might well have joined a stream in her biography whose initial portion was very similar to that of *B*. Nor, presumably, are *A'* and *B* *indirectly* joinable (i.e. connected by a series of total streams whose successive members are directly joinable). So *A'*-experiences and *B*-experiences are not potentially co-conscious.

One thing which might seem to complicate the first part of this example is that, if I had been kept awake in the way envisaged (e.g. by the traffic on the bypass or by the party next door), I may well have done something (such as got up earlier or reset my alarm) which would have deprived me of the subsequent auditory experiences I actually had. In other words, the continuation of *A* may well have led not to a *joining up with B*, but to the latter's *replacement* – and indeed I regard this as the more likely outcome. But whatever conclusions we may reach on this matter, they do not affect the validity of the example or the purpose for which we are using it. For it is entirely irrelevant whether the hypothetical situation we have to envisage, to illustrate the potential for joining, is a plausible one. The crucial point is simply that the two streams are so related in the actual world as to ensure that, *if* (however improbably) *B* had remained and *A* had been appropriately extended, they would have joined.

If we now say that two experiences are *consciousness-related* (*C-related*) if and only if they are either strictly co-conscious or serially co-conscious or potentially co-conscious, then my proposal is that we take experiences to be co-personal if and only if they are C-related in this sense. At least, I make this proposal relative to the two assumptions constitutive of the general strategy of the Lockean approach: (i) that persons are non-physical, and (ii) that co-personality is to be defined in terms of the psychological relations between mental items (or between basic-subject stages), rather than as the common attachment of items to the same persisting basic subject. Admittedly, the account I have so far offered only covers the co-personality of *experiences*, not of mental items in general. But for reasons which will become clear presently, this restriction does not matter.

It is time now to take a closer look at this general Lockean strategy in the light of the conclusion to which it has led. The main reason why (even when they are construed as wholly non-physical) it seemed inappropriate to equate persons with basic subjects, and thus to equate co-personality with (basic) consubjectivity, was that we could apparently envisage situations in which the distribution of basic subjects over bodies and mental items was systematically at variance with what, employing our ordinary criteria, we would normally take to be the distribution of persons. The point then was that we would find it more plausible to interpret these situations as ones in which co-personality and consubjectivity came apart, rather than as ones for which our ordinary criteria were shown to be erroneous. However, the proposed equation of co-personality with C-relatedness, in the sense defined, forces us to view things in a quite different way, as I shall now explain.

The first point which needs to be made is that if co-personality is defined in the way proposed, then it is logically impossible for two experiences to be co-personal without being consubjective – to belong to the same person without being attached to the same basic subject. This can be established as follows. Let E_1 and E_2 be two C-related experiences (nothing, of course, to do with the 'E_1' and 'E_2' of my original auditory example), with E_1 belonging to basic subject S_1 and occurring in total stream A, and with E_2 belonging to basic subject S_2 and occurring in total stream B. There are then four cases to be considered:

(i) There is the case in which E_1 and E_2 are strictly co-conscious. Here, the two experiences must be parts of a single experience. But we have already established that any experience belongs to a basic subject. So it immediately follows that the experiences are consubjective.

(ii) There is the case in which, while not strictly co-conscious, E_1 and E_2 are serially co-conscious. Here, the two experiences are linked by a series of experiences whose successive members are strictly co-conscious and therefore consubjective. But since an experience is just the realization of some experiential state in a particular basic subject at a particular time, we know that any experience belongs to only one basic subject and hence know that the relation of consubjectivity is transitive. So again it follows that E_1 and E_2 are consubjective.

(iii) There is the case in which, while E_1 and E_2 are neither strictly nor serially co-conscious, streams A and B are directly joinable; and, for the sake of argument, let us assume that A is earlier than B. Now since an experience is just the realization of some experiential state in a particular basic subject at a particular time, we know that the identity of an experience logically depends on the identity of its basic subject. So we know that there is no possible world in which E_1 occurs without being attached to S_1 or in which E_2 occurs without being attached to S_2. Now envisage a possible world W (and let us make this a world which is both logically and nomologically possible[12]) in which B exists and in which A is continued to the time when B begins. Given that A and B are directly joinable, we know that, in W, the continuation of A would join up with B, making the two experiences serially co-conscious. So, from case (ii), we know that, in W, E_1 and E_2 would be consubjective. But since it is impossible for S_1 and S_2 to be identical in W unless they are identical in the actual world, and since each of the experiences has the same basic subject in W as it has in the actual world, it follows that, in the actual world, S_1 and S_2 are identical.[13] In other words, it follows that E_1 and E_2 are consubjective.

(iv) There is the case in which A and B are merely indirectly joinable. Here the two streams are connected by a series of total streams whose successive members are directly joinable. But we know from case (iii) that experiences belonging to directly joinable streams are consubjective, and we established in case (ii) that consubjectivity is transitive. So again we can conclude that E_1 and E_2 are consubjective.

In each case, then, the particular form of their C-relatedness suffices to establish that E_1 and E_2 are consubjective. And this means that experiences cannot be co-personal in the sense defined unless they are attached to the same basic subject.

It immediately follows from this that we cannot, as we had initially supposed, envisage a situation in which a single personal biography is distributed over a series of basic subjects. It may be logically possible for the basic subject which is initially attached to a certain body to be replaced by another, which inherits its psychological attributes; and it may even be possible that this sort of thing happens quite regularly, without anyone realizing that it does. But if co-personality is defined as C-relatedness, then each such change in the identity of the resident subject will be a change in the identity of the person too. For while the experiences before and after the change may pass as co-personal, they cannot be genuinely C-related unless they are consubjective, which *ex hypothesi* they are not. It should also be stressed that the fact that such changes would go undetected does not mean that we have no grounds for believing that (in general) they do not occur – any more than the fact that we would be none the wiser if the world had been created five minutes ago (complete with all the apparent memories and apparent traces of a fictitious past) proves the groundlessness of our ordinary historical beliefs.[14] But the epistemological issues of consubjectivity are not ones which I can explore in detail here. All I shall say, as a gesture towards a solution to the sceptical problem, is that, first, in default of any positive evidence to the contrary, the ordinary canons of theoretical simplicity favour the hypothesis that each brain is permanently attached to a single basic subject; and secondly, assuming that we can only account for the attachment of a subject to a brain in terms of some system of scope-restricted laws (laws which make reference to a particular brain and a particular basic subject[15]), it is hard to envisage a form of attachment which is nomologically credible but vulnerable to change.

We have established that C-relatedness, and hence (as we are proposing to define it) co-personality, entails consubjectivity. But we have not established that this entailment holds in reverse. We have not established that all the experiences which belong to the same basic subject are C-related. In fact, for all we have established so far, it is possible that all experiences belong to just one basic subject, who is attached to a multiplicity of separate bodies and has a multiplicity of separate mental lives.

One way of trying to establish that consubjectivity entails C-relatedness would be by invoking the principle (call it P) that simultaneous consubjective experiences must be strictly co-conscious. For suppose that an experience E_1, occurring in stream A, and an experience E_2, occurring in stream B, are consubjective. If these experiences are simultaneous, then it immediately follows from P that they are strictly co-conscious, and hence C-related. If they are not simultaneous, we have two possibilities: either they are serially co-conscious or they are not. If the former obtains, then *a fortiori* they are C-related. So only the second case is crucial. But now, taking this case, assume that E_1 is the earlier experience, and that there is an interval between the streams, and envisage a possible world W in which, with B held constant, A is continued to the time when B begins. Let E_3 be the last experience in this continuation and let E_4 be the simultaneous item which forms the first experience in B. Since serially co-conscious experiences are necessarily consubjective, we know that, in W, E_1 would be consubjective with E_3, and E_2 would be consubjective with E_4. And since E_1 and E_2 are consubjective in the actual world, and since an experience stays attached to its actual-world subject in all possible worlds in which it occurs, we can conclude that E_3 and E_4 would also be consubjective. But since these latter experiences are simultaneous, it follows, by P, that they would be strictly co-conscious. And this shows that, in the actual world, E_1 and E_2 are *potentially* co-conscious, and hence C-related. All ways, then, the supposition that E_1 and E_2 are consubjective, together with the envisaged principle, results in the conclusion that E_1 and E_2 are C-related. So, if it is a conceptual truth, P would ensure that consubjectivity entails C-relatedness.

But can principle P itself be validated? It might seem that we can establish it very simply. For suppose basic subject S has experiences E_1 and E_2 at time t. In having E_1, S is in some experiential state Σ_1, and in having E_2, S is in some experiential state Σ_2. So presumably, at t, S is in the complex experiential state $\Sigma_1 + \Sigma_2$. But since there is nothing more to the having of an experience than being in some experiential state, then, in being in the complex state $\Sigma_1 + \Sigma_2$, S is presumably the subject of the complex experience $E_1 + E_2$. And this makes E_1 and E_2 components of a single experience and therefore strictly co-conscious.

However, this argument is fallacious. For in the sense which is relevant to the definition of strict co-consciousness, it is clear that the realizations of Σ_1 and Σ_2 in S will only combine to yield the realization of a complex experiential state if the complex, qua complex, is accessible to S's introspective awareness. And the argument does nothing to show that, because E_1 and E_2 are simultaneous and consubjective, they form an introspectively detectable complex. Thus, for all the argument shows, E_1 might be *my* present experience and E_2 *my wife's* present experience, with S as the common basic subject which underlies our introspectively separate biographies. To say of such a case that there is a single complex experience $E_1 + E_2$ attached to S is to employ the notion of a single experience in a very weak sense – certainly not the sense needed for the definition of strict co-consciousness as the latter functions in the envisaged analysis of co-personality.

However, I think there is a better way of defending P. For it seems to me that, even when we take account of the fact that a single experience has to be introspectively unified, we cannot (with one qualification which I shall mention in a moment) avoid conceding that the simultaneous experiences of a single basic subject are unified in the requisite way. The point is simply that we lose our grip on what it is for something to qualify as a single basic subject unless we think of it as having, at any time, an integrated mind, whose contents are accessible to a single centre of introspective awareness. An analogy with the physical realm might help here. There is no *formal* objection to saying, with respect to the class of tables, that there is only one space-occupying physical particular, which can simultaneously occur in a variety of places, with a variety of (tabular) shapes, sizes, and types of material composition. I say that there is no *formal* objection to this; and I mean that there is nothing in the logic of particulars, properties, and identity, abstracted from any specific subject-matter, which reveals a contradiction in such a scheme. None the less, the scheme would not be consistent with our actual concept of a table, nor indeed with our more general concept of a material object. For our concept of a table (material object) requires us to think of anything to which it applies as *particularized with respect to space*, so that, at any time, a single entity of the relevant type can only have different spatial positions in so far as it is divisible into different spatial parts. Now, as I see it, something analogous applies in the mental realm. There is no formal contradiction in saying, with respect to the class of persons, that there is only one basic mental individual, which simultaneously occurs in one introspective context as me, in another as my wife, in another as the person next door, and so on. But something which was in this way universal with respect to introspective contexts would not qualify as a basic mental *subject* in any recognizable sense: it would not be something which could fill the role defined by our intuitions about ownership, when we say that, for each experience, there must be something whose experience it irreducibly is. Just as it is essential to our conception of a material object that, except in so far as it is spatially divisible, it should have, at any time, a single spatial position, so it is essential to our conception of a mental *subject* that it should have, at any time, a single consciousness.

As I indicated, there is one qualification I would make to this. For we can, I think, make sense of a case in which a single mental biography divides into two introspectively separate branches, such that the simultaneous experiences drawn from the different branches are consubjective but not strictly co-conscious. The easiest way to envisage such a case is to think of it as resulting from the bisection of a living human brain.[16] Let me explain.

For the sake of argument, let us assume: (i) that a human person's experiences directly causally depend only on the states and activities of his brain; (ii) that each cerebral hemisphere of a human brain is capable of generating experiences without the functional help of the other; (iii) that, in a normal brain, the simultaneous experiences generated by the different hemispheres are strictly co-conscious; and (iv) that, in a normal brain, the members of any uninterrupted sequence of experiences that are generated by either hemisphere, or by the two in combination, are serially co-conscious. Now, in the framework of these assumptions, envisage a case in which, for some particular human individual, we sever the neural connections (in the *corpus callosum*) between the two hemispheres of his brain, thereby removing the possibility of any direct causal traffic between them. We can plausibly suppose that the effect of this bisection will be to create two introspectively separate centres of consciousness, so that the simultaneous experiences generated by the different hemispheres cease to be strictly co-conscious. At the same time, we can also plausibly suppose that there will be no impairment to the links of consciousness that connect the experiences of each hemisphere with one another and with the experiences prior to the division. Thus if we assume that the whole operation is conducted with only a local anaesthetic, so that there is no break in the continuity of consciousness, we can plausibly suppose that, at the moment of bisection, a single stream of experience divides into two branches, in such a way that, on the one hand, the simultaneous experiences of the different branches are not strictly co-conscious, but, on the other, the experiences of each branch are serially co-conscious both with one another and with those of the original integrated stream. Since serially co-conscious experiences are consubjective, and since consubjectivity is transitive, such a case would constitute a counter-example to principle P. It would be a case in which simultaneous consubjective experiences failed to be strictly co-conscious.

The point I want now to stress, however, is that although this case would constitute a counter-example to P, it does not affect our acceptance of the thesis which the principle was invoked to support. For if the experiences in both the branches are serially co-conscious with the experiences of the original stream, then they are, by definition, serially co-conscious with one another. So although we have a case in which simultaneous consubjective experiences are not strictly co-conscious, we do not have a case in which consubjective experiences are not C-related. Admittedly, we have made things easy for ourselves by supposing that there is no break in the subject's consciousness. The situation would be less straightforward if we instead supposed the operation to be performed with a *general* anaesthetic, so that the initial stream (A) and the two later streams (B_1 and B_2) become separated by an interval of unconsciousness. In this case too, however, we are going to end up with the same conclusion. For we clearly want to be able to say that (in any sense relevant to co-personal grouping) both B_1 and B_2 qualify as directly joinable with A, and so as indirectly joinable with each other. And this commits us to saying that all the experiences in the three streams are both consubjective and C-related. The only complicating factor is that, before we can reach this conclusion, we need to adjust our definition of direct joinability to cover the peculiar circumstances of the envisaged case. Thus because there is no guarantee that *any* continuation of A to the time of the later streams will merge with *both*, we need to make the definition more liberal: we need to say that two streams qualify as directly joinable not only in the case where, with the later stream held constant, joining would be ensured by an appropriate forward continuation of the earlier, but also in the case where, with the earlier stream held constant, joining would be ensured by an appropriate backward continuation of the later.

Putting all the points together, then, the overall conclusion to which we are led is that C-relatedness and consubjectivity necessarily coincide. It is logically impossible for experiences to be C-related without being consubjective; and, notwithstanding the slight qualification to P, it is also logically impossible for them to be consubjective without being C-related. This means, remarkably, that, ignoring the trivial issue of whether persons should be construed as wholly non-physical, even the Lockean strategy, when properly executed, leads back to the simple view, which equates persons with basic subjects. It means that, despite what Locke himself believed, we cannot envisage cases in which stages of the same person belong to different thinking substances or in which stages of the same thinking substance belong to different persons.

Two further things now fall into place. First, we can see that the potential for streamal joining is grounded on consubjectivity itself. Thus, in the example of my period of dreamless sleep, it is the fact that the two streams belong to the same basic subject which ensures that, with the appropriate form or forms of continuation, they would join. Moreover, this ensuring is clearly of a *logical*, rather than a *nomological*, kind: it is a matter of what consubjectivity itself entails with respect to the unity of consciousness, rather than of its contingent effects in the framework of natural law. Secondly, we can see why, as I earlier remarked, it does not matter that we have so far only defined co-personality for the domain of *experiences*. For if persons are basic subjects, then other mental items can be assigned to their correct personal biographies simply on the basis of their attachment to such subjects. Indeed, now that we know where it leads, we are in a position to discard the Lockean strategy altogether and redefine co-personality (quite generally) as consubjectivity.

Finally, I should point out that, although I accept the possibility of a single mental biography dividing into two introspectively separate, but still consubjective, branches, I do not accept the possibility of two non-consubjective biographies fusing to form a single one. For any such envisaged fusing would make the two earlier biographies C-related, and, as we have seen, C-related experiences must be consubjective. The only way in which it would be possible for two biographies to fuse would be if, independently of the fusion, they belonged to the same basic subject – a situation which would presumably only arise if the fusion were merely the undoing of an earlier fission. This is not to deny that it may one day be possible to fuse the hemispheres drawn from separate brains and form something which (at least if we ignore any causation from mind to body) will function at the physical level like a single brain. My point is only that, whatever (if anything) psychologically results from such an operation, it will not be a case of there being a single biography whose experiences are C-related to the earlier experiences of different basic subjects.

3 EMBODIMENT

Although the basic subjects involved in human mentality are wholly non-physical, each subject is, at least for a certain phase of its history, intimately linked with a particular biological organism. It is this link which makes it appropriate to speak of the subject as *having a body*, or as *embodied*. It is this link too which both makes it natural, for ordinary purposes, to think of the basic subject as a member of a certain animal species (and hence as something which, in addition to its psychological endowments, has a corporeal nature and location in physical space) and allows us, even from the standpoint of our Cartesian philosophy, to recognize a derivative subject (what we earlier referred to as a 'person$_2$'[17]) to which both physical and psychological attributes can be ascribed. Finally, it is this link which enables the basic subject to qualify as *human*. For nothing could count as a human subject unless it lived (however brief) a human life, and a life could not count as human unless, at least in its first phase, it was suitably united with the animal life of an organism of the appropriate (*homo sapiens*) type.[18]

But what, then, is the nature of this link? What is the connection between the non-physical subject and the biological organism which embodies it? Because of the multiplicity of factors involved, anything approaching an adequate answer to this question would be lengthy and complicated. Moreover, at a certain level of micro-psychophysical detail, it would become the business of the neuroscientist rather than the philosopher.[19] I shall confine myself here to making a few general points about the basic structure of embodiment.

To begin with, it is clear that the connection between the non-physical subject and the biological organism is, fundamentally, a functional one: it is a matter of there being a psychophysical arrangement whereby each partner is equipped to have the right sorts of direct causal influence on the other. This arrangement will be secured by the respective natures of the two entities concerned, together with some framework of physical and psychophysical laws; and the relevant psychophysical laws will presumably be of the scope-restricted sort we discussed earlier (6.3, pp. 167–72) – laws which have an irreducibly singular concern with the particular subject and the particular organism (or relevant organism-part) in question. It should be noted that, although it equips the subject and the organism to interact, the arrangement may pre-date the time when such interaction is physically possible; for the relevant psychophysical laws may be in place before the organism's neural structures have become sufficiently complex to feature in psychophysical causation. One plausible view, indeed, would be that the arrangement gets established at biological conception, when the organism comes into existence. This, of course, would require accepting that the subject himself exists (at least) from biological conception; and, presumably, it would lead one to say that, along with the organism, the subject *comes into existence* at conception.[20]

Embodiment, then, takes the form of a direct functional

connection between the basic subject and a biological organism. It must not be thought, however, that just *any* sort of direct functional connection would suffice; for a moment's reflection shows that this is not so. To take just one example, suppose there is a basic subject *S* and an organism *O* such that the only direct functional link between them consists in the fact that (i) it is a law of nature that any change in the blood-temperature of *O* directly causes a corresponding change in the strength of *S*'s belief in the existence of God and (ii) it is a law of nature that any change in the strength of *S*'s desire to be a professional philosopher directly causes a corresponding change in the size of the mole on *O*'s chin. Clearly, such a psychophysical arrangement would not make it appropriate to speak of *S* as *embodied* by *O* nor make it natural to think of *S* as himself the possessor of a corporeal nature.

One obvious reason why such an arrangement would fail to secure embodiment is that the functional linkage it creates is simply too sparse: we need a much richer system of psychophysical connections before we can begin to think of the subject as possessing a body. But the paucity of the functional system is not the only relevant factor. In order to secure embodiment, a system must not only be sufficiently rich, but must also be, in a distinctive way, *appropriate*, or at least *in general appropriate*, to the subject's psychology: it must be a system which, at least for the most part, enables the relevant mental states to function, in relation to the organism and to one another, in ways that, as we might put it, *reflect*, or *fit*, or *suit*, or *harmonize with*, their psychological character. The system envisaged above fails on this count too: there is clearly nothing about *S*'s belief in the existence of God which makes it distinctively appropriate that its strength should depend on *O*'s temperature nor anything about his desire to be a professional philosopher which makes it distinctively appropriate that its strength should determine the size of *O*'s mole. And this lack of appropriateness would not be altered by simply having a more extensive set of psychophysical connections of a similarly arbitrary sort.

This raises the question of what makes a functional system appropriate to the subject's psychology. How is one to decide whether a given functional role does or does not reflect (fit, suit, harmonize with) the psychological character of the mental state to which it is assigned? Well, putting it succinctly, we can say that a system is appropriate in so far as it meets the norms of epistemic and rational efficiency. In our own case, this appropriateness is exemplified by such things as: (i) the human perceptual system, whereby the subject's sense-experiences are controlled by the organism's sensory input in ways that enable him to perceive (and thereby gain information about) the physical world from the organism's viewpoint; (ii) the human behavioural system, whereby the subject exercises volitional control over the organism's motor output in ways that enable him to act on (and thereby fulfil his purposes with respect to) the physical world through the organism's bodily movements; and (iii) the human belief-system, whereby the subject's set of beliefs at any time is rationally controlled by the immediately preceding set, together with any *new* experiences, insights, and items of putative information he may receive. Of course, this third instance of appropriateness only *directly* contributes to the subject's embodiment in so far as the system depends for its working on the organism's central nervous hardware.[21] But, irrespective of the extent of this dependence, the system *indirectly* contributes, by forming a component both of that larger (perception-including) system which enables the subject to have physical knowledge, and of that larger (action-including) system which enables him to achieve his physical purposes.

At certain points, such appropriateness helps to promote a feeling of embodiment in the subject himself: it helps to make it seem to the subject, experientially, as if he and the organism are one.[22] Thus the fact that he perceives the physical world from the organism's viewpoint (i.e. from that perceptual viewpoint which coincides with the organism's physical location) makes it seem to the subject that he is really located at that point. Likewise, the smoothness with which his decisions and intentions translate themselves into appropriate behavioural responses (themselves part of what he perceives) makes it seem to the subject that these responses are actions he directly performs. Moreover, I think we can take such feelings of oneness with the organism to be part of what creates the subject's objective embodiment – part of what makes it correct to speak of the non-physical subject as having a body and allows us to recognize a derivative subject with a corporeal nature. However, the main way in which appropriateness contributes to embodiment, and indeed the reason why it is necessary for it, is that it is what allows the organism to be the subject's representative in third-person (public-observational) perspective. It is what allows an external observer to discern the subject's mentality in the organism's behaviour, bodily condition, and physical circumstances. This, indeed, is why we have to work on the assumption of appropriateness in ascribing mental states to others. For there is simply no rationale for making one ascription rather another, or indeed for making any ascriptions at all, unless we assume that the functional role of the subject's mental states (if he has any) is in general accord with their psychological character. It does not follow from this that the assumption is warranted: its being required by our ascriptive practice is not as such evidence of its truth. At the same time, the very fact that it makes the behaviour of other human organisms systematically amenable to psychological interpretation is something which calls for explanation, and arguably the only satisfactory explanation would be that both it and the ascriptions it licenses are correct. Obviously, much more needs to be said on this epistemological issue, but I shall not pursue the matter here.

In claiming that embodiment requires the appropriateness of the functional system to the subject's psychology, I do not mean, of course, that it requires *perfect* appropriateness. It obviously leaves room for areas in which there is, or is to some degree, a mismatch between between psychological character and functional role. For example, a subject could be embodied and yet his visual system be very unreliable as a way of conveying correct information about his environment. Or he could be embodied, and yet have impaired control over his bodily movements. Indeed, some measure of inappropriateness is the common lot of everyone. This may prompt the question of how much inappropriateness (e.g. as a proportion of the whole system) embodiment can tolerate. But, as with almost any concept where the underlying factors admit of degrees, our concept of embodiment is not sufficiently precise (inflexible) to yield any definite answer to this. Nor, of course, would it be as useful, or have as much theoretical rationale, if we imposed such precision on it. For any *sharp* dividing line between the tolerable and intolerable degrees of inappropriateness would inevitably represent some virtually insignificant difference as having a theoretical importance which it clearly lacks. As in so many other areas, we have to think *vaguely* to think *big*.

Finally, we should note that this account of embodiment sheds an interesting new light on analytical functionalism. The analytical functionalist claims that psychological concepts are to be analysed in functional terms, i.e. in terms which define someone's being in a certain mental state as his being in a state which has a certain functional role, or cluster of roles, in the relevant causal system. This is a position which we rejected some time ago, and nothing in our recent discussion gives us any reason to alter our verdict. But what is now of interest, in the light of that discussion, is that the functionalist's mistake is beginning to look understandable. The point is that the role, or role-cluster, which the functionalist takes to be definitive of a given mental state is just what, in any case, counts as appropriate to its psychological character. Consequently, since the general appropriateness of the functional system to the subject's mentality is logically required for embodiment, and since we think of *human* subjects (who are conspicuously embodied) as the paradigm, it is not difficult to understand how the functionalist could be led to his erroneous view. His error, in effect, would be to mistake the functional requirements of embodied mentality for requirements of mentality as such.

4 FREEDOM AND AGENCY

This functionalist account of embodiment might encourage us to suppose that the whole psychophysical system, including (in so far as we can think of it separately) the psychological subsystem, is purely mechanistic: it might encourage us to think that, both internally and in relation to the physical organism which embodies it, the human mind works by laws of ordinary cause and effect, no different in their general character from the causal laws which govern (the inanimate portions of) the physical world. Traditionally, however, Cartesian dualists have taken human subjects to enjoy a *freedom of the will*, of a sort not compatible with a purely mechanistic account of human psychology. Thus they have held that, at least in normal circumstances, the non-physical subject has a genuine power of choice, whose operation is not constrained by prior physical or psychological conditions, and which enables him to exercise an ultimate control over the movements of his body. And they have seen this power of choice, in combination with his knowledge of right and wrong, as the basis of the subject's moral accountability. All this, moreover, is thought of as contributing to man's distinctive glory. As Descartes himself put it:

> it is the greatest perfection in man to be able to act by its [the will's] means, that is freely, and by so doing we are in a peculiar way masters of our actions and thereby merit praise or blame.[23]

In embracing this libertarian position, Cartesians are simply endorsing the common-sense view – the view which we all accept prior to philosophical reflection. It is possible that, in part, our ordinary acceptance of this view reflects the fact that a belief in moral responsibility is socially useful: it helps to sustain the system of praise and blame, reward and punishment, by which people are conditioned to behave in socially acceptable ways. But the main reason why the libertarian position has the backing of common sense is that the feeling of volitional freedom is an essential element in our ordinary experience of decision-making. For whenever we are conscious of having to take a decision – of having to make a choice between alternative courses of action – we cannot help thinking of the outcome as resting with us rather than as already fixed by prior conditions. This does not mean that we never feel under any pressure to choose in one way rather than another, much less that we are wholly indifferent to the promptings of our own desires. But it does mean that we feel the final decision to be in our own hands; that whatever the external pressures or internal promptings, we feel it is ultimately up to us whether we yield to them or not. This is so even when the case in favour of a particular decision is overwhelming. Thus, taking account of both my self-interest and my moral duty, I now recognize an overwhelming case against jumping out of the (second-floor) window. None the less, I feel that I have the power to do it; and not just the power to do it *if I choose*, but the power, irrationally and gratuitously, *to choose in that way*.

The fact that decisions feel free, and cannot be felt as decisions without being felt as free, is obviously congenial to the libertarian doctrine. But it does not suffice to *prove* it. For it could still be argued that this feeling is illusory. True, the feeling may be essential to the experience of decision-making; and it may be that, for this reason, we cannot avoid believing in libertarianism when we focus on our situation from the inside. But it does not follow from this that the libertarian doctrine cannot be challenged from a more objective standpoint; nor that such a challenge is bound to be ineffective. All that follows is that there is a prima facie case for accepting the doctrine and that the onus is on its would-be opponents to advance some counter-argument. Let us then try to see what counter-arguments may be forthcoming, and what resources the libertarian has for meeting them.

Traditionally, the main attack on libertarianism has come from the advocates of determinism, who insist that our actions and decisions are causally determined by prior conditions – whether physical conditions, or psychological conditions, or a combination of the two. But if this were the sole threat to his position, the libertarian could afford to shrug it off, since there is no convincing argument for determinism in any of its forms. The only way of arguing for *physical* determinism would be by arguing for an especially strong version of the closed-system view discussed earlier (6.5). But we have already seen that the case for this view is weak; and, even from its standpoint, there is much to suggest that the fundamental system is not deterministic.[24] As for any other form of determinism, the case is even weaker. For whatever the situation in the physical realm, there is simply no empirical evidence at all to suggest the presence of deterministic laws elsewhere. It is true that we can usually find some psychological explanation for the decisions we take. But, typically, these explanations represent the subject as responding to reasons, and (by construing such responses as free) this is something which the libertarian is happy to accept.

However, although the libertarian can rebut the challenge of the determinist, there is another way of attacking his position which is both more subtle and harder to resist. As the libertarian conceives it, the relevant freedom is something which gives us ultimate control over our actions and renders us morally responsible for them. But, even on the assumption

268

that determinism is false, it is difficult to see how such freedom could be achieved. For the failure of causal determination only seems to leave us at the mercy of chance. As A. J. Ayer forcefully put this point in his essay 'Freedom and necessity':

> What he [the libertarian] wishes to imply is that my actions are the result of my own free choice: and it is because they are the result of my own free choice that I am held to be morally responsible for them. But now we must ask how it is that I come to make my choice. Either it is an accident that I choose to act as I do or it is not. If it is an accident, then it is a matter of chance that I did not choose otherwise; and if it is merely a matter of chance that I did not choose otherwise, it is surely irrational to hold me morally responsible for choosing as I did. But if it is not an accident that I choose to do one thing rather than another, then presumably there is some causal explanation of my choice: and in that case we are led back to determinism.[25]

If this argument is right, then the real challenge to the libertarian comes not from determinism, but from the fact that there seems to be no way of even conceiving of the freedom which he ascribes to us. If our choices are causally determined by prior conditions, they are unavoidable and thus not within our control. If they are not causally determined, then, to that extent, they seem to be the product of chance and again no more within our control than if they were causally imposed on us. Either way, we would be the helpless victims (or I suppose sometimes the helpless *beneficiaries*) of the choices which occur within us and in no sense morally responsible for the actions to which they lead.

It might be objected that Ayer has overlooked the distinctively rational character of human deliberation and choice. His argument assumes that there is no middle ground between the tyranny of causation and the arbitrariness of chance. But why should not choice-for-a-reason be what falls in between? Thus suppose I decide to go to the cinema to see what is reputed to be a particularly interesting film. The libertarian will say that my decision was not causally determined by prior conditions: at the time I took it, I had it in my power to decide differently. But equally, it was not in the ordinary sense accidental, since I took it for a reason: I wanted to see the reputedly interesting film. But this seems to show that the libertarian can avoid both horns of Ayer's dilemma. For, in characterizing it as both causally undetermined and rationally explicable, he can represent my decision as neither the product of necessity nor the outcome of chance.

The trouble with this reply is that, unless reasons are taken as causes, the rational explanation of a decision does not seem to remove its accidental character. Let us grant the libertarian that my desire to see the film gave me a reason for taking my decision. And let us also grant him that, independently of causal considerations, there is a sense in which this desire counts as the *operative* reason for my decision; for, in taking the decision, it was this desire which I was intending to fulfil. But the question remains as to why I yielded to it? Either the desire was causally overriding, in which case we are back with determinism. Or it was not, in which case (Ayer will insist) it must have been, to that extent, a matter of chance that I decided to satisfy it. Nor will it help to suppose that the desire was, in some non-causal sense, stronger than any rival desire which I had the opportunity to satisfy. For while this may render my decision more rational than the possible alternatives, it still does not explain it in a way that avoids the dilemma. Either I was causally made to pursue the most rational course or (as Ayer will see it) it was left to chance. Either way, it seems that I, as such, have no control over, nor responsibility for, what happens.

Another way of trying to avoid the dilemma would be to appeal to the fact that, even in terms of causal explanation, complete determination and total randomness are not exhaustive alternatives. Thus we can envisage a situation in which the prior conditions causally restrict the range of available decisions, without necessitating any particular one. Then whatever decision the subject takes will be neither fully determined (since a different decision could have occurred) nor wholly a matter of chance (since the range of alternatives has been causally restricted). As a further refinement, we could suppose that, while the prior conditions do not determine which of the relevant decisions occurs, they do make some more likely than others. For example, we could suppose that there are just two decisions, D_1 and D_2, such that the prior conditions assign a probability of $9/10$ to D_1 and a probability of $1/10$ to D_2. If D_1 then occurs, its occurrence is even less a matter of chance than it would have been, had the probabilities been even.

However, none of this will be of any use in meeting Ayer's argument. For even where the occurrence of a certain decision is neither completely determined nor wholly a matter of chance, it is still, for all we have shown, exhaustively covered by a combination of these two factors. To the extent that the causal pressures towards it fall short of sufficiency, Ayer would insist that its occurrence is purely accidental; to the extent that its occurrence is not purely accidental, he would take it to be causally explicable. And if causality and chance are the only factors, there seeems to be no room for freedom of choice or moral responsibility. It seems that the subject will just be the passive recipient of the decisions which, in combination, these factors impose on him.

In the face of all this, we might be tempted to adopt a 'compatibilist' position, in which we retain a belief in freedom, but construe it in a way which removes its conflict with determinism. The standard approach here, and indeed the position taken by Ayer himself, is to say that what conflicts with freedom is not causality as such but constraint, where the latter is something which either deprives the subject of his power of choice or makes the exercise of this power behaviourally inefficacious. In effect, such compatibilists endorse Hume's definition of liberty as 'a power of acting or not acting, according to the determinations of the will'.[26] Thus construed, liberty becomes something which we always possess, so long as we retain our capacity to make decisions and to translate them into actions. And, crucially, it becomes something which leaves open the possibility that the events of decision-taking are causally determined by prior conditions.

The reason why we might be tempted to adopt this compatibilist position is not that it provides a plausible account of freedom *as we ordinarily conceive of it*. Far from it. For it seems clear that our ordinary concept of freedom is of something contra-deterministic – something which would be eliminated if a subject's decisions were ones which it was causally impossible for him to avoid. Rather, what makes the compatibilist position tempting is that it seems to be the only way of making freedom comprehensible: it alters our ordinary concept of freedom, but in a fashion required to achieve coherence. The point here, of course, is that if Ayer's argument is correct, we cannot make sense of the contra-deterministic freedom of our ordinary scheme: the only alternative to causal determination is chance, and chance does not give the subject control over his decisions in the way that freedom requires. In effect, the closest we can get to envisaging the subject himself as in control is to suppose that his decisions have an appropriate functional role in the relevant causal system; that they are both appropriately responsive to the subject's psychological condition and exert an appropriate influence on his behaviour. How far this kind of control would go towards making the subject morally responsible for his actions, and hence worthy of praise or blame, is a further question. But to the extent that it fails to secure such responsibility, as we ordinarily conceive of it, this may be thought a reason for revising our notion of responsibility to accord with the sort of freedom available.

Before we think of embracing compatibilism, however, we need to make quite sure that our ordinary concept of freedom *is* defective – that there really is no way of making sense of the libertarian view in its orthodox, contra-deterministic form. Does Ayer's argument really succeed in showing that the freedom postulated by this traditional view is unattainable? Can the idea of such a freedom be dismissed quite so simply? For reasons which I shall now explain, it seems to me that Ayer's reasoning here, though superficially plausible and widely endorsed, is fallacious, and that the orthodox libertarian position can be satisfactorily defended. (The arguments I now develop follow very closely my earlier discussion of this topic in my book on Ayer's philosophy.[27])

The orthodox libertarian denies that, in normal circumstances, our decisions are causally determined by prior conditions, since that would mean that we have no control over them. Ayer's retort is that, to the extent that our decisions are not causally determined, they must occur by chance, which still puts them beyond our control. But what does Ayer mean when he speaks of a decision as occurring by *chance*? If he just means that it is not causally determined by prior conditions, then it becomes a tautology that decisions which are not thus determined occur by chance; but equally, it has not been shown that decisions which are chance in that sense lie outside the subject's control. On the other hand, if he means that, as well as not being causally determined by prior conditions, the decision is something which just happens to the subject, something of which he is just a passive recipient, then it is clear that decisions which occur by chance lie outside the subject's control; but equally, it has not been shown that decisions which are not causally determined by prior conditions occur by chance in that sense. In other words, the apparent cogency of Ayer's argument stems from a concealed equivocation. The self-evidence of the claim that a decision which is not causally determined by prior conditions occurs by chance depends on interpreting chance as no more than the failure of such determination. The self-evidence of the claim that a decision which occurs by chance lies outside the subject's control depends on interpreting chance as additionally implying the subject's passivity. This means that Ayer's argument never comes to grips at all with the orthodox libertarian position. For the libertarian understands a free decision to be an event which is not only not causally determined by prior conditions, but also something for which the subject himself is, at the time of its occurrence, directly causally responsible.

It does not follow, of course, that the (orthodox) libertarian position is correct or even coherent. And there is no denying that it is philosophically perplexing. For what could it mean to say that the subject *himself* is, at the time of its occurrence, directly causally responsible for his decision? We know that one of the implications is that the decision is not causally determined by prior conditions; for such determination would prevent the causal initiative from resting with the subject himself at the time in question. But this negative condition must be a consequence of something positive in the notion of the subject's causal role. And it is here that the libertarian position seems so perplexing. For how can the subject *himself* be the cause of something? It seems that the only way in which an event could be caused by the subject would be by being caused by some event in, or state of, the subject's mind, and this, of course, is just what is excluded by assigning causal responsibility to the subject *himself*. Admittedly, we could take the notion of causation-by-a-subject as primitive and claim that it is only perplexing when we try to reduce it to something else.[28] But if we can accept a primitive notion of causation by a *subject*, why not also accept a primitive notion of causation by a *table* (i.e. a table *itself*) or causation by a *number* (a number *itself*)? And surely these latter notions are manifestly absurd. But then why is it not equally absurd to speak of a subject as the cause of something, unless this is just a misleading way of saying that the event is caused by some aspect of the subject's psychological condition?

The libertarian is likely to reply that the causal responsibility of the subject is to be understood in terms of the familiar notion of agency. Quite apart from the philosophical issue over free will, we ordinarily draw a distinction between two types of mental events. Thus, on the one hand, there are those mental events with respect to which the subject is *passive*: events which just happen to the subject, events of which he is merely the *recipient*. On the other, there are those mental events with respect to which the subject is *active*: events of the subject's doing something, events in which he is the *agent*. Let us call events of the first type *passivity* (*P*) events, and those of the second type *agency* (*A*) events. Among events which we would classify as P-events are sensations, sense-experiences, and emotions; and among events which we would classify as A-events are decisions, acts of trying, and the framing of mental images. Some mental activities, of course, combine elements of both kinds – for example, reflective thinking, in which the subject both *actively* determines the direction of the thought-process (e.g. by pursuing a certain line of investigation) and, at various points within it, finds himself *passively* persuaded that something is the case. In this sense, the two categories are not exhaustive, since an event which contains both A and P components falls into neither. It is important to stress that we apply the distinction solely in virtue of the intrinsic character of the events in question. Someone may deliberately induce in himself a certain sensation; we can even suppose that he induces it *directly*, just by willing it to occur. But we would still classify the sensation itself as a P-event (as something which just happens to the subject), even though the subject is active with respect to the volition which brings it about. Conversely, in taking a certain decision, someone may be yielding to psychological pressure, such as might come from a threat or a strong desire. But we would still classify the decision-taking itself as an A-event (as an event of the subject doing something), even though the subject is passive with respect to the pressure to which he responds.

Now the libertarian is likely to claim that it is the notion of agency, as it features in this ordinary distinction, which explains the notion of the subject's causal responsibility. In cases where the subject *himself* is directly causally responsible for some mental event, such as the taking of a decision, it is not that he causes it in the way in which one event may cause another; nor, of course, that the event is caused by some aspect of his psychological condition. Rather (the libertarian will claim), it is that the event is, in itself, an event of subject-agency. The causal initiative rests with the subject because the event is, by virtue of its intrinsic nature, the subject's own mental action, an event of the subject doing something. If the libertarian adopts this position, he will not, of course, speak of some decisions as free and others as unfree. He will claim that *all* decisions are free in the relevant sense, since all decisions are events of subject-agency and thus events for which the subject himself is, in the requisite way, causally responsible. And this will be his position with respect to A-events quite generally.

I think that this response is on the right lines. The only problem is that, *philosophically*, the ordinary notion of subject-agency is hardly less perplexing than the notion of causal responsibility it is intended to explain. For what does it mean to speak of a mental event as an event of agency? In what sense is decision-taking (trying, image-framing, etc.) a case of the subject doing something, in a way which contrasts with the passive reception of sensation? And if sensations and decisions are equally mental and equally events in the subject's biography, how is there room for any distinction in the manner of the subject's involvement in them? It seems that any answers to these questions would have to fall back on the nature of the subject's causal role: the events of agency are the events of which the subject himself is the causal initiator. But then we are just going round in circles, explaining the subject's causal role in terms of agency and explaining agency in terms of this causal role.

However, there is another possibility. The libertarian needs to be able to interpret the notion of agency in a way which puts the causal initiative for events of agency in the hands of the subject, and we know that, for this initiative to rest with the subject, it is at least required that the events be not causally determined by prior conditions. We also know that, if there are events of agency, they qualify as such solely in virtue of their intrinsic character. Thus if some particular event of decision-taking qualifies as an A-event, it is not because, on this occasion, the subject happens to play the appropriate causal role in its production – a role which he may fail to play on other occasions when events of the same kind occur. Rather, it qualifies as an A-event because, by its intrinsic nature, it is a mental *action*, an event of the subject *doing* something. Finally, it is clear that if something is a P-event, it is either causally determined by prior conditions or it is logically possible for there to be an event of exactly the same intrinsic type which is. A mental event of which the subject is a passive recipient, such as a pain or a visual experience, may fail to be thus determined, but there is nothing in its intrinsic nature by which such determination is logically precluded.

Putting these points together, we have three crucial propositions which the libertarian's account of agency must accommodate. If we abbreviate the phrase 'causally determined by prior conditions' to 'PC-determined', and if we use the expression 'intrinsic type' to mean *fully specific* intrinsic type, these three propositions can be formulated as follows:

(1) It is logically necessary that if anything is an A-event, it is not PC-determined.

(2) If something is an A-event and if T is its intrinsic type, it is logically necessary that any event of type T is an A-event.

(3) If something is a P-event and if T is its intrinsic type, it is logically possible for there to be an event of type T which is PC-determined.

Let us say that an event is *intrinsically non-determinable* if and only if, if T is its intrinsic type, it is logically impossible for there to be an event of type T which is PC-determined; and let us say that an event is *intrinsically autonomous* if and only if it is intrinsically non-determinable and does not contain any component event which is not intrinsically non-determinable. Granted that we do not classify something as an A-event if it contains a P-component (as we said above, complexes of A and P events do not fall into either category), we can immediately deduce from (1) and (2) that all A-events are intrinsically autonomous. Moreover, (3) can be reformulated as the claim that no P-event is intrinsically non-determinable. But since any mental event must be either a P-event or an A-event or something wholly composed of events of these types, it follows that, between them, the three propositions entail that a mental event is an A-event if and only if it is intrinsically autonomous. So the libertarian could define agency in terms of intrinsic autonomy. He could say that for an event to be an event of subject-agency is just for it to be mental and intrinsically autonomous. This would avoid any circularity, since intrinsic autonomy is defined solely in terms of concepts which can be grasped independently of the notions of agency and the subject's causal responsibility. In describing an event as intrinsically autonomous, we are merely saying that its intrinsic nature excludes the possibility that either it or any of its components is causally determined by prior conditions.

One drawback of this definition, as it stands, is that the notion of intrinsic autonomy omits the role of the subject altogether. In saying that the subject is active with respect to a certain mental event, we are surely saying something about the nature of the subject's involvement in that event, even if this involvement is in some way tied up with the event's intrinsic autonomy. The trouble with defining agency as autonomy is that this makes no reference to the subject's involvement at all: the definition may be extensionally accurate (for it may be logically necessary that a mental event is an event of subject-agency if and only if it is intrinsically autonomous), but, without some explicit mention of the subject's involvement, it does not fully capture what, in speaking of agency, we actually mean.

Now, at first sight, it might seem that this weakness is irremediable. For how can we specify the subject's involvement without re-importing the circularity? How can we characterize it except in terms of the subject's role as agent or causal initiator of the event in question? But in fact there is an answer. For we can specify the involvement in terms of the intrinsic autonomy which it sustains. We can say that for a subject to be the agent of a certain mental event is for him to be involved in it in whatever way it is which makes events of that type intrinsically autonomous. More precisely, given a mental event E and a (basic) subject S, we can offer as an analysis of 'S is the agent of E' – or put better, as an analysis of 'E is an event of S's agency':

(1) S is the subject of E (i.e. the subject in whose biography E occurs).

(2) There is some mode M of involvement such that, for any component mental event X of E (where E counts as a component of itself):

    (a) S is M-involved in X;

    (b) if T is X's intrinsic type, then it is logically necessary that, for any event Y of type T, the subject of Y is M-involved in Y;

    (c) it is logically impossible for there to be a mental event Y such that the subject of Y is M-involved in Y and Y is PC-determined.

In other words, agency is a special involvement of the subject which qualifies as agency because it sustains intrinsic autonomy. And it sustains intrinsic autonomy because, where it obtains, it is both part of the intrinsic nature of the mental event in question and what puts that event, along with its components, beyond the reach of PC-determination.

But now there seems to be a new problem. For if the libertarian defines agency, not as intrinsic autonomy, but as that form of subject-involvement which sustains autonomy, surely he owes us an account of what such involvement is in itself. Surely he has to tell us what sort of involvement it is which pertains to the intrinsic natures of the relevant types of event and which makes it logically impossible for events of these types to be causally determined by prior conditions. And how can he do this without appealing to the very notions of the subject's agency and causal responsibility which he is trying to define? But the answer is that the libertarian does not need to meet this challenge at all. With any kind of conscious state, as we have often stressed, there is bound to be an aspect of its intrinsic nature which we cannot specify – an aspect which we can only grasp introspectively, by knowing what it is like, subjectively, to be in that state. This is why we cannot fully communicate to a congenitally blind person what it is like to see or to a congenitally deaf person what it is like to hear. The case of mental agency is no different. There is nothing to be *said* about the nature of the subject's special involvement in A-events other than that it is what renders them intrinsically autonomous, thereby making them his *actions* rather than events which merely happen to him. What more there is to be known is known introspectively – by the subject's knowing, from the inside, what it is like to be involved in that way, i.e. to be mentally doing something. The availability of this introspective knowledge does not, of course, make the suggested analysis of the concept of agency redundant. The point of the analysis is to reveal the sense in which the involvement, whose intrinsic nature is known introspectively, qualifies for the theoretical description 'agency', with all that this description implies concerning the causal role of the subject.

It might still be thought that the very notion of intrinsic autonomy is incoherent, not because we have failed to give it a clear meaning, but because (allegedly) it is inconceivable that an event should be autonomous in that way. For how could any event be of an intrinsic type such that it was logically impossible for something of that type to be causally determined by prior conditions? Surely, whatever the type, there is the logical possibility of its being a law of nature that whenever certain conditions obtain, an event of that type subsequently occurs in a certain locational (space-time or mind-time) relation to them. And if there were such a law and the relevant conditions occurred, the resulting event would presumably qualify as causally determined.

But if we take intrinsic autonomy to be inconceivable, this is only, I think, because we are failing to take account of the special character of the events for which autonomy is being claimed. Considered in the abstract, intrinsic autonomy may seem inconceivable, because our ordinary conception of an event makes no provision for it. Moreover, for all ordinary kinds of event such autonomy *is* inconceivable: in particular, we cannot envisage a type of *physical* event whose intrinsic nature precludes its PC-determination. However, when we focus on such events as decision-takings, image-framings, and acts of trying, our intuitions pull us in a different direction. Our intuition is that these events are, by virtue of their intrinsic natures, events of subject-agency, and the very notion of agency involves the assignment of causal responsibility to the subject himself. But this surely means that our intuitive understanding of these events already implicitly characterizes them as intrinsically autonomous. For how can we interpret the claim that the subject's causal responsibility for an event is part of its intrinsic nature except as the claim that this nature includes some form of subject-involvement which makes it logically impossible for events of this type (or of the types of its components) to be PC-determined?

My conclusion, then, is that, by invoking the notion of intrinsic autonomy in the way envisaged, we can successfully defend the libertarian position against the arguments which arise from Ayer's dilemma. And this means that the original prima facie case for libertarianism still stands. Moreover, we have now added a further and strengthening element to this case. For, if I am right, we cannot explain the distinction between A-events and P-events except by pressing the autonomy-account – an account which itself sustains the libertarian position. Admittedly, the opponent of free will could still claim that this supposed distinction is spurious – that, at least at the level of the philosophically basic account, there are no events of subject-agency in the relevant (contrasting-with-passivity) sense. But given that the distinction has the support of ordinary intuition, the onus is clearly on the anti-libertarian to find some adequate argument against it. And now that we have shown how to make philosophical sense of the notion of agency, and have already established a suitable ontology of entities to serve as the relevant agents (non-physical mental subjects to exercise a non-physical mental agency), there is not the slightest reason to suppose that such an argument will be found.

NOTES

1 THE DUALIST DOCTRINE

1 In Locke 1959, II viii.
2 The point of this qualification is to allow for the possibility of a 'metaphysical' reduction of colour-facts to dispositional facts, in the manner explained presently.
3 In 5.3, pp. 139–41.
4 This is slightly loose. For strictly speaking, as we shall see in the next chapter (2.3, pp. 27–31), the claim that colour-statements are to be construed dispositionally does not entail that they can be exactly re-expressed in dispositional terms.
5 I am thinking, in particular, of the analytical functionalist, who, having analysed psychological concepts in functional terms, is likely to accept that the relevant functional facts are wholly constituted by physical facts.
6 When I speak of conceptual analysis or metaphysical stratification *within* the framework of the mental realm, I do not wish to imply that the concepts employed as primitive, or the facts cited as constitutive, are *entirely* mental.
7 See Leibniz 1898.
8 See Berkeley 1949a and b. For a discussion of how Berkeley should be interpreted, see Foster 1985b.
9 My discussion of the issues of the physical world, and, in particular, my defence of the relevant form of phenomenalistic idealism, can be found in Foster 1982.

2 NIHILISM AND ANALYTICAL BEHAVIOURISM

1 The precise meaning of 'basic subject' will be explained in 7.1, pp. 203–4.
2 See especially Rorty 1965, 1970.
3 In 1.4, p. 15.
4 See, for example, Stich 1983.
5 Quine (1953, 1960) has launched a vigorous, though in my view

wholly unconvincing, attack on these notions of *propositional content* and *translation*, along with other intensional notions like *meaning* and *analyticity*. For some effective replies to Quine, see Grice and Strawson 1956, Strawson 1957, and Blackburn 1975.

6 Of course, it will only be possible for *B* to reveal how *S* is to be construed if *B* itself can be fully understood. And presumably *B* will only be fully understandable if, despite its infinite complexity, there is a finite way of *specifying* its composition.

7 See Carnap 1934, 1959, Hempel 1949, and Ryle 1949.

8 The school founded by J. B. Watson and subsequently led by B. F. Skinner.

9 See Wittgenstein 1958 Part I: sections 258–65.

10 Foster 1985a, Part I.

11 It is essentially this problem which is exhibited in Putnam's examples of the 'super-spartans' and the 'X-worlders' (Putnam 1965).

12 I do not, of course, intend the subjunctive mood of the conditional to imply that Smith does *not* have the relevant belief.

13 Though in this case, I think, the corrective would be so radical as to amount to mental nihilism.

3 ANALYTICAL FUNCTIONALISM

1 Metaphysical functionalism in this sense has no connection with the position to which Block gives this title in his 'Introduction: what is functionalism?' in Block 1980a.

2 See, in particular, Armstrong 1968, 1970 and Lewis 1966, 1980.

3 See Block 1978. Hilary Putnam is an obvious example of a psychofunctionalist in this sense. See, for example, Putnam 1967.

4 See Shoemaker 1984, especially ch. 12.

5 I am using the expression 'sensory input' to signify any kind of input to, or process within, the body which typically produces some kind of sensation or sense-experience. For example, it covers all such things as photic input to the eye, vibrations in the ear, pressure on the skin, and palpitations of the heart, along with the afferent neural processes which they initiate.

6 I briefly discuss this later, in 6.5, pp. 196–8.

7 Admittedly, as we shall see in 4.4, the same problem arises for the conception of the nature of physical objects.

8 The problems associated with the *inflexibility* of type-identity will be exposed in 4.3.

9 I am thinking of such activities as trying to move one's arm or leg.

10 This is because of the interpretative component in perceptual experience. See my discussion of this in Foster 1985a, pp.161–3.

11 Cf. Lewis 1966, 1972.

12 One reason, of course, why these clusters will tend to be infinite is that the set of types relevant to the specification of the given type will tend to be infinite.

13 This point is pressed against the functionalist by, amongst others, Block and Fodor 1972, section III, and Block 1978, pp.304–5. For a possible functionalist response, see Shoemaker 1975, 1982.

14 See Block 1978, 1980b and (on behalf of the functionalist) Shoemaker 1975, 1981.

15 Jackson 1982, 1986; Robinson 1982, ch. 1, section 2. Nagel (1974) developed a closely related line of argument.

16 I first appealed to this case in my reply to Daniel Dennett's paper 'Quining qualia' at the Oxford Philosophical Society in 1979. Dennett's paper was eventually published, through in a substantially revised form, as Dennett 1988.

17 For example, Robinson's case (see note 15) is of a congenitally deaf scientist.

18 Putnam 1975a, p. 136. Putnam does not himself endorse this assumption.

19 Both Churchland 1985 and Tye 1986 invoke a distinction of this sort in their attempts to rebut the knowledge argument, but in a context where the dispute does not focus sharply on the issue of analytical functionalism.

20 Given that the image involved in the identification is auditory rather than visual, it is obvious why, apart from the quote marks, I leave my graphical representation of the quotational designator blank. What I intend is that the designator should semantically function in relation to the pitch in the way that, for example, we would take ' "Δ" ' to function in relation to the displayed triangular shape.

21 Tye 1986, p. 12. Incidentally, Tye uses the name 'Jones' for my 'Smith' and uses 'Smith' as a name for someone sighted.

22 Lewis's position is described in detail in chapter 4.

23 Lewis 1983, p. 131.

24 See particularly, Wittgenstein 1958 Part I, sections 243–363.

25 Jackson 1982. Robinson too (see note 15) directs his version of the knowledge argument against the physicalist, but he seems to see it, at this stage, as constituting merely a prima facie rather than a conclusive objection.

26 Jackson 1982, p.130.

27 Jackson 1982, p.127.

28 e.g. Horgan 1984 and Churchland 1985.

29 See Leibniz 1898, section 17.

30 The reason for the scare-quotes is simply that, if my interpretation of the example is correct, the input in question does not induce sensory experience.

31 Block 1978.

32 Searle (1980, 1984, 1990).

33 Searle uses the term 'syntactic' in an unusual sense.

34 Searle 1990, p. 24.

35 Thus see Searle 1984, ch. 1.

36 This would bring the functionalist close to the position of Lewis

1980. As I explain in 4.2, however, Lewis's position is not itself a form of analytical functionalism.

4 THE TYPE-IDENTITY THESIS

1 I do not want to deny that, in addition to this notion of an *objective* property, there is also the notion of an *intensional* property, whereby two predicates signify the same property if and only if they have the same meaning.

2 On this whole issue, see Kripke 1972, III and Putnam 1975a.

3 For convenience, I am here ignoring the very unusual form of type-identity discussed in section 4.

4 Lewis 1966, 1972, 1980; Armstrong 1968, 1970.

5 Smart 1959. Admittedly, Smart himself came to adopt a more flexible approach in subsequent writings, according an equal theoretical importance to stimulus and response. Thus see Smart 1963.

6 I continue to use 'sensory input' in the broad sense used in the previous chapter (See note 5).

7 Lewis 1983, p. 101, note 6.

8 Lewis 1983, p. 125.

9 Lewis 1983, p. 125.

10 This indeed is Lewis's strategy. See in particular Lewis 1972.

11 In each case, of course, its being *more* does not exclude its also being, in another respect, *less*.

12 Thus see Putnam 1967 and McGinn 1978.

13 This sort of presupposition would be present in natural-kind terms as construed by Putnam (1975a).

14 See my discussion of this in 3.5, pp. 84–7.

15 Lewis 1969, 1980. Cf. Kim 1972.

16 Or if we prefer to construe the space, not as a concrete thing, but as the abstract system of ways in which physical objects could be geometrically arranged, then what we cannot find out is the nature of the distance-relations which form the building blocks of these arrangements.

17 See 1.2, pp. 2–7.

18 For such an elaboration and defence (within the framework of a physical realism later abandoned), see Foster 1982, chs 4–6.

19 See Lockwood 1981, and 1989, ch. 10, though the second of these only appeared after I had completed my work on this section. Russell's views are found in the *Analysis of Mind* and the *Analysis of Matter* (1921, 1927).

20 In a personal communication, Lockwood has hinted that these experiential pegs and structural holes may not be so mismatched *in the context of quantum theory*. However, I have yet to see how a quantum-mechanical account of the holes (even under Lockwood's interpretation of quantum theory) would make any difference to the fundamentals of my argument.

21 See Foster 1982, especially Part II.

5 TOKEN-IDENTITY AND METAPHYSICAL REDUCTIONISM

1 Kripke 1972, p. 335. Because Kripke is mainly concerned with *type*-identity, this short argument is sometimes overlooked altogether (e.g. by McGinn 1977).
2 In 1.2.
3 See 2.3, pp. 27–31.
4 This was the account in 1.2, p. 5.
5 On this point, see Kripke 1972, pp.303–8.
6 There is an analogy here between the way in which logical necessitation lacks the essential asymmetry of constitution and the way in which nomological necessity (the necessity of natural law) lacks the essential asymmetry of causation.
7 For a more detailed discussion of this point, see Foster 1982, ch. 3. Incidentally, I there use the term 'logical sustainment' to mean what 'constitution' means here.
8 Thus see 3.2, pp. 53–4.
9 On the cases of water and heat, see the discussion in 4.2, pp. 100–1.
10 This is the term I use in Foster 1982, pp. 229 ff., and Foster 1985b, pp. 105 ff. In both these places, however, I speak of retrospective (and prospective) *sustainment*, rather than *constitution*.
11 As well as the intuitive objections to this identity-account, there are problems of identification and variable realization analogous to those which vitiated the *psychophysical* type-identity thesis (see 4.3, pp. 110–19).
12 Thus see 2.2.
13 In 2.2, pp. 19–24.

6 TOKEN-IDENTITY AND PSYCHOPHYSICAL CAUSATION

1 In a sense, this second way overlaps with the first, since, as we have seen, the type-identity theorist is likely to invoke a form of analytical reductionism (i.e. the functional-profile theory) as part of the defence of his position.
2 This seems to be what Thomas Nagel identifies as the problem in his essay 'Panpsychism'. Thus see Nagel 1979, p. 187.
3 I am here, of course, endorsing one aspect of the structuralist thesis discussed in 4.4.
4 Foster 1968; 1979, III; 1985a, III 7.
5 Hume 1978, p. 170
6 Strawson 1959, ch. 3. The theory was at one time endorsed by A. J. Ayer (1963, ch. 4).
7 I used it before in both Foster 1979 and Foster 1985a.
8 In fact, this point is not limited to the psychophysical case. Thus the irreducibility of causation also makes it plausible to suppose

that many fundamental physical laws are explicitly causal – e.g. laws about causal forces.

9 Originally in Davidson 1970. There are elaborations and developments in Davidson 1973 and Davidson 1974. All three essays are republished in *Actions and Events* (Davidson 1980), and, for convenience, I shall cite the page numbers in this volume.

10 In any case, as well as rejecting psychophysical laws, Davidson thinks he can show that there are no purely psychological laws.

11 See particularly Davidson 1963 (Davidson 1980, ch. 1) Although Davidson's argument has some plausibility, the construal of reasons as (mechanistic) causes cannot be reconciled with the libertarian position I defend in 8.4.

12 See especially Davidson 1967.

13 Davidson 1967. See especially section III.

14 Davidson 1980, p. 208.

15 Davidson 1980, p. 208.

16 I have put the term 'reducible' in scare-quotes here because what is envisaged is not *real* reduction, even in the relatively broad sense in which I use the term: it does not involve saying either that psychological concepts are analysable in physical terms or that psychological facts are wholly constituted by physical facts.

17 Davidson 1980, p. 222.

18 Davidson 1980, p. 231.

19 We discussed this phenomenon of context-dependence in 2.5, pp. 40–6.

20 Such a law would not, of course, be available for a belief which was irreducibly about (and hence depended for its existence on) some concrete external particular. But this has no bearing on the present issue. In any case (though I realize the matter is controversial), I would argue that where a belief appears to have this irreducibly *de re* character, there is always a more basic way of describing the subject's cognitive condition such that the reference to the relevant particular disappears. (For a good discussion of the general issue of *de re* thought, see Blackburn 1984, ch. 9.)

21 Quine's thesis is elaborated in Quine 1960. For further discussion of how Davidson's reasoning is to be interpreted, see Elgin 1980, Lycan 1981, Honderich 1981, Loar 1981, pp. 20–5, Gulick 1983, Stanton 1983, and Kim 1985.

22 See Davidson 1980, p. 214. Cf. Kim (1978, 1982).

23 Perhaps this is why, in one place (1980, p. 253), Davidson seems to equate the supervenience thesis with the claim that the psychological characteristics of a situation (if it has any) are always *determined by* its physical characteristics.

24 For versions of this argument, see Hopkins 1978, section I and Peacocke 1979, III: 3. See also Lewis 1966, where a very similar argument is used in defence of the *type*-identity thesis.

25 I shall discuss the libertarian position itself in 8.4, pp. 266–80.

26 The classic exposition and defence of this epiphenomenalist view

can be found in T. H. Huxley's essay 'On the hypothesis that animals are automata, and its history' (in Huxley 1893).

27 Presumably even such introspective knowledge would not be available if, as well as denying their causal influence on the physical world, the epiphenomenalist denied that mental items have any causal influence on the occurrence of other mental items.

28 See Wittgenstein 1958, Part I, 243–363.

29 The echo, of course, is from Hume 1978, I iv 2 (p. 187).

30 This situation is only slightly reminiscent of the more thorough-going 'pre-established harmony' postulated by Leibniz. Leibniz was led to adopt this more radical theory because he excluded the possibility of causal interaction between different finite substances.

31 Strictly speaking, this last position does not make psychological properties causally operative, since they become properties *of* (actually and potentially) *causing*, rather than properties *which cause*. But it would certainly prevent one from thinking of them as *irrelevant* to the causal influence of mental items on the physical world.

32 I am grateful to Andrew Jack for encouraging me to consider this possibility.

33 See 8.4, pp. 266–80.

7 THE MENTAL SUBJECT

1 The Council of Chalcedon (AD 451), defining orthodox Christology, affirmed Christ to be one individual (hypostasis) with two (the divine and the human) natures.

2 This was the position adopted by A. J. Ayer in his essay 'The concept of a person' (1963, ch. 4).

3 Hume, 1978, I iv 6.

4 Hume 1978, p. 252.

5 Hume 1978, p. 252.

6 Thus see Hume 1978, I iii 14.

7 Ayer 1946, p. 122.

8 For a fuller discussion of Ayer's Humean approach to personal identity, see Foster 1985a, Part III, section 8.

9 Hume himself seems to endorse such a view in his dispositional account of general ideas (1978, I i 7).

10 See 3.5, pp. 84–5.

11 See, for example, McGinn 1982, p. 23, and Churchland 1984, p. 19.

12 Descartes 1931, Volume I, p. 190.

13 *Principles of Philosophy*, Part I, XXXII (Descartes 1931, Volume I, p. 232).

14 For example, Williams 1978.

15 *Principles of Philosophy*, Part I, IX (Descartes 1931, Volume I, p. 222). By 'feeling', Descartes means sense-experience.

16 See, in particular, Locke 1959, II. xxiii. 1–4, together with further

relevant remarks in his letters to Stillingfleet. The full text of these letters can be found in Locke 1801, Volume IV, but the main relevant passages are given in Woozley 1964, pp. 448–52.

17 I discuss the physical case in 4.4.

18 See my concluding remarks in 4.4, pp. 129–30. For a fuller elaboration of this point, see Foster 1982, ch. 7.

19 Thus see Foster 1982, Part III.

8 PERSONAL IDENTITY, EMBODIMENT, AND FREEDOM

1 I take it up again in section 3.

2 Locke 1959, II xxvii.

3 See Flew 1951, and Mackie 1976, pp. 177–89.

4 A 2-place relation R is transitive if and only if, for any x, y, and z, if x is R-related to y and y is R-related to z, then x is R-related to z.

5 See Thomas Reid 1941, III. 6.

6 Cf. Wiggins 1976. The ancestral of a relation is that relation which stands to it in the way that *being an ancestor of* stands to be *being a parent of*. In effect, the ancestral of a relation is what this relation turns into if it is made transitive.

7 Cf. Foster 1979, V.

8 From James 1950, Volume 1, ch. XV.

9 When I speak here of a 'colour-pervaded region', I do not insist that the pervasion be homogeneous. I allow for the possibility that the pervasion varies continuously in shade from point to point (varying in hue along one spatial axis and in brightness along the other). Likewise, in speaking of a 'sound-filled period', I allow for the possibility of a continuous variation in pitch or loudness from moment to moment.

10 The point I am here making is not to be confused with the claim that any auditory experience must be, or be part of, a period of continuous auditory awareness. This latter claim may well be correct. But what I am here claiming, and what seems to me indisputable, is that, irrespective of its own temporal properties, any auditory experience must be the awareness *of* a phenomenal period.

11 The complication arises in connection with the case of fission, and it is dealt with at the end of this section.

12 Because in our definition of direct joinability, we left open the option that the relevant 'ensuring' was merely nomological.

13 On the fact that identity-relationships hold constant through all possible worlds, see Kripke 1972, 303–42.

14 This example about the past comes from Russell 1921, ch. IX.

15 See 6.3, pp. 167–72.

16 A much discussed case. See, in particular, Nagel 1971, Parfit 1984, ch. 12, and Swinburne 1984.

17 In section 1.

18 Notice that this leaves open both (i) the possibility of a human life continuing after biological death and (ii) the possibility of a human subject pre-existing the start of his human (= the start of his biological) life.

19 Of course, it would have to be a neuroscientist, like Sir John Eccles, with the right (dualist) philosophical views about the mind. See, e.g., Eccles 1953, and Eccles in (= Part II of) Popper and Eccles 1977.

20 On this last point, orthodox Christianity would take Jesus Christ (who, as the second person of the Trinity, pre-existed his biological conception) to be an exception.

21 On the issue of such dependence, see Robinson 1989.

22 Descartes is describing this feeling of embodiment when he says in *Meditation* VI: 'I am not only lodged in my body as a pilot in a vessel, but ... am very closely united to it, and so to speak so intermingled with it that I seem to compose with it one whole.' (Descartes 1931, Volume I, p. 192.)

23 Descartes 1931, Volume I, pp. 233–4.

24 I am thinking here, of course, of the alleged failure of determinism at the level of quantum mechanics. Russell (1948, pp. 54–6) pointed out the possibility of the libertarian trying to exploit this indeterminism.

25 Ayer 1954, p. 275. The essay first appeared in *Polemic* 1946, No. 5.

26 Hume 1975, p. 95.

27 Foster 1985a, III: 9. The main change of substance is that I give a slightly more restrictive (and I think, for the relevant purposes, a better) definition of *intrinsic autonomy*. (Note that what used to qualify for the title 'intrinsic *autonomy*' in my earlier book, I now refer to as 'intrinsic *non-determinability*'.)

28 This is the line taken by Roderick Chisholm. See, for example, Chisholm 1966.

BIBLIOGRAPHY

Armstrong, David 1968: *A Materialist Theory of the Mind* (London: Routledge & Kegan Paul).

Armstrong, David 1970: 'The nature of mind' in C. V. Borst (ed.) *The Mind-Brain Identity Theory* (London: Macmillan).

Ayer A. J. 1946: *Language, Truth, and Logic*, 2nd Edition (London: Victor Gollancz).

Ayer A. J. 1954: *Philosophical Essays* (London: Macmillan).

Ayer A. J. 1963: *The Concept of a Person and Other Essays* (London: Macmillan).

Berkeley, George 1949a: *Principles of Human Knowledge*, in A. A. Luce and T. E. Jessop (eds) *The Works of George Berkeley*, Volume 2 (London: Thomas Nelson). First published 1710; 2nd Edition 1734.

Berkeley, George 1949b: *Three Dialogues between Hylas and Philonous*, in A. A. Luce and T. E. Jessop (eds) *The Works of George Berkeley*, Volume 2 (London: Thomas Nelson). First published 1713; 2nd Edition 1725, 3rd Edition 1734.

Blackburn, Simon 1975: 'The identity of propositions' in Simon Blackburn (ed.) *Meaning, Reference, and Necessity* (Cambridge: Cambridge University Press).

Blackburn, Simon 1984: *Spreading the Word* (Oxford: Clarendon Press).

Block, Ned, and Fodor, Jerry 1972: 'What psychological states are not', *Philosophical Review* LXXXI. Reprinted in Block 1980a.

Block, Ned 1978: 'Troubles with functionalism' in C. W. Savage (ed.) *Perception and Cognition: Issues in the Foundations of Psychology, Minnesota Studies in the Philosophy of Science* Volume IX (Minneapolis: University of Minnesota Press). Reprinted in Block 1980a.

Block, Ned (ed.) 1980a: *Readings in the Philosophy of Psychology* Volume I (Cambridge, Massachusetts: Harvard University Press and London: Routledge & Kegan Paul).

Block, Ned 1980b: 'Are absent qualia impossible?' *Philosophical Review* LXXXIX.

Carnap, Rudolf 1934: *The Unity of Science* (London: Kegan Paul).

Carnap, Rudolf 1959: 'Psychology in physical language', translated by George Schick, in A. J. Ayer (ed.) *Logical Positivism* (Illinois: Free Press).

Chisholm, Roderick 1966: 'Freedom and action' in K. Lehrer (ed.) *Freedom and Determinism* (New York: Random House).

Churchland, Paul 1984: *Matter and Consciousness* (Cambridge, Massachusetts: MIT Press).

Churchland, Paul 1985: 'Reduction, qualia, and the direct introspection of brain states', *Journal of Philosophy* LXXXII, No. 1.

Davidson, Donald 1963: 'Actions, reasons and causes', *Journal of Philosophy* LX. Reprinted in Davidson 1980.

Davidson, Donald 1967: 'Causal relations', *Journal of Philosophy* LXIV. Reprinted in Davidson 1980.

Davidson, Donald 1970: 'Mental events' in L. Foster and J. W. Swanson (eds) *Experience and Theory* (Minneapolis: University of Minnesota Press. Published in Great Britain by Duckworth, 1970). Reprinted in Davidson 1980.

Davidson, Donald 1973: 'The material mind' in P. Suppes *et al.* (eds) *Logic, Methodology, and Philosophy of Science* IV (Amsterdam: North Holland). Reprinted in Davidson 1980.

Davidson, Donald 1974: 'Psychology as philosophy' in S. C. Brown (ed.) *Philosophy of Psychology* (London: Macmillan). Reprinted in Davidson 1980.

Davidson, Donald 1980: *Actions and Events* (Oxford: Clarendon Press).

Dennett, Daniel 1988: 'Quining qualia' in A. J. Marcel and E. Bisiach (eds) *Consciousness in Contemporary Science* (Oxford: Clarendon Press).

Descartes, Ren 1931: *Philosophical Works*, in two volumes, translated by Elizabeth S. Haldane and G. R. T. Ross (Cambridge: Cambridge University Press). Haldane and Ross edition first published 1911.

Eccles, John 1953: *The Neurophysiological Basis of Mind* (Oxford: Clarendon Press).

Elgin, C. Z. 1980: 'Indeterminacy, underdetermination, and the anomalous monism', *Synthese* 45.

Flew, Antony 1951: 'Locke and the problem of personal identity', *Philosophy* 26.

Foster, John 1968: 'Psychophysical causal relations', *American Philosophical Quarterly* V, No. 1.

Foster, John 1979: 'In *self*-defence' in G. F. Macdonald (ed.) *Perception and Identity* (London: Macmillan).

Foster, John 1982: *The Case for Idealism* (London: Routledge & Kegan Paul).

Foster, John 1985a: *Ayer* (London: Routledge & Kegan Paul).

Foster, John 1985b: 'Berkeley on the physical world' in John Foster and Howard Robinson (eds) *Essays on Berkeley* (Oxford: Clarendon Press).

Grice H. P. and Strawson P. F. 1956: 'In defence of a dogma', *Philosophical Review* LXV, No. 2.

Gulick, Robert Van 1983: 'Rationality and the anomalous nature of the mental', *Philosophy Research Archives*.

Hempel, Carl 1949: 'The logical analysis of psychology' in Herbert Feigl and Wilfrid Sellars (eds) *Readings in Philosophical Analysis* (New York: Appleton-Century-Crofts).

Honderich, Ted 1981: 'Psychophysical lawlike connections and their problem', *Inquiry* 24.

Hopkins, James 1978: 'Mental states, natural kinds, and psychophysical laws', symposium with Colin McGinn, *Aristotelian Society*, Supplementary Volume.

Horgan, Terence 1984: 'Jackson on physical information and qualia', *Philosophical Quarterly* Volume 34, No. 135.

Hume, David 1975: *An Enquiry Concerning Human Understanding* edited by L. A. Selby-Bigge, 2nd Edition revised by P. H. Nidditch (Oxford: Clarendon Press). First published 1748.

Hume, David 1978: *A Treatise of Human Nature*, edited by L. A. Selby-Bigge, 2nd Edition revised by P. H. Nidditch (Oxford: Clarendon Press). First published 1739.

Huxley, T. H. 1893: *Collected Essays Volume I: Method and Results* (London: Macmillan).

Jackson, Frank 1982: 'Epiphenomenal qualia', *Philosophical Quarterly* Volume 32, No. 127.

Jackson, Frank 1986: 'What Mary didn't know', *Journal of Philosophy* LXXXIII, No. 5.

James, William 1950: *Principles of Psychology* (New York: Dover). First published 1890.

Kim, Jaegwon 1972: 'Phenomenal properties, psychophysical laws, and the identity theory', *Monist* LVI, No. 2.

Kim, Jaegwon 1978: 'Supervenience and nomological incommensurables', *American Philosophical Quarterly* XV, No. 2.

Kim, Jaegwon 1982: 'Psychophysical supervenience', *Philosophical Studies* 41.

Kim, Jaegwon 1985: 'Psychophysical laws' in E. LePore and B. McLaughlin (eds) *Actions and Events: Perspectives in the Philosophy of Donald Davidson* (Oxford: Basil Blackwell).

Kripke, Saul 1972: 'Naming and necessity' in D. Davidson and G. Harman (eds) *Semantics of Natural Language* (Dordreht: Reidel). Republished as *Naming and Necessity* (Oxford: Basil Blackwell, 1980).

Leibniz, Gottfried 1898: *Monadology*, in Robert Latta (tr. and ed.) *Monadology and Other Philosophical Writings* (Oxford: Clarendon Press).

Lewis, David 1966: 'An argument for the identity theory', *Journal of Philosophy* LXIII, 1. Reprinted, with additional material, in Lewis 1983.

Lewis, David 1969: 'Review of *Art, Mind, and Religion*', *Journal of Philosophy* LXVI. Reprinted in Block 1980a.

Lewis, David 1972: 'Psychophysical and theoretical identifications', *Australasian Journal of Philosophy* 50. Reprinted in Block 1980a.

Lewis, David 1980: 'Mad pain and Martian pain' in Block 1980a. Reprinted, with an additional 'Postscript', in Lewis 1983.

Lewis, David 1983: *Philosophical Papers* Volume I (New York: Oxford University Press).

Loar, Brian 1981: *Mind and Meaning* (Cambridge: Cambridge University Press).

Locke, John 1801: *Works*, in ten volumes (London: printed for J. Johnson *et al.*).

Locke, John 1959: *An Essay Concerning Human Understanding*, edited by A. Campbell Fraser (New York: Dover, 1959). First published 1690.

Lockwood, Michael 1981: 'What *was* Russell's neutral monism?' in Peter A. French, Theodore E. Vehling, Jr, and Howard K. Wettstein (eds) *Midwest Studies in Philosophy Volume VI: The Foundations of Analytic Philosophy* (Minneapolis: University of Minnesota Press).

Lockwood, Michael 1989: *Mind, Brain, and the Quantum: The Compound 'I'* (Oxford: Basil Blackwell).

Lycan, William 1981: 'Psychophysical laws', *Philosophical Topics* 12.

Mackie, J. L. 1976: *Problems from Locke* (Oxford: Clarendon Press).

McGinn, Colin 1977: 'Anomalous monism and Kripke's Cartesian intuitions', *Analysis* 37, No. 2.

McGinn, Colin 1978: 'Mental states, natural kinds, and psychophysical laws', symposium with James Hopkins, *Aristotelian Society*, Supplementary Volume.

McGinn, Colin 1982: *The Character of Mind* (Oxford: Clarendon Press).

Nagel, Thomas 1971: 'Brain bisection and the unity of consciousness', *Synthese* 20. Reprinted in Nagel 1979.

Nagel, Thomas 1974: 'What is it like to be a bat?', *Philosophical Review* LXXXIII, No. 4. Reprinted in Nagel 1979.

Nagel, Thomas 1979: *Mortal Questions* (Cambridge: Cambridge University Press).

Parfit, Derek 1984: *Reasons and Persons* (Oxford: Clarendon Press).

Peacocke, Christopher 1979: *Holistic Explanation* (Oxford: Clarendon Press).

Popper, Karl and Eccles, John 1977: *The Self and its Brain* (Berlin: Springer-Verlag and London: Routledge & Kegan Paul).

Putnam, Hilary 1965: 'Brains and behaviour' in R. J. Butler (ed.) *Analytical Philosophy*, Second Series (Oxford: Basil Blackwell). Reprinted in Putnam 1975b.

Putnam, Hilary 1967: 'Psychological predicates' in Capitan and Merrill (eds) *Art, Mind, and Religion* (Pittsburgh: University of Pittsburgh Press). Reprinted as 'The nature of mental states' in Putnam 1975b.

Putnam, Hilary 1975a: 'The meaning of "meaning" ' in K. Gunderson (ed.) *Language, Mind, and Knowledge, Minnesota Studies in the Philosophy of Science* Volume VII (Minneapolis: University of Minnesota Press). Reprinted in Putnam 1975b.

Putnam, Hilary 1975b: *Philosophical Papers* Volume 2: *Mind, Language, and Reality* (Cambridge: Cambridge University Press).

Quine, Willard Van Orman 1953: 'Two dogmas of empiricism' in Quine *From a Logical Point of View* (Cambridge, Massachusetts: Harvard University Press).

Quine, Willard Van Orman 1960: *Word and Object* (Cambridge, Massachusetts: MIT Press).

Reid, Thomas 1941: *Essays on the Intellectual Powers of Man*, edited by A. D. Woozley (London: Macmillan). First published 1785.

Robinson, Howard 1982: *Matter and Sense* (Cambridge: Cambridge University Press).

Robinson, Howard 1989: 'Embodiment' in John R. Smythies and John Beloff (eds) *The Case for Dualism* (Charlottesville: University of Virginia Press).

Rorty, Richard 1965: 'Mind-body identity, privacy, and categories', *Review of Metaphysics* 19.

Rorty, Richard 1970: 'In defense of eliminative materialism', *Review of Metaphysics* 24.

Russell, Bertrand 1921: *Analysis of Mind* (London: George Allen & Unwin).

Russell, Bertrand 1927: *Analysis of Matter* (London: Kegan Paul).

Russell, Bertrand 1948: *Human Knowledge: Its Scope and Limits* (London: George Allen & Unwin).

Ryle, Gilbert 1949: *The Concept of Mind* (London: Hutchinson).

Searle, John 1980: 'Minds, brains, and programs', *Behavioural and Brain Sciences* Volume 3, No. 3.

Searle, John 1984: *Minds, Brains, and Science* (London: British Broadcasting Corporation).

Searle, John 1990: 'Is the brain's mind a computer program?', *Scientific American* (January).

Shoemaker, Sydney 1975: 'Functionalism and qualia', *Philosophical Studies* 27. Reprinted in Block 1980a and Shoemaker 1984.

Shoemaker, Sydney 1981: 'Absent qualia are impossible – a reply to Block', *Philosophical Review* XC, No. 4. Reprinted in Shoemaker 1984.

Shoemaker, Sydney 1982: 'The inverted spectrum', *Journal of Philosophy* LXXIX, No. 7. Reprinted in Shoemaker 1984.

Shoemaker, Sydney 1984: *Identity, Cause, and Mind* (Cambridge: Cambridge University Press).

Smart, J. J. C. 1959: 'Sensations and brain processes', *Philosophical Review* LXVIII.

Smart, J. J. C. 1963: 'Materialism', *Journal of Philosophy* LX.

Stanton, William 1983: 'Supervenience and psychophysical law in anomalous monism', *Pacific Philosophical Quarterly* 64.

Stich, Stephen 1983: *From Folk Psychology to Cognitive Science* (Cambridge, Massachusetts: MIT Press).

Strawson, P. F. 1957: 'Propositions, concepts, and logical truths', *Philosophical Quarterly* Volume 7.

Strawson, P. F. 1959: *Individuals* (London: Methuen).

Swinburne, Richard 1984: 'Personal identity: the dualist theory' in S. Shoemaker and R. Swinburne *Personal Identity* (Oxford: Basil Blackwell).

Tye, Michael 1986: 'The subjective qualities of experience', *Mind* XCV, No. 377.

Wiggins, David 1976: 'Locke, Butler, and the stream of conscious-ness: and men as a natural kind', *Philosophy* 51.

Williams, Bernard 1978: *Descartes* (Harmondsworth, Middlesex: Penguin).

Wittgenstein, Ludwig 1958: *Philosophical Investigations*, translated by G. E. M. Anscombe (Oxford: Basil Blackwell).

Woozley, A. D. 1964: 'The controversy with Stillingfleet' in his *Appendix* to John Locke *An Essay Concerning Human Understanding*, abridged and edited by A. D. Woozley (London: Fontana/Collins).

INDEX